IMPROVING SOCIAL COMPETENCE

IMPROVING SOCIAL COMPETENCE
A Resource for Elementary School Teachers

Pam Campbell
The University of Connecticut

Gary N. Siperstein
The University of Massachusetts

Allyn and Bacon
Boston   London   Toronto   Sydney   Tokyo   Singapore

Copyright © 1994 by Allyn and Bacon
A Division of Paramount Publishing
160 Gould Street
Needham Heights, Massachusetts 02194

Library of Congress Cataloging-in-Publication Data

Campbell, Pam
    Improving social competence:a resource for elementary school
teachers/Pam Campbell, Gary N. Siperstein.
        p.   cm.
    Includes bibliographical references and index.
    ISBN 0-205-13757-1
    1. Social skills—Study and teaching (Elementary) 2. Social
skills in children.   I. Siperstein, Gary N.   II. Title.
    HQ783.C36   1993
    302´.14´07—dc20   93-31685
                                                     CIP

Printed in the United States of America
10 9 8 7 6 5 4 3 2 1   98 97 96 95 94

DEDICATION

This book is for teachers—those who recognize the importance of friendship and acceptance in a child's life.

We dedicate this book to our own children—Debbie, Mark, and Stevie—who have shown us the importance of being a friend as well as a parent.

ABOUT THE AUTHORS

Dr. Pam Campbell is an Assistant Professor of special education at The University of Connecticut. She has taught a range of university courses including instruction, curriculum, and classroom management for both general and special educators. She has been a teacher of students in regular education, Chapter I, and special education. In addition, she has collaborated with parents and school systems in dealing with issues related to special education, school reform, and professional development.

Dr. Campbell has written numerous articles, and chapters, as well as curriculum and training materials in the areas of collaboration, social competence, technology, instruction, and transition. Along with Dr. Stan Shaw, she coordinated a statewide symposia on special education in the 21st century and co-edited a special issue of *Remedial and Special Education* that focused on the future of special education. Her current interests include issues related to dealing with diversity in mainstream classrooms and the delivery of effective instruction to all students.

Dr. Gary Siperstein is a professor of psychology at The University of Massachusetts at Boston. He is also director and founder of the Center for the Study of Social Acceptance that carries out research, curriculum development, and training designed to improve the quality of life of individuals with disabilities. Dr. Siperstein's major focus is on the social aspects of individuals with disabilities, particularly students in the classroom.

Dr. Siperstein has developed In-service training programs that focus on improving teachers' knowledge and skills in areas including children's social skills, school stress, and the pre-referral process. These programs are designed to enable students with disabilities to become a part of the social fabric of the classroom and school. He has written numerous articles and chapters on the critical aspects of children's social cognition in children with disabilities. Dr. Siperstein is Editor of the *Monograph Series of the American Association on Mental Retardation* and serves as Associate Editor and Consulting Editor for other journals. His current interests include reducing the stress that children and teachers experience in the classroom, and the social problems experienced by children with Attention Deficit Disorder.

CONTENTS

APPENDICES

LIST OF FIGURES

PREFACE

Teachers are concerned about students who are rejected or ignored by their peers; yet they are better prepared and expected to address the academic, rather than social, competence of their students. Researchers have long recognized the importance of peer relations for children's social development; yet their findings have not always been effectively translated into classroom practice. Meanwhile, students who lack social competence continue to deal with the feelings and negative self-perceptions associated with being left out or ignored by their peers and teachers. Further, they must return day after day to the very school settings in which those feelings are perpetuated. These circumstances have provided the impetus for this book.

Improving Social Competence: A Resource for Elementary School Teachers is designed to bridge the gap between classroom practice and research findings. Our intent has been to develop a tool that provides the skills, information, and activities that teachers can use to address the social competence of their students in elementary school.

This book is intended primarily for those who teach in general education classrooms. However, it can also be a useful resource for those who work in other settings or fulfill other roles in an elementary school. Teachers in special education classrooms, libraries, music rooms, gymnasiums, and playgrounds can easily adapt the materials and ideas presented in this book to enable any student to interact more productively in these settings. Other educational professionals, including school psychologists, guidance counselors, social workers, speech/language clinicians and other support staff who work with students may consider many of the ideas in this book useful in their work.

This book is the product of many years of development in elementary classrooms. Practicing teachers, together with their students, have shared their concerns and frustrations. They have helped us focus on the issues and problems present in their classrooms and develop useful effective materials and techniques to address social difficulties. They have allowed us to field-test materials and activities designed to promote social competence. They have given us feedback and suggestions for modifications to these materials. This book is the result of their efforts; we hope that our response justifies their investment.

OVERVIEW OF THE BOOK

In keeping with our intent to bridge research and practice, we have designed this book and its activities on a model derived from current theory and respected research. The model for improving social competence that provides the framework for this book is based on the notion that socially skilled children who are self-confident in social situations can become more socially competent within classrooms that are rich in social opportunities. Such classrooms promote social competence because peers can interact with one another and there are many opportunities for students to practice social skills and enhance their social self-confidence. This book is divided into two major sections that reflect this model: Section 1 focuses on the opportunities that a classroom may provide and Section 2 focuses on developing the social skills and self-confidence that students might bring to the classroom environment.

Section 1, *Focusing on the Classroom,* encourages teachers to provide a supportive classroom climate that will increase the opportunities for productive interactions. By first creating opportunities for change at the classroom level, teachers can affect individual students in the most efficient and least blameful manner. Changes in the overall educational environment are often so successful that they preclude the need for intervention with individual students.

In four chapters, Section 1 guides teachers through an examination of the factors that determine opportunities for social interaction—the teacher, the environment, instruction, and their integration into an overall classroom climate. Each of these factors may either limit or promote the development of social competence.

Chapter 1 shows teachers how to examine their own expectations and teaching styles. The expectations that teachers hold for students as a group and as individuals set the tone and the standards for what happens in the classroom. First teachers learn to recognize their own expectations and to identify how the students perceive those expectations. Suggestions are then given on how to modify and communicate expectations more effectively to students.

Chapter 1 also shows teachers how to determine their preferred teaching style to see whether the ways in which they use their authority impede or promote interactions in the classroom. While a teacher's preferred style is often related to one's personality, teachers can reflect on their own previous learning experiences that might have had an influence on their present teaching style. The chapter offers encouragement to teachers who might want to try other styles that could better support student interactions.

Chapter 2 discusses three elements of the classroom environment—rules, space, and time—that affect the opportunities for social interaction. Classroom rules can give students limits and consequences for behavior, as well as expectations for how to behave. For students whose home environment lacks consistent limits, classroom rules may provide a sense of safety for at least part of their day. The organization and arrangement of the physical space of the classroom—including furniture, dividers, and equipment—can promote a smooth flow of productive student interactions. In addition, the efficient management of instructional and transition time can enable students to be on-task more often and consequently more productive and less disruptive.

Chapter 3 enables teachers to examine the ways in which they deliver academic instruction and determine whether there might be additional opportunities for students to interact and develop social competence during these activities. Most of the skills necessary for academic work, such as communicating, working with others, and problem-solving are also necessary for social interactions. Cooperative learning is recommended as an instructional strategy to bring about not only the visible motions of interaction, but also to enable students to build peer relationships through sharing challenges and achievements.

Chapter 4 considers how the teacher, the environment, and instruction combine to determine the overall classroom climate. When a classroom climate is positive, students respect each others' differences and feelings and support one another in their efforts to succeed. Chapter 4 enables teachers to assess the climate of their classroom and suggests ways for improvement. Chapter 4 also looks at the variety of classrooms in which students function throughout the day, from the general education classroom to the gymnasium, the playground, the resource room, and the cafeteria. It offers guidelines for evaluating and modifying any classroom in order to provide consistency to meet the needs of individual students.

Section 1 is best used by first reading through all four chapters to gain a sense of the interrelationships among the teacher, the environment, and instruction, as they contribute to the classroom, regardless to its location or ostensible purpose. Having acquired this overview, teachers can then choose an area in which to begin. Some will intuitively recognize the area of greatest opportunity in their classroom. In some instances, this might be an area that is easily changed; while, in others, this might be an area of greatest need. Other teachers may want to carry out assessments across several areas before setting their priorities for intervention. The goal of this section is to enable students who are socially skilled and self-confident to have the opportunities they need to become socially competent.

For some students, however, providing opportunities may not be enough. They may know the appropriate social skills, but lack the confidence to use them; others have neither skills nor self-confidence. For these students, direct teacher intervention is needed.

Section 2, *Focusing on the Student*, provides ways for teachers to identify these students to develop social skills and increase their self-confidence in social situations. The activities in this section have been designed to complement the spirit and intent of those contained in Section 1. They are designed to be used as part of an holistic approach to improving social competence within the opportunities provided by the student's classroom.

Chapter 5 provides assessment tools to identify students who lack social skills, as well as two instructional techniques for teaching social skills: modeling and coaching. Modeling teaches the progressive steps that make up a social behavior. Coaching helps students develop the social knowledge needed to utilize their social behaviors appropriately within a social context. Students can then combine social behaviors and social knowledge into the social skills needed to interact productively. Students also need self-confidence to use their skills in situations that provide opportunities.

Chapter 6 provides information and activities so teachers can identify students who may know a social skill but seem unwilling to use it; this hesitancy may be due to their lack of self-concept, self-esteem, and self-efficacy. Suggestions are provided to enable these students to become self-confident enough to use the social skills they have learned to interact more frequently and productively with their peers.

The ideas in Section 2 take advantage of practices that are effective with all students, regardless of situation, difference, disability, or experience. The techniques are designed to help students acquire, maintain, and use social skills and, consequently, have greater confidence in their efforts to be successful in social situations.

Within Sections 1 and 2, each chapter provides basic information, as well as assessments and activities. Materials for assessment before, during, and after interventions have been provided. These tools incorporate the three components of informed assessment—multiple instruments, multiple sources, and multiple occasions—to enable teachers to make appropriate, effective, and efficient decisions.

The activities enable teachers to put the information gained from assessments directly into practice. Charts are also provided as aids for organizing information and solidifying plans. The activities are easily modified according to specific classrooms, grade levels, or student populations.

Four appendices are also included: Appendix A: *Modeling Activities* and Appendix B: *Coaching Activities* provide many additional examples of using these methods for specific behaviors and situations. Appendix C:

Additional Resources includes many sources of information and research on related topics. It also includes additional assessments and planning activities. Appendix D: *Instructional Goals and Objectives for Individualized Educational Plans (IEPs)* is intended to aid in coordinating the activities suggested by this book into educational goals for individual students with disabilities.

INTRODUCTION

Most students are socially competent. They are socially skilled and confident in social interactions. Consequently, they make acquaintances, gain acceptance, develop and maintain social relationships, and have friends. Their social relationships are productive and meaningful not only to themselves, but also to their peers and the classroom as a whole. They contribute to positive classroom climates in which everyone is able to get along and accomplish both social and academic objectives.

Unfortunately, not all students are socially competent. For some, the acquisition of social skills is more difficult, and they often do not feel confident in social situations. These students experience problems not only in the classroom, but throughout the school—in the hallway, in the lunchroom, and on the playground. These are frequently the students who argue, throw things, tease peers, or storm out of the classroom. They are also the students who simply seem awkward, fearful, hesitant, and ill-at-ease. As a result of their behavior, their peers either blatantly reject or simply ignore them. Consequently, they have fewer opportunities for peer interactions in which they might learn and practice the behaviors and knowledge needed for social competence.

Students who experience problems in their social relationships are at a distinct disadvantage. They may become trapped in a cycle that precludes their ever becoming as socially skilled or self-confident as their peers and fosters their continued exclusion from social interactions. Lacking social interactions, they fail to develop social relationships in which they might practice social skills. Lacking social relationships, students lack opportunities to interact with others. Lacking opportunities to interact with others, students fail to develop the social skills needed to become socially competent. Students deficient in social skills are often labeled as maladjusted. They become delinquent or drop out of school as adolescents and are more likely to experience problems as adults. These outcomes are predicted for a growing body of students who are at-risk in today's elementary schools because of their lack of social competence.

There may be many factors that contribute to students' being at-risk (due to their lack of social competence). Often, the same factors—learning and/or behavioral disabilities, hunger, distress, cultural differences, poverty—that interfere with academic achievement preclude social achievement as well. For example, students may not perceive situations correctly, remember information accurately, problem-solve successfully, or use known solutions spontaneously and appropriately.

Difficulty with language or inexperience with the customs of the dominant culture present additional complications. Initiating and maintaining a conversation are skills that are dependent on both verbal and nonverbal language. These situations present challenges to students with language disabilities or those whose primary language differs from that of the dominant culture. For example, in some cultures, eye contact is viewed as a disrespectful, rather than socially appropriate, behavior.

Finally, social learning is often more difficult than academic learning because interactions always differ and tend to happen very rapidly. In many cases, more than one of these factors may interact. The interplay of the factors that contribute or undermine social competence is complex.

Teachers who wish to help their students become more socially competent can benefit from understanding that the acquisition of social competence is dependent on an individual's cognitive development and the interplay between individuals and their social environment. Becoming and remaining socially competent is a complex, dynamic, interactive process in which the social skills—behaviors and knowledge—that are needed vary according to the individual and the situation. It is a lifelong process that children begin as infants. Most learn from their successes and failures and apply their social skills in age-appropriate ways. For example, socially competent teenagers still need to make friends and are able to apply the new strategies and behaviors they have learned as they matured.

For the teachers and peers who deal with these students throughout the school year, the benefits of developing the social competence of individual students are clear. With improved social competence, students who have previously interfered with the effectiveness of the group can instead become valued participants and contributors. Their individuality can become an appreciated asset rather than a perceived liability. With less time spent on behavioral management, there is more time for academic endeavors and a greater likelihood of personal satisfaction. These students need and deserve the opportunity to reverse the cycle of failure and move more fully and productively into the community of their school.

ACKNOWLEDGMENTS

This book is the product of the exceptional dedication and expertise of many talented individuals. We acknowledge the work of John Bak, who helped provide the impetus for this project, as well as Harriet Nezer and Barbara Nezer, who addressed the need for a resource such as this over ten years ago. We are indebted to the contributions of Adrianne Smith, Sue Gately, Pat Willott, and Tim Reagan; each has helped us link theory with practice in the field. We thank Carol Elizabeth Biancardi and Rebecca Teevan for their editorial and technical assistance. We clearly recognize that this task could not have been completed without the excellent and efficient efforts of the editor of this current version, Maida Tilchen. The practical wisdom, attention to detail, and insistence on excellence of each of these talented professionals is reflected in the content and form of this book.

We also wish to thank Max Mueller, Norm Howe, Don Blodgett, Frank King, and others from the Office of Special Education and Rehabilitative Services in the U.S. Department of Education; as well as Rose Crawford and her associates at the National Center for Learning Disabilities. They provided us with exceptional opportunities and support for our training activities.

Thank you to our reviewer, Patricia Nettles, Oswego Public Schools, Oswego, New York. Her suggestions were constructive and her feedback encouraging. Finally, we express our gratitude to Mylan Jaixen, our editor at Allyn and Bacon, and his assistant, Sue Hutchinson for their ongoing support and continued encouragement during the final phases of this endeavor.

Guiding all our work has been the belief that every student can be a vital member of the school community. The activities in our book are designed to provide teachers with the knowledge, skills, and materials so that each student has the opportunity to participate most fully and productively.

Pam Campbell
Gary N. Siperstein

IMPROVING SOCIAL COMPETENCE

FOCUSING ON THE CLASSROOM

The classroom provides a natural setting in which teachers can foster social competence. Elementary school students spend most of their school day in the classroom, and it is there that opportunities for productive interactions can be arranged and encouraged by the teacher. By considering how the influence of the teacher, the environment, and instruction contribute to the classroom as a whole, teachers can set up classrooms in which students know that they are expected to work together, to learn from one another, and to interact socially in a safe and supportive way.

Classrooms that foster social competence are busy, yet carefully organized. Limits are clearly defined; consequences are clear and consistent; and teacher expectations are realistic and expressed to students as part of the classroom routine. Students can communicate their needs effectively because they have opportunities to be heard and to listen to one another. They can work and play cooperatively because they learn how to share activities, materials, and interests in order to achieve shared goals. In sum, students can go about their day knowing what to expect in terms of behavior and instruction, and be keenly aware of the need to interact appropriately and effectively with one another. This clarity and consistency contributes to the achievement of both individual and group goals.

There are several benefits to addressing social competence at the classroom level. First, when students are practicing their social skills, they are simultaneously using skills that enable them achieve academic objectives. Sharing materials or working cooperatively in a small group are social skills that contribute to task completion as well as peer relationships. Second, focusing on the classroom enables teachers to promote the social competence of many students at the same time within the context of academic instruction. Third, since students spend most of their school day in the classroom, the classroom provides the most time and greatest number of opportunities. Finally, the peer relationships that develop in the classroom frequently carry over to other areas of life. Students who work together in the classroom might also share lunch or play together during recess; they might participate in after school activities or ride the bus together.

When opportunities to interact are limited by the classroom environment, students who lack social competence are at-risk for both academic and social failure. Teachers play a critical role in reducing that risk. By structuring the classroom to foster social competence, teachers can give all their students time and activities with which to practice their social skills in a natural setting among their peers.

THE TEACHER

OVERVIEW

As the teacher, you control what happens in your classroom. Your own behavior is a powerful determinant in whether or not students succeed. Your actions reflect your expectations and attitudes. By examining the expectations you have for your students and your style of teaching, you can consider changes that will enable your classroom to be a place that faciliates the positive interactions that foster social competence. Chapter 1 will guide you through several assessments and activities that may suggest changes in your behavior that you might wish to consider.

Teachers set the tone for what occurs in their classrooms. They do this most powerfully through the expectations they have for their students and through their teaching style. Regardless of a teacher's level of awareness, expectations and styles affect all aspects of the classroom. This happens for the following reasons. First, because teachers are powerful authority figures, students tend to accommodate themselves to teacher expectations. When students believe their teachers expect the best, they perform better, feel better about themselves, and contribute to a classroom environment in which everyone gets along and is more productive. However, when students believe that teachers do not think well of them, they often perform only to the low level that they assume is expected and do not strive for greater achievement.

Second, a teacher's style in the classroom determines how the environment is organized and how instruction is delivered. This determines the likelihood of interactions among students and, consequently, the degree to which students will have opportunities to practice and refine social skills to become more socially self-confident.

It is appropriate that teacher expectations and styles be considered first, for they strongly influence the classroom environment (see Chapter 2), instruction (see Chapter 3) and the overall type and climate of the classroom (see Chapter 4). This first chapter will define expectations and teacher styles and describe their impact on the classroom and students. It will outline ways for teachers to examine their own expectations and styles in order to organize their classrooms and deliver instruction in ways that will help their students improve their social competence.

EXPECTATIONS

DEFINITION AND DEVELOPMENT

Expectations are the hopes and aspirations that people have for the behavior of others. Expectations may be based on previous experiences, observations, hearsay, and personal biases. When certain behaviors become associated with a person, others may develop expectations for similar behavior in the future. They then communicate these expectations—sometimes subtly through a look or tone of voice and sometimes openly through such words as *I expect you to* . . . . Once communicated, expectations influence behavior—the behavior of those holding the expectations, as well as that of the person for whom the expectation is held. It is also important to recognize that variations in communicative style and behavior may reflect cultural differences (Asante & Gudykundst, 1989). Thus, behavior not only reflects current expectations, it also portends future expectations and subsequent behavior. This cycle of expectations and behavior forms the basis for all interpersonal interactions whether personal or professional, academic or social. It influences how well individuals are able to achieve their goals and get along with one another.

Expectations are formed based on roles, behaviors within those roles, stereotypes, and social norms. In our society, people assume many different roles such as parent, child, sister, teacher, student, doctor, grandmother. Individuals can fill more than one role simultaneously (teacher, parent, brother, son, and coach) and over the course of a lifetime (daughter, sister, lawyer, wife, mother, and grandmother). Some younger students may have difficulty understanding that people can fulfill more than one role at a time. For example, they are frequently surprised when they meet their teacher in the supermarket. It is also important to understand that what is entailed in performing a particular role is, to a very great extent, culturally specific. For instance, being a *daughter* in some cultures carries with it a set of behaviors and expectations that are quite different from what most members of the dominant culture in our society would expect.

Expectations are also based on the ways in which individuals fill or behave within their roles. Every role has expectations associated with it. In school, teachers are expected to teach, principals to supervise, custodians to maintain the school, and students to learn. Teachers, principals, custodians, and students are expected to behave *accordingly;* in other words, as teachers, principals, custodians, and students are supposed to behave.

While people expect individuals to behave in certain prescribed ways within specific roles, it is obviously possible to fill similar roles very differently. For example, while all teachers are expected to teach, individually they behave differently within that role. They have very different expectations and styles, organize their classrooms in very distinct ways, and use different instructional methods. Most students learn to associate behaviors with roles and also to differentiate ways in which individuals may fulfill the same role.

Expectations are also based on stereotypes related to a particular group's behavior, appearance, and ability. Frequently, people base expectations about individuals or groups on such stereotypes as social class (poor, rich, middle class), minority group membership (Native American, Hispanic, Asian-American, African-American), disability (learning disabilities, emotional problems, behavior disorders, mental retardation, physical disabilities), age, and gender. Teachers may establish expectations for entire classes based on a general sense of socio-economic status or past reputation such as, "This is a bad class. They're all from the projects; so we know what to expect. . . ." Sometimes stereotypes that may seem positive are actually negative generalizations; for example, "She'll do fine in the advanced math group; she's Asian." Regardless of whether a stereotype seems positive or negative however, it is inevitably harmful because it places unrealistic expectations and limitations on both the holder and the recipient.

Stereotyped expectations are learned. Students can learn them from one another, from their parents, or from their teachers. Although teachers hope that students will learn to base expectations for others on individual behavior rather than stereotypes, misinformation and peer pressure commonly result in the categorization of others. This leads to the formation of cliques and closed groups. It is particularly harmful when teachers let the label of a disability or cultural difference determine their own expectations for behavior and performance because students may model teacher behaviors and develop similar expectations. The labeled students—*burnouts, jocks, nerds,* etc.—will then subscribe to group designations or the cultural stereotypes they learn from adults or other students.

Finally, expectations are based on the norms of social situations. Social situations define appropriate behavior and the expectations that individuals learn to associate with that behavior. The school situation itself dictates behavior—being on time, walking in lines, raising hands, respecting authority, etc. When teachers or students deviate from norms, they may be viewed negatively by others. For example, teachers who are frequently late or absent may be viewed as unprofessional by their peers. Similarly, students who disrupt the classroom routine may be viewed negatively by some of their peers. Most students accept norms as appropriate guidelines for behavior and learn that conforming to norms is expected.

EXPECTATIONS FOR THE TEACHER

Expectations of the teacher are extremely powerful determinants of teacher behavior. Therefore, teachers spend a great deal of time trying to meet the expectations of others. When these expectations conflict with each other or with an individual's ability to meet them, performance suffers. Figure 1.1 can be used as a first step toward appreciating the power of these expectations. This activity is an opportunity for you to identify the expectations of others and to evaluate their effect on your own behavior.

The expectations of others affect not only how you behave, but how you feel about your behavior. Conflicting expectations, or expectations that cannot realistically be satisfied, may be causing you to feel inadequate and guilty. Being aware can help you to eliminate or at least reduce the stress associated with these feelings. By planning and trying concrete responses to expectations, you can reduce your anxieties as well as increase your understanding of how others see your role. Figure 1.2 will help you develop your response.

Completing Figures 1.1 and 1.2 may increase your respect for the power of expectations. You can harness this power by developing expectations for your students that reflect your appreciation of the impact of your expectations on student performance.

TEACHER EXPECTATIONS OF STUDENTS

Students have expectations for teachers and for other students that form the basis for the way teachers and students behave in school. However, it is the expectations that teachers have for their students that are the most influential in the classroom. Teacher expectations become the norm of the classroom and an accepted part of the routine. Teacher expectations shape the ways in which classmates perceive and act toward each other. As expectations become established over time, they become less subject to question and form an integral part of the classroom operation and ultimately determine the social norms. These norms help students know what is expected of them and what they can expect from others.

Expectations can determine whether individual students will succeed. Teachers and students who expect success and enable one another to succeed support one another to attain higher levels of achievement and greater feelings of self-worth. In contrast, when teachers and students expect less than the best from one another, success is more difficult to achieve and low self-worth can result. Students, especially those with special needs, are more likely to be affected by low, rather than high, expectations. When students are not expected to read well because they are learning disabled, they may actually underachieve in order to fulfill the low expectations that others have of them. When expectations are low, students achieve less, feel less competent, and are less confident of their ability to accomplish academic and social tasks.

It is natural for teachers to have expectations for students and unavoidable that they behave in ways that reflect those expectations. It is also natural for students to respond to their teacher's behavior by trying to meet the expectations associated with that behavior. To ensure that students have the opportunity to succeed, teacher expectations that motivate and encourage competence are needed. In addition, these expectations must be known to the students. Too often teacher expectations are not readily apparent in the classroom, but rather the unwritten rules of the classroom. Teacher expectations must be delineated, specified, and then communicated to students.

DELINEATING EXPECTATIONS

Many teachers fail to communicate their true expectations to themselves, let alone to their students, because they are simply unaware as to what those expectations actually are. By delineating expectations, they can at least increase their level of self-awareness. This can be accomplished in two ways: first, by examining their expectations for the class as a whole using Figure 1.3, and then by considering those expectations in terms of individual students using Figure 1.4. Some students have difficulty meeting these expectations. Figure 1.4 will guide you to compare your expectations for the whole class to the ability of an individual student to meet these expectations. Together, Figures 1.3 and 1.4 can help you delineate your expectations, determine their relative importance, and then differentiate the ability of individual students to meet them.

SPECIFYING EXPECTATIONS

Once you are more in tune with your expectations and their potential effect on your students, you can think more specifically about the expectations you might specify for your class. If all students are able to meet current expectations, you may go directly to the next section of this chapter on teacher styles. However, be sure to periodically reassess your expectations for your students. Evaluating your expectations throughout the school year will help you become aware of how your expectations change, frequently without notice. As students achieve, expectations can be raised, although it is important to keep the need to set expectations that are realistically high in mind. For students with a history of problems in learning and behavior, attention to seemingly insignificant increments of positive change can provide powerful motivation for continued improvement. To specify expectations that are appropriate for your students, you may find the guidelines below helpful.

FIGURE 1.1 Assessing What Others Expect of the Teacher

PUROSE:
To identify and categorize the effects of expectations of others on the teacher.

DIRECTIONS:
For each item, list at least two expectations that you believe others have of you.

1. My principal expects me to:
   1.
   2.
2. My fellow teachers expect me to:
   1.
   2.
3. The parents of my students expect me to:
   1.
   2.
4. My students expect me to:
   1.
   2.
5. The specialists expect me to:
   1.
   2.
6. The custodians expect me to:
   1.
   2.
7. My own family expects me to:
   1.
   2.
8. I expect myself to:
   1.
   2.

Asking yourself these questions may help you realize that you really do not know what the expectations of certain people are. In fact, you may have been trying to read their minds and operating under unsupported assumptions. You may decide to ask some people what they do expect of you.

When you are satisfied that your list is as accurate as possible, categorize the expectations listed as follows:

1. These expectations are fair and can realistically be met:

2. These expectations are in conflict:

3. These expectations are unreasonable and cannot be met:

INTERPRETATION:
Doing this exercise probably made you aware of the stress and misdirected energy caused by your perception of the expectations of others. All expectations, whether fair, conflicting, or unreasonable, demand a response. Planning that response, based on your increased awareness, will help you reduce your anxieties. Talking with others about reasonable and realistic expectations should increase the understanding others have of your role.

FIGURE 1.2 Responding to Expectations

PURPOSE:
To plan a response to the expectations others place on the teacher.

DIRECTIONS:
Using the lists of three categories of expectations placed on you (developed in Figure 1.2: *Assessing What Others Expect of the Teacher*), answer the following questions.

1. *These expectations are fair and can realistically be met:*

   For expectations I want to meet, what are some of the concrete steps I can take (or am now taking) to meet them?

2. *These explanations are in conflict:*

   For expectations that conflict,
   • Are both expectations fair and realistic?

   • Why do I believe others have these expectations and how can I support others to attain higher levels of achievement and validate this assumption?

   • If these expectations are real, what can I do that will relax the situation?

   For example, can I talk over the conflict with each person?
   • How can I choose which expectation to satisfy first?

   • What are the consequences of failing to satisfy each expectation? Which consequence is least desirable?

   Can I now make a choice?

3. *These expectations are unreasonable:*
   • Why do I believe others have these expectations and how can I validate this assumption?

   • Can I do anything to relax the situation, such as talk to the person involved in order to seek alternatives, accommodations, or compromise?

   • Can I accept that I acknowledge these expectations but cannot meet them?

INTERPRETATION:
This activity should lead you to greater awareness of the stress and energy demands put on you by expectations. By planning and trying concrete responses to expectations, you can not only reduce your anxieties but also increase communication and understanding of others. This activity may also have increased your respect for the power of expectations. You can harness this power by developing expectations for your class that reflect your empathy for the impact of expectations on student performance.

FIGURE 1.3 Teacher Expectations for the Whole Class

PURPOSE:

This activity can help you delineate the expectations you have for your class as a whole.

DIRECTIONS:

1. On a separate piece of paper, list nine expectations you have for your class as a whole. Some areas to consider are: behavior, attitude, academic or social competence, values, communication skills, cooperation, and tolerance.
2. Use the form below to prioritize your expectations in terms of their importance to you: Most Important (1), More Important (2), Important (3), Less Important (4), Least Important (5).
3. Write one of your nine expectations in each of the boxes below. Notice that you will have one expectation that is Most Important (1) and one that is Least Important (5), two expectations that are More Important (2) And Less Important (4), and three expectations that are Important (3). Allow adequate time to make careful decisions about the relative importance of each expectation. This is not easy because each of the expectations has value to you. It may be helpful to determine the one you absolutely could not give up and then decide on one that you might be able to teach without. Enter these expectations into the Most and Least Important categories. Then, continue this process with the remaining categories.
4. When you are satisfied that you have placed each expectation in the proper space, study the display.
5. Consider how well your priorities overlap instructional goals and whether revisions might make sense.

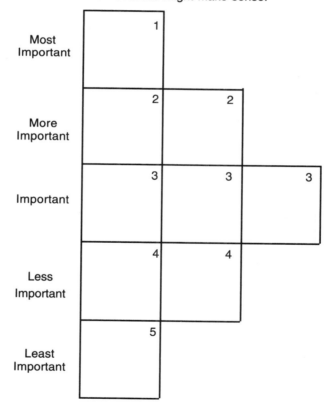

FIGURE 1.3 Teacher Expectations for the Whole Class *(Continued)*

INTERPRETATION:
You have identified nine expectations that are important to you in terms of the whole class. Within those nine expectations, you have identified those that are more and less important to you. Your behavior reflects these expectations. If you believe that all students in your class are able to meet these expectations, and then you have successfully communicated those expectations to students, you might go on to the next section on teaching styles.

If, however, there are students who do not seem to be succeeding in your classroom, you might first wish to examine these expectations in terms of an individual student's ability to meet the expectations that are important to you.

FIGURE 1.4 Teacher Expectations and the Individual Student

PURPOSE:
This activity can help you evaluate the ability of an individual student to meet your expectations as stated in Figure 1.3: *Teacher Expectations for the Whole Class.*

DIRECTIONS:
1. Select a student who seems to be having difficulty.
2. Look at the list of expectations you have for your class as a whole.
3. Study the expectation categories below; they range from *Easiest* (to meet) to *Difficult* (to meet). You will place each of your nine expectations in a category that best represents that student's ability to meet each expectation.
4. Think about how easily the student might meet each of your nine expectations. As you decide, write each expectation in the corresponding space, one expectation per box. Allow yourself adequate time to make careful decisions about the student's relative ability for each expectation.
5. When you are satisfied that you have placed each expectation in the proper space, study the display.
6. Change the position of individual expectations until you are satisfied.

Student _____

	1		
Easiest			
Easy	2	2	
Easier	3	3	3
A little difficult	4	4	
Difficult	5		

7. Use the Comparison Form below to clarify differences between your expectations for the class as a whole and the ability of this individual student to meet those expectations important to you.

FIGURE 1.4 Teacher Expectations and the Individual Student *(Continued)*

COMPARISON FORM

Expectation	Ranking for Teacher	Ranking for Student	Difference
	1		
	2		
	2		
	3		
	3		
	4		
	4		
	5		

8. Write each of your nine expectations on the Comparison Form according to its position in Figure 1.3.
9. In the column under Ranking for Student, write the number of the category (1-5) of each expectation in Figure 1.4.
10. Calculate the difference as follows:
   a. In each row, subtract the smaller number from the larger, regardless of order.
   b. Enter that number in the Difference column.
   c. Place a plus (+) sign in front of a difference score if the student ranking is larger than that of the teacher.
   d. Place a minus (−) sign in front of a difference score if the teacher ranking is larger than that of the student.

INTERPRETATION:
Note differences of +2 and more and −2 and less.
   +2 and more:
      These are areas of significant difference and strength for the student.
      Praise and reinforce the student for meeting these expectations.
   −2 and less:
      These are areas of significant difference and potential difficulty for both you and the student. Decide whether you might be able to reprioritize your expectations. Can they be omitted or rearranged in terms of their importance for this student? If not, clarify these expectations and teach the student how to meet them. Another possibility might be to set more appropriate expectations for individual students. Figure 1.3 can be used for individual students as well as the whole class.

- *Recall Past Experiences.* Use knowledge of previous student performance to design expectations that will enable individual students to succeed.

- *Use Multiple Data Sources.* Interview previous teachers, peers, parents, custodians, and the students themselves. Determine what it is that students *can* do by asking questions, observing, and reviewing records. Use more than one source to improve the chances of gathering accurate data.

- *Minimiize Bias.* Be wary of hearsay and conversation, particularly in the teacher's lounge, as a source of information about individual students. These sources may result in inaccurate information or stereotyping. The fact that an older brother had a learning disability does not necessarily mean that his younger siblings will have similar problems.

- *Set Expectations for the Class.* Teach individual students who may have difficulty how to meet general class expectations.

- *Set Expectations for Individual Students.* Consider individual differences and needs. Incorporate smaller sets of expectations for individual students into contracts and written agreements with individual students.

- *Align Rules and Expectations.* Make it easier for your students by incorporating expectations into classroom rules. The systems used to encourage adherence to rules can also be used to encourage meeting teacher expectations. Stating expectations as rules also helps clarify and communicate teacher expectations to students.

- *State Expectations Positively.* Positively stated expectations encourage appropriate behavior and success because they tell students what to do. Students then know the exact behaviors that are expected, e.g., *Speak in soft voices* rather than *Never yell.*

COMMUNICATING EXPECTATIONS

Once appropriate expectations have been set, they must be clearly communicated to every student. When teachers' expectations are not communicated clearly, students may be confused and unsure as to how to behave. In their confusion, students may appear to be challenging teachers or attempting to take control of situations while they ae actually trying to detemine what is expected of them. They may actually be *asking* teachers to set limits and be more explicit as to their expectations. Clear expectations give students a structure within which to function. Students relax and feel more comfortable as they learn how to contribute appropriately in the classroom. Figure 1.5 can be used to determine whether you have clearly communicated your expectations to your students.

Teachers communicate their expectations to students through verbal and nonverbal interactions. Spoken and written words communicate expectations verbally. Stating expectations several times during the day can remind students of teacher expectations and guide them toward more successful performance. In communicating expectations to students verbally, eliminate vocabulary that reflects stereotyical views. Phrases such as "girls always," "boys never," "learning disabled students can't," "students with disordered behavior always" are indicative of thinking that is based on stereotypes and not individual potential. This may be particularly difficult for some adults to modify, especially if these habits have been practiced for many years. Gender-biased words such as mailman, fireman, stewardess, policeman, and newspaper boy can be replaced by more encompassing terms such as letter carrier, firefighter, flight attendant, police officer, and news-

FIGURE 1.5 Communicating Expectations to Students

PURPOSE:
To determine whether students are aware of expectations the teacher has for them.

DIRECTIONS:
Administer to a group or individual students in verbal or written form.
1. Ask students to list or tell you expectations (you choose the number) that you (as teacher) have for them (as students) in your class. For students who cannot generate responses, present your own list of expectations in random order and ask students to rank them in the order they think is most important to you the teacher.

2. Ask students to pick the most and least important expectation that the teacher has for them.

3. Compare students' lists to your own (either Figure 1.3 or Figure 1.4).

INTERPRETATION:
If the students' lists are similar to your own, then your expectations are known to your students. Your behavior reflects those expectations and students are clear on how to respond. If the students' lists differ, then your expectations are not known and your behavior may be confusing to your students. The following discussion will help you plan ways to better communicate your expectations.

paper carrier. Constant self-monitoring is an effective way to reduce and eventually eliminate terms that may be offensive and discriminatory. Translating expectations into written rules can help students who might have difficulty remembering two bodies of information (expectations and rules). Teaching and posting expectations on the wall in the classroom, on a student's desk, or in a notebook can improve compliance. Chapter 2 offers guidelines on how to choose and implement rules in the classroom.

Gestures, tone of voice, posture, and body language communicate expectations nonverbally. This can sometimes pose special problems. There are students who are unable to read subtle cues and understand innuendo. They may miss a gesture or misinterpret a tone of voice meant to impart a message that differs from the words that are spoken. This is particularly true of some students with special needs. Similarly, cultural differences may play an important role in interfering with nonverbal cues. For instance, in some Asian cultures, touching a student's head is considered insulting and inappropriate; while in our dominant culture, this technique is frequently used to provide supportive feedback or let a student know that the teacher is monitoring behavior. Eye contact patterns also differ dramatically from one culture to another. Many Native American children, for example, are taught that it is rude to look an adult in the eye—behavior that is commonly misunderstood by Anglo teachers who assume (based on their own cultural norms) that students who fail to maintain eye contact may be lying or avoiding a response. Students with hearing impairments, on the other hand, generally require more eye contact than some teachers find comfortable. In a classroom of students with different cultural experiences or special needs, everyone should try to be aware of the subtle, yet critically important differences.

The organization of the classroom environment can also reflect the expectations that teachers have for students. When students are seated closer to the teacher, they typically have more frequent interactions with the teacher and fewer interactions with other students. It may be necessary to change seating arrangements during the course of the school year to ensure that the same students are not always in the front (or back) of the room. Another alternative is for teachers to move around the classroom to increase teacher/student interactions. (See Chapter 2).

Instruction can also be delivered in ways that reflect appropriately high expectations. By giving students reasonable choices about instructional activities, materials, and methods; they learn to be more independent learners. Opportunities to think through outcomes and make choices teach students that there is more than one way to meet a teacher's expectations. Multicultural and nonsexist materials as well as those that highlight the accomplishments of individuals with disabilities, promote identification with the content and help raise the expectations that students hold for themselves.

When teachers are aware of their expectations, the ways in which they develop, their appropriateness, and how they are communicated to students, they can evaluate their impact on students both as members of the group and as individuals. They will know whether they can or should change their expectations of their students. They can also change their own behavior to reflect more appropriate expectations.

With appropriate and well-communicated expectations, students will behave in ways that please not only themselves but also their teachers. Then, teachers will view their students as more competent learners who contribute to a positive classroom climate. In such an environment, students interact with each other and provide support and encouragement to one another. Such environments naturally lend themselves to students becoming more competent academically and socially.

TEACHING STYLES

Teaching styles are the ways in which teachers use authority—the degree to which teachers share power, leadership, and control with students. Teaching styles can be characterized very broadly as autocratic, democratic, or laissez faire. They determine the types of interactions students have with their teacher and with one another. Teaching styles influence all aspects of the classroom—its organization, the instruction, and the interactions that take place there.

AUTOCRATIC

Autocratic teachers *control* the authority in the classroom. They make the decisions regarding classroom organization and the delivery of instruction. Students know they are expected to behave in orderly ways and typically follow a rigid and consistent schedule. They come to depend on their teacher for organization and direction. While many students respond well to such structure, few opportunities exist for independent thinking, thoughtful choice-making, taking responsibility for their own behavior, and practicing social skills. There may be fewer informal interactions unless the teacher decides that such activities are worthwhile. While some students with behavior problems or cognitive deficits succeed in a highly controlled, teacher-directed classroom, others achieve more in a freer atmosphere in which they are given some responsibility for decisions.

DEMOCRATIC

Democratic teachers *share* authority with students. Teachers and students develop rules and expectations together. The classroom atmosphere is freer because students have a voice in the organization of the classroom and in the delivery of instruction. Sharing leadership does not enable a teacher to abdicate responsibilities but gives some of the decision-making power to the students, and provides an opportunity for students to take greater responsibility for their own behavior. The teacher's role then centers around selecting students to whom choices might be given, determining how much decision-making power should be given, and monitoring the ability of these students to make decisions wisely.

Some students thrive in classrooms that are less structured and provide opportunities for accomplishing tasks in alternative ways. They learn to make decisions and develop independence. Others have more difficulty adjusting to such openness and flexibility. For those who either hesitate to join group activities or lack the skills to do so appropriately, opportunities for interactions among students may be problematic. At such times, democratic teachers may decide to step in, be more autocratic, and make decisions for students.

LAISSEZ FAIRE

Laissez faire teachers, like their democratic counterparts, also *share* authority with students, but in much less structured ways. Both allow students to share responsibility for the organization and management of classroom activities, but laissez faire teachers do not specify who is in charge or when or how students may make decisions. Laissez faire teachers and their students capitalize on spontaneous learning experiences in ways that are not possible with democratic or autocratic teaching styles. Activities may seem to occur without planning. On a particular day, a reading lesson might be scheduled first, followed by a math lesson. The following day, based on students' needs or requests, reading might be followed by a spelling lesson that incorporates reading vocabulary. A major drawback of this teaching style is that some students become confused or anxious about unclear or inconsistent expectations and changing roles. These students need greater structure or more consistent supervision.

Consider for a moment your own personal experiences with different teaching styles. Use Figure 1.6 to recall your teachers and how their styles affected your own academic and social achievement.

Teachers rarely use one style *exclusively*. While they tend to use one style more *frequently* than another, they tend to shift back and forth, depending on the needs of their students, the demands of the situation, or their own moods or tolerance levels. Within a single day, a teacher may deliver a directed reading lesson followed by a science lesson that permits greater student decision-making power. Some teachers use an *authoritative* style in the morning and a *democratic* style in the afternoon to better manage the behavior of their students. Most teachers can move comfortably between at least two teaching styles whenever their students, the situation, or their own needs suggest the need for a change. In assessing your own teaching style, this fluidity must be considered. Use Figure 1.7 to identify how different styles are used with different results throughout a typical school day.

In addition to assessing your own style, observing the interactions (teacher/ student and student/student) that take place in other classrooms can also help identify the styles that seem most effective or detrimental for individual students. Mainstream teachers may see that the teaching style of the resource room teacher enables the student with special needs to make decisions about how work is to be completed. Allowing the same flexibility in the mainstream classroom may help the student successfully complete more work. On the other hand, when students with special needs are placed in the mainstream for art, music, or physical education, variations in teaching styles may interfere with the ability of students to survive—academically and socially. Chapter 4 will help you compare teaching styles in different classrooms.

Having become aware of one's own style, and of the effectiveness of other styles on individual students, teachers can then decide whether a change in teaching style might make their students more successful. The following guidelines may be helpful if you decide to try another style of teaching.

GUIDELINES
FOR USING
DIFFERENT
TEACHING STYLES

- *To Use an AUTHORITATIVE Teaching Style*

    Make decisions alone.

    Explicitly define rules, expectations, and goals.

    Establish a regular schedule and follow it.

    Create an orderly, goal-directed classroom.

    Tell students how to complete tasks.

    Assign students to pairs and groups.

    Assign seats to students.

    Tell students when and how to move to other areas of the classroom.

- *To Use a DEMOCRATIC Teaching Style*

    Develop classroom rules, expectations, goals, and schedules *with* students.

    Work with individual students to develop individual rules, expectations goals, and schedules.

FIGURE 1.6 Familiar Teaching Styles

PURPOSE:
To recall how the styles of different teachers you encountered as a learner affected your own success in school.

DIRECTIONS:
1. In column 1, list the names of your own past teachers who stand out in your mind for positive or negative reasons.
2. In column 2, enter grade levels or subject areas.
3. In column 3, without judging, describe their effect on your learning, and the relationships you had with other students.
4. In column 4, consider the techniques and strategies they used. Based on the descriptions of teacher styles in this chapter, identify the one or two styles that seem to have been predominant for each teacher.
5. In column 5, judge how this style affected your self-concept, social competence and self-confidence.

1	2	3	4	5
Teacher	Grade Level/ Subject Area	Effects of Style	Teacher Style	Your Reaction

INTERPRETATION:
By identifying the teaching styles and judging their impact on your own classroom experience, you can begin to appreciate how aspects of your own teaching style may have a positive or negative impact on your students. You may decide that a change in your style for part of the school day might benefit your students.

FIGURE 1.7 Assessing One's Own Teaching Style

PURPOSE:
To survey your own style/s in the classroom and evaluate whether changes might improve the achievement of students in your class.

DIRECTIONS:
1. Recall times when your students seem to have had greater success in your classroom.

Date	Activity	Student Behaviors (What were they doing?)	Teacher Behaviors (What were you doing?)

2. Recall times when your students seem to have had greater difficulty in the classroom.

Date	Activity	Student Behaviors (What were they doing?)	Teacher Behaviors (What were you doing?)

INTERPRETATION:
Examine the two charts for patterns. Is there a relationship between your style and the student's behavior? If so, you may want to test your theory and apply the results. If your style does not seem to affect the students' behavior, you can also use this chart to look for patterns in the effects of time or activity.

Let the class develop rules for special situations that might involve their working together.

Ask students to present their own plans for completing a task; then, give them the time and opportunities to do so.

Ask students to help you decide on whether to work individually or in groups or pairs.

Ask students to help you decide on partners and groups.

Ask students to help you decide where to place their desks or complete assignments.

Ask for student input when determining how to deliver instruction and structure assignments.

- *To Use a LAISSEZ FAIRE Teaching Style*

    Explain or demonstrate the value of spontaneous learning experiences.

    Work with students to encourage spontaneous learning experiences that will satisfy the needs of all students.

    Do not follow a schedule.

    Together with students, develop long-term goals and expectations.

    Plan how these goals and expectations can be met within a spontaneous atmosphere.

    Let students decide whether to work in groups or pairs.

    Let students pick their own partners and groups.

    Let students decide where they wish to place their desk or complete their assignments.

    Establish a system for students to express confusion or anxiety resulting from a less structured classroom.

In this chapter, you have seen how teacher expectations and teaching styles influence the delivery of instruction and the potential for students to succeed. In the next chapter, *The Environment,* we will examine these factors in greater depth. As you read Chapter 2, you will find that what you have learned about your expectations and teaching styles will help you choose and implement appropriate rules and use time and space more effectively in your classroom.

THE ENVIRONMENT

OVERVIEW

This chapter discusses ways to evaluate and manipulate, rules, time, and space—three components of the classroom environment—to minimize classroom disruptions and maximize opportunities for productive interactions that enhance both academic and social achievement. It is important to reduce classroom disruptions as much as possible. When students cause disruptions that interfere with learning and task completion, their peers typically respond with disapproval, avoidance, and in some cases rejection. Rejection and separation from the peer group preclude further opportunities for students to learn or practice acting appropriately. Students with special needs or those lacking information about classroom behavioral norms are frequently the ones who are disruptive and end up reinforcing negative perceptions that peers and teachers may already have.

On the other hand, appropriate interactions provide opportunities for students to practice social skills. When classmates are getting along, they naturally reinforce one another with acceptance and, in some cases, friendship. They take one another into groups where they have many more opportunities to practice and refine their social skills.

When rules, time, and space are used effectively, they can promote appropriate interactions. Clearly stated rules give students limits and positive consequences for appropriate behavior and can mirror teacher expectations. Efficiently managed time increases time-on-task and limits opportunities for non-productive behavior. Thoughtfully organized physical space enables students to interact academically and socially while moving smoothly through the day. Each of these environmental factors is considered in the following sections.

RULES

Interruptions detract from instruction and interfere with the attainment of instructional objectives. Appropriate rules that are consistently and effectively implemented can decrease interruptions and the amount of time spent managing student behavior, while increasing instructional time and time-on-task.

All students benefit from well-organized classrooms, but the success of certain students actually depends on clearly defined and consistently enforced rules. Some students do not know how to behave appropriately in the classroom, either in getting along with others or attending to academic tasks. In recognizing that they simply do not know how to interact with their peers or their teachers, there are several factors to consider.

In some cases, there may be conflicting cultural norms. For example, one student might take another student's pencil without asking because property is communal in her culture. Rules and expectations that students have learned at home, in the community, or in other schools, classrooms, and social settings often contradict one another. Students may need one set of rules to survive in the classroom and another to survive in the streets. For these students, rules clarify the classroom situation.

Another group of students may know what is expected but do not seem to apply this knowledge. They may lack the experience of having received a positive response for behaving appropriately in the past or lack the self-confidence to put their knowledge into action. For these students, rules and consequences provide guidelines and assured recognition of appropriate behavior so they can practice experiencing positive responses and build their confidence. For both groups, rules provide the *how to's* for behavior that help them to be consistent with the behavior of their peers.

To create and implement rules in your classroom, you may find the following guidelines helpful.

GUIDELINES
FOR CREATING
RULES

- *Involve Students.* On the first day of school, discuss why rules are important. Work collaboratively with students to develop a set of classroom rules. Be sure that rules that are important to you are included.
- *Keep Rules to a Minimum.* Use five to eight rules to cover most aspects of classroom life. Too many rules require students to remember too much.
- *Use Simple Wording.* State rules as observable behaviors that all students recognize. Use terms such as: *listen, walk, raise your hand.* Avoid ambiguous or vague terms, such as *talk at a reasonable volume* or *play fairly.*
- *Use Positive Terms.* State rules as behaviors that students *can* do, not as something they must remember *not* to do. Examples of positively stated rules that teachers have found effective are:

   Always walk in the classroom.

   Listen when the teacher is talking.

   Leave gum at home.

   Leave quietly during group time.

   Bring a pencil to class every day.

   Raise your hand during class discussions.

   Clean your desk after lunch.
- *Establish Consequences.* Help students determine simple consequences for obeying, as well as disobeying rules. For example, consequences for obeying the rules the first time: *praise;* the second time: *name written down;* the third time: *removal of a chore.* Consequence for disobeying the rules the first time: *warning;* the second time: *name written down;* the third time: *loss of a privilege.* Ask students to affirm their agreement and commitment to the rules and consequences by signing or committing to the rules.
- *Post Rules Prominently.* Post rules and consequences so that they are clearly visible to all students. Simply pointing to posted rules or asking students to review posted rules can help enforce rules.
- *Enforce Rules Consistently.* Be vigilant. Catch students as frequently for *obeying* as for *disobeying* rules. Implement consequences for either circumstance immediately. Focus on the rules, the behavior, and the agreed-upon consequences.
- *Vary Rules According to Special Situations.* Alter rules and consequences for special situations such as visitors and field trips or for individual students according to their needs and abilities.

- *Monitor Rules.* Changes in teaching style, expectations, or classroom organization require changes or modifications to rules or consequences. Review classroom rules periodically. If students seem to break or follow a particular rule consistently, examine whether it (or its consequence) is still appropriate.

Use Figure 2.1 to work with your students to identify the stated and unstated rules of the classroom and determine their effectiveness. Then use Figure 2.2 to establish classroom rules.

While the guidelines provided earlier in this chapter can be helpful in creating and using rules, there may be individual situations that require alternative strategies. In these instances your own judgments of student needs and abilities are your best guide.

Well-designed and consistently enforced rules result in a significant reduction in the amount of instructional time that is wasted attending to and managing undesirable behavior. There are also additional steps that can be taken to use time more productively in the classroom.

TIME

The effective use of time is critical to student achievement, yet, somehow it often seems to continually slip away. Careful documentation of how time has been spent during a school day may reveal that a shockingly small portion of the day has been used productively for instruction. In a typical day, a great deal of time is taken up by noninstructional activities such as lunch, assembly, and managerial tasks. Walking from room to room, taking books out and putting them away, and moving from one activity to the next within the classroom all take time away from instruction and learning activities.

By recognizing, reducing, and eliminating intrusive factors, you can make more instructional time available. This can be accomplished by changing your own procedures as well as those of your students, while addressing the limitations imposed by administrative policies and procedures.

To improve the use of time in your classroom, begin by assessing the time that is actually available for instruction. Instructional time is that which remains after all other demands such as lunch and recess, managerial tasks, and transitions have been met. Use Figure 2.3 to determine how much time you really have for instruction in your school day.

To increase available instructional time, reconsider your classroom schedules, streamline transitions, and increase student time-on-task. The classroom schedule can provide the first clues as to where losses and gains in available instructional time may be found. To design the best classroom schedule, use the following guidelines.

GUIDELINES
FOR DESIGNING SCHEDULES

- *Examine Your Current Schedule.* Consider the order of activities during each school day. Are there times of the day that seem to move more or less efficiently? Does your schedule accommodate high and low energy patterns for whole classes and yourself?
- *Identify Areas in Need of Change.* Target those activities within your classroom that might be rearranged. Are there other teachers who would team teach or switch special activities with your class?

FIGURE 2.1 Assessing Classroom Rules

PURPOSE:
To identify and evaluate stated and unstated classroom rules.

DIRECTIONS:
1. Write down classroom rules.

2. Write down additional spoken or unspoken rules.

3. Write down the consequences for obeying classroom rules.

4. Write down the consequences for disobeying classroom rules.

5. Consider each rule:

    Is it important for the whole class?

    If not, for which students is it important?

    Is it effective for the whole class?

    If not, for which students is it effective? ineffective?

    Do all students understand the need for this rule?

    Are the consequences effective for this rule?

    Is the rule important at all times during the day?

6. Consider the whole list of rules:

    Are there unstated rules that should be stated?

    Are there rules that are missing?

7. Ask students to state the rules of the classroom.
    Say (for example): *Let's take a little time to review the rules of our classroom. What are the rules of this classroom?*
    Write their responses on the board or an overhead transparency. (You may want to remove the posted rules during the exercise. . . .) Keep a permanent list of their suggestions.

8. Compare the student list with your own. Ask yourself:

    Are there differences?

    Are there rules of which many students are unaware?

    Are there rules that students have failed to mention?

    Are only certain students unaware of certain rules?

    Have students stated your expectations as rules?

INTERPRETATION:
If individual students are confused about the rules, you may choose to work with them individually or in a small group to review the existing rules. If the whole class seems to have a view of the rules that is different from your own, you may want to review and re-establish the rules.

FIGURE 2.2 Establishing Classroom Rules

PURPOSE:
To help students determine rules for the classroom.

DIRECTIONS:
Remind students of the list of rules they generated during the assessment activity (See Figure 2.1). Try whichever of the following activities applies to the needs of your class.

1. Choose the five to eight rules that are most important to you. State them negatively, and present the list to students. Ask them to restate the rules positively. Discuss the reason for each rule.

2. Choose the five to eight rules that are most important to you. Ask students to illustrate each rule with two drawings: one showing the rule being followed, another showing the rule being broken. By having students work in groups for this activity, you can provide more opportunities for them to think about and discuss the rules.

3. Give students the entire list of rules and ask them to choose the five to eight most important rules.

4. Ask students to list rules and consequences they find in other classrooms or school environments. Compare their lists to your classroom rules. Discuss strategies for coping with different sets of rules and consequences.

5. Determine a final list of rules and post them for the class to see.

6. Using Figure 2.1, review the rules.

INTERPRETATION:
This activity gives students the opportunity to have a hand in creating the rules by which they must abide in the classroom. Such input affords the students ownership of the rules and should make it easier for them to follow the rules. This activity also makes the reasons behind the rules clearer. Many students find it easier to follow rules when they know the rationale.

FIGURE 2.3 Assessing Available Instructional Time

PURPOSE:

To determine actual instructional time.

DIRECTIONS:

Use this worksheet to calculate the time that is typically available for instruction during an average classroom day. Available instructional time will be the difference between the time that is allocated for instruction and the time lost due to all non-instructional activities. Time is calculated in minutes.

To calculate Allocated Time:

1. Select a day of the week at random (_____)
   Obtain the schedule for that day.
2. Enter the length of that school day (in minutes)   _____
3. Subtract time scheduled out of the classroom
   (lunch, recess, special subjects, etc.)   _____
4. Enter Allocated Time: _____

To calculate Managerial Time:

5. Estimate the time taken for: lunch count   _____
                                           attendance   _____
                                        announcements   _____
                                                other   _____
6. Enter Total Managerial Time: _____

To calculate Interruption Time:

7. Estimate the time typically taken for: visitors   _____
                                            disruptions   _____
                                                  other   _____
8. Enter Total Interruption Time: _____

To calculate Transition Time:

9. a. Time an *in-seat* transition (between two
       activities in the classroom);   _____
    b. Multiply by the estimated number of *in-seat*
       transitions.   _____
    c. Enter total *in-seat* transition time.   _____
10. a. Time an *out-of-seat* transition (between two
       activities in the classroom).   _____
    b. Multiply by the estimated number of *out-of-
       seat* transitions.   _____
    c. Enter total *out-of-seat* transition time.   _____
11. a. Time a *between classroom* transition (between
       two classrooms: homeroom to art; classroom
       to lunch);   _____
    b. Multiply by the number of *between classroom*
       transitions.   _____
    c. Enter total *between classroom* transitions.   _____
12. Total lines 9c, 10c, and 11c.   _____
13. Enter Total Transition Time: _____

To calculate Available Instructional Time:

14. Enter Allocated Time (from line 4):   _____
15. Total Managerial Interruption, and Transition
    Time (Sum of lines 6, 8, and 13).   _____
15. Subtract line 15 from line 14.   _____

Enter Available Instructional Time: _____

INTERPRETATION:

The difference between Allocated time and Available Instructional Time is the time that is lost to non-instructional activities during a typical school day. This information can be used as a starting point to evaluate the use of time in the classroom by you as the teacher.

- *Consolidate Managerial Tasks.* When possible, combine activities such as attendance, announcements, and lunch count into one regularly scheduled block of time. Develop a scheduled time or system for minimizing or eliminating interruptions from public address systems or other teachers (e.g., leave a note on the door saying *Stop back later—Learning Zone* or *Teaching in Progress*).
- *Post the Class Schedule.* Post the weekly and daily schedules. Inform students of time allocated for each activity.
- *Provide Individual Schedules.* For students who leave the classroom for other instruction and activities, provide individual schedules.
- *Provide Support.* For students who have difficulty following their schedule, provide supportive cues such as a picture of a clock. Give warnings, such as a hand signal or verbal reminder, when changes in activities are pending. Reward students who follow schedules efficiently.

As schedules are adjusted to improve the use of time and students learn to follow schedules, they will move within and between classrooms more efficiently and instructional time will increase. This time may be expanded further when transition time is managed efficiently.

TRANSITION TIME

Transition time is the time *between* tasks and activities. Transitions may occur in one place or require movement within the classroom or to a new environment. For example, students may be putting away one book and taking out another (in-seat transition), moving from a desk to the reading table (out-of seat transition), or stopping a math lesson to line up for art (between classroom transition). Most transitions average five to ten minutes, and there may be as many as ten transitions per day—a total of eighty minutes. It is easy to lose more than twenty percent of a six hour school day to transitions between instructional segments.

Transitions can be managed to enable students to move efficiently from one activity to another and also provide opportunities for student interactions. When these times are not planned or monitored, students can get in each other's way, misuse materials, make inappropriate comments, and otherwise delay and interfere with classroom routines. By evaluating and planning structured use of transition times and giving students clear rules for expected behavior, the problems typically associated with these unavoidable periods can be minimized as they become opportunities for students to act appropriately.

For many students, transitions are especially risky. Those who leave the classroom for other activities deal with transitions more frequently as they change settings. These transitions are also often more complex, involving multiple sets of peers, procedures, and expectations. It is important for the teacher to understand that transitions of this sort may be especially difficult for precisely those children who may be most vulnerable to feeling different. Further, where differences of culture or language are also present, the potential for misunderstanding is compounded. The role of the teacher in these situations is to minimize the difficulty by making the process of transition as simple and straight forward as possible. There are several ways to approach this task. Use Figure 2.4 to calculate transition time in your classroom.

To make use of the information calculated in Figure 2.4, use the following guidelines to significantly reduce transition time.

GUIDELINES
FOR TRANSITION
TIME

- *Establish Transition Rules.* Establish rules that are appropriate for all transitions: *Move quietly* or *Keep hands and feet to yourself.* Also establish rules that are unique to specific transitions such as *Put _____ away* and *get_____* , or *Move chairs quietly.* Discuss these rules with students and post them so they are seen easily.
- *Provide Cues.* As a transition time nears, provide signals and cues for students. Tell them: *The period will end in _____ minutes,* or *We will be moving to a new activity.* Ring a warning bell; put the remaining time on the board; have peers remind one another when a period is ending. Move closer to students to provide additional verbal (whispered reminders) and nonverbal cues (touch, pointing) when necessary and/or culturally appropriate.
- *Use Student Names.* Call students by name to prompt a pending transition or to enable the class to make a smooth transition. Remind students of appropriate transition behavior.
- *Teach Transition.* Model and practice transitions, especially the more difficult ones.
- *Make Transitions a Group Effort.* Reward the class for reducing transition times.
- *Facilitate Transitions.* Keep resources (books, sharpened pencils, paper, erasers, chalk, etc.) accessible.
- *Facilitate Transitions Between Classrooms.* Develop and implement similar transition procedures in both settings. If only some students are changing rooms, schedule within-classroom transitions to coincide with those that take place between classrooms. Allow sufficient time for students to make transitions. Monitor behavior in hallways. If necessary, ask peers to accompany students from one setting to another.
- *Foster Independent Management.* Have students monitor and evaluate how well they make transitions.
- *Use Transition Time to Change Moods.* Give students the opportunity to relax and shift their focus.

Use Figure 2.5 to further evaluate and plan new ways to manage transition time in your classroom.

A systematic reconsideration of your schedule and the management of transition time can help you increase available instructional time. Now you are ready to consider ways to utilize that time most efficiently and maintain high rates of student time-on-task.

TIME-ON-TASK

Time-on-task, also referred to as engaged time and academic learning time, is the time a student spends actively involved in learning. On-task students spend less time interacting inappropriately and more time interacting productively through activities such as sharing materials, exchanging ideas, and working together on complex tasks. These students are consequently perceived by their peers as competent—often a prerequisite for acceptance

FIGURE 2.4 Assessing Transition Time

PURPOSE:
To examine the use of transition time in order to plan for its reduction.

DIRECTIONS:
Using the Transition Time Journal form provided, keep a log for one or two typical days. The log is divided into fifteen minute intervals so that exact start and stop times are not necessary. Use a stopwatch to get the most accurate record of the duration of a transitional event and note it in the appropriate column: in-seat; out-of-seat; and between classroom. The column on the right is for any observations or thoughts you have on student behavior during transitions. Note any students who stand out and why.

TRANSITION TIME JOURNAL

Using the stopwatch, record the duration of each transitional event in its appropriate time period and category.

	In-Seat Transitions	Out-of Seat Transitions	Between Classroom Transitions	Notes
8:00				
8:15				
8:30				
8:45				
9:00				
9:15				
9:30				
9:45				
10:00				
10:15				
10:30				
10:45				
11:00				
11:15				
11:30				
11:45				
12:00				
12:15				
12:30				
12:45				
1:00				
1:15				

FIGURE 2.4 Assessing Transition Time *(Continued)*

	In-Seat Transitions	Out-of-Seat Transitions	Between Classroom Transitions	Notes
1:30				
1:45				
2:00				
2:15				
2:30				
2:45				
3:00				

INTERPRETATION:

When your transition observations are complete, study records and comments in the journal. Note whether there are any patterns in the types of problems students are having with transitions.

Are there certain students who experience difficulty with all transitions.

What are these students doing during transitions?

Are there certain activities or types of transitions with which many students experience difficulty?

Are there specific times of the day during which students experience more difficulty with transitions?

Are there certain subject areas that seem to cause greater transition problems?

Are there areas of the classroom in which students have greater difficulty making transitions?

Are there certain materials that students must put away or prepare that seem to lengthen transition times?

With increased awareness of transitions and their effect on students' ability to learn and interact, you can design a plan to help students manage transitions more efficiently.

FIGURE 2.5 Managing Transition Time

PURPOSE:
To teach a transition time behavior to your students.

DIRECTIONS:

1. Select one transition from those you observed in Figure 2.4.

2. Develop two to four steps to structure student behavior during this transition time. Make sure that these steps reflect the needs of your students and the constraints of your instructional space. Watch students who do manage the transition efficiently to determine the behaviors/steps needed.
   Sample:
   Transition from an individual math activity to a large group instructional session. When you hear the signal it is time to:
   1. Put away your math materials.
   2. Take out materials for reading.
   3. Stand and quietly push in your chair.
   4. Walk to the next work area.
   5. Wait quietly for instructions.

3. Have students act out these steps, then discuss their overall purpose.

4. Ask students for suggestions on how the class might make smoother transitions. If possible, incorporate their ideas into the plan.

5. Provide opportunities for guided and independent practice in making the transition. Over the next few days, remind students of the steps prior to each transition.

6. Monitor transitions.

7. Provide corrective feedback/praise. Repeat until you are satisfied that students are improving.

8. Direct students to use the same behavior for similar transitions.

INTERPRETATION:
As students become more efficient, use this method to teach and monitor other types of transitions. Frequent practice will lead to maintenance and generalization.

into groups. As a result, they are more successful both academically and socially.

As you learned from completing Figure 2.3, actual instructional time is limited. Because not all instruction succeeds in keeping all students appropriately engaged, time-on-task can be even less than total instructional time. Teachers can increase time-on-task by monitoring students during instruction. There are many aspects of on-task behavior that are easily measurable. These include verbal responses, writing, and hand raising. The Observation and Recording techniques provided in Section 2 and Appendix C are appropriate for chronicling those aspects of time-on-task that are observable and measurable. However, bear in mind that some behaviors are not easily defined as off- or on-task. For example, students looking out a window may appear to be off-task, yet they may actually be thinking through a problem. Use the following guidelines to increase time-on-task.

GUIDELINES
FOR INCREASING TIME-ON-TASK

- *Plan Starting and Stopping Times.* Select specific starting and stopping times for activities. Use a timer or stopwatch to increase student awareness of time limitations.

- *Monitor On-Task Behavior.* Ask students to help by recording their own on-task behavior or that of their peers during cooperative activities (See Chapter 3). Arrange for students who waste time to finish incomplete work at other times.

- *Match Tasks to Student Abilities.* Students are more likely to remain on-task when they are able to accomplish the task. Frustration with tasks that are too difficult or unclear and boredom with tasks that are too easy or repetitive lead to off-task behavior. When you see signs of frustration or boredom, evaluate how well the activity matches the student's ability.

- *Increase Opportunities for Active Participation.* Students who are involved in learning remain on-task. Giving students opportunities to be actively involved through cooperative learning activities, for example, increases the likelihood they will be focused on learning and completing the task.

- *Teach On-Task Behavior.* For students who experience problems remaining on-task, model appropriate on-task behavior. Help students monitor their on-task behavior. (See Section 2 for in-depth guidance on teaching individual student behaviors.)

- *Praise/Reward On-Task Behavior.* Notice and call attention to students who are on-task and complete assignments on time. Reward teams within the class or the class as a whole for improvements in time-on-task.

In monitoring the use of time in your classroom, you have undoubtedly observed how it is affected by the arrangement of space and furniture. This will be examined further in the next section.

SPACE

By determining movement patterns, creating instructional areas, and placing student desks to reflect expectations and teaching styles, teachers can help students remain on task longer, work more efficiently in cooperative groups, make smoother transitions, and minimize distractions. Students who have difficulty getting along with others and participating in class activities can benefit most from the thoughtful use of space in the classroom because furniture placement and the location of activities influence how and with whom students interact. Sufficient work space can also contribute to fewer instances of disruptive behavior.

Teachers can encourage or discourage socially appropriate behavior by seating students near or away from certain peers. For students who lack the skills to interact with their peers, or who simply need to practice social skills, sitting near those who are socially competent may provide opportunities to observe, model, and receive cues and feedback for appropriate behavior. Seating students with friends or role models can provide a natural motivation to work together in more socially appropriate ways. Students who hesitate to approach and work with others can benefit from arrangements where they can watch more socially skilled peers. On the other hand, physically separating students who tend to have conflicts with one another may reduce disruptions and provide fewer models of inappropriate social behavior. (See Chapter 3 for additional information on ways to group students.)

Although space arrangements are limited by the fixed locations of doorways, electrical outlets, storage areas, the number of students, and the amount of space available, teachers can still arrange their moveable classroom furniture and plan activities to take advantage of their teaching style and to also accommodate student needs. Activities to determine your preferred teaching style should be completed before redesigning your classroom space (See Chapter 1).

Teachers generally arrange their classrooms into distinctive but customary patterns that reflect their preferred teaching style. Figure 2.6 shows four typical classroom arrangements and the influence each might have on the focus of attention, instruction, activities, movement, and opportunities for student collaboration. By evaluating your own needs and those of your students, you can select features from the different arrangements that will enable you to reach instructional goals more effectively and promote the acquisition of social skills.

Teachers who use an authoritarian style often prefer to be the focus of attention and use large group instruction and teacher-directed activities. These teachers might arrange student desks in ordered rows with students facing the teacher (Types 1 and 2). Such arrangements offer students fewer opportunities to talk and interact with one another.

Less structured arrangements (Types 3 and 4) are more suitable for less authoritarian teachers who feel comfortable with letting students be the focus of attention and permitting more interaction. Small clusters of desks, open spaces, or tables spaced throughout the classroom are suitable for these types of teachers. They may not even have a desk of their own in the classroom.

When teachers arrange desks in rows (Types 1 and 2), students might be physically closer but less able to move around without distracting one another. It may be more difficult, for example, to get to the pencil sharpener without bothering other students. On the other hand, classrooms with more open spaces (Types 2, 3, and 4) may enable students to move around too freely. Carefully evaluate how and when students need to move around and then try to accommodate their needs without creating opportunities for disruptive behavior.

Classroom arrangements can also create opportunities for students to work together. When desks are separated (Type 1), opportunities to look at each other and interact are minimized. Students have fewer opportunities to talk and will be forced to work more independently. When desks are side

FIGURE 2.6 Classroom Arrangements

TYPE OF CLASSROOM

CHARACTERISTICS

1.

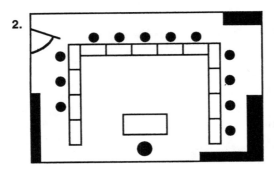

- Focus: teacher
- Instruction: large group
- Activities: teacher-directed
- Movement: restricted
- Student collaboration: minimized

2.

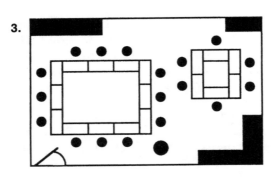

- Focus: teacher
- Instruction: large group
- Activities: teacher-directed
- Movement: less restricted
- Student collaboration: limited

3.

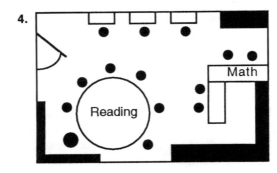

- Focus: student and teacher
- Instruction: individual: small/large group
- Activities: teacher- or student-directed
- Movement: possible
- Student collaboration: frequent

4.

- Focus: students
- Instruction: individual or small group
- Activities: teacher- or student-directed
- Movement: required
- Student collaboration: maximized

by side or arranged in clusters so that students face one another (Types 2, 3, and 4), students have more opportunities for eye contact and talk with peers while they work. With such arrangements, students can take advantage of opportunities to observe and practice social skills. They may be able to sit with their friends and interact socially while accomplishing academic tasks.

Being mindful of changing academic and social needs—sometimes within the same day—and differing student abilities in adjusting to changing arrangements is important when planning the arrangements of space. It is also important to pair students who are competent and cooperative with those who may hesitate to join group activities. Some students may function better alone for one type of activity, but benefit from interacting with peers during another. Use the following guidelines to plan space arrangements in your classroom.

GUIDELINES
FOR ARRANGING
CLASSROOM
SPACE

- *Be Aware of the Location of Each Student.* Monitor the placement of students who may be more difficult to manage or teach. Students who are seated farther from the focus of instruction tend to receive less positive and more negative teacher attention.

- *Maintain a Clear View.* Arrange the classroom so that students and teachers have a clear view of each other and teachers can monitor activities and changing needs.

- *Monitor Peer Relationships.* Remain flexible and open to changes in seating arrangements since student friendships and alliances change frequently. Change seating arrangements to encourage or discourage relationships among students. Group students who will work/play with one another to foster productive interactions.

- *Accommodate Individual Needs.* Survey students about their personal preferences and needs. They may need a quiet corner or a place to use the tape recorder. Notify students of changes in classroom space before they occur. You should also take into account the cultural preferences or needs of students who may be unwilling or unable to articulate them.

- *Monitor Traffic.* Keep heavily trafficked areas free of congestion. Students should be able to reach pencil sharpeners, group work areas, bookshelves, computers, and the teacher's desk easily. Seat students who are easily distracted or who disrupt others away from heavily trafficked areas.

Careful planning can enhance opportunities for students to act more appropriately and prevent a variety of problems from occurring. By assessing the use of space in the classroom, teachers can both accommodate its limits and maximize its potential. Figure 2.7 will help you to determine the uses of your classroom and the needs of the users. Additionally, it helps you to consider limitations and whether these can be changed. You can use Figure 2.8 to try out different space arrangements.

Classroom rules, time, and space can all be used to improve social competence without requiring intervention for individual students. Student input can be used to assess the current use of these factors and to incorporate changes. Decisions should be made on the basis of student needs, your teaching styles, and the physical and administrative requirements of the school. Whatever choices are made, clear guidelines will help students to act more appropriately and productively. In the next chapter you will learn how the delivery of instruction may inhibit or promote productive student interactions as well as academic achievement.

FIGURE 2.7 Assessing Space

PURPOSE:
This activity can be used to assess the physical environment of your classroom and the needs of its users.

DIRECTIONS:
Consider the following questions:
1. Who uses the classroom?

   students

   adults

2. What activities take place in this classroom?

   instruction

   indoor recess

   afterschool programs

   other classes or tutoring

3. Are there factors that enhance or interfere with classroom activities?
   fixed/movable items such as doors, closets, built-in furnite, chalkboards, bulletin boards, sinks)

   lighting

   ventilation

   heat

   noise

   electrical outlets

   movement patterns

   other

4. Are special accommodations needed?
   wheelchairs

   equipment

   bathrooms

   other

INTERPRETATION:
This activity will give added insight on how the use of classroom space may enhance or hinder instruction, learning, and social interactions.

FIGURE 2.8 Creating a Classroom Model

PURPOSE:
To use a model to consider alternative arrangements of classroom space.

DIRECTIONS:
Copy the models of classroom furniture. Cut apart and use with graph paper to create different classroom arrangements. Label moveable and stationary features, instructional areas, students' desks, etc. Consider movement patterns.

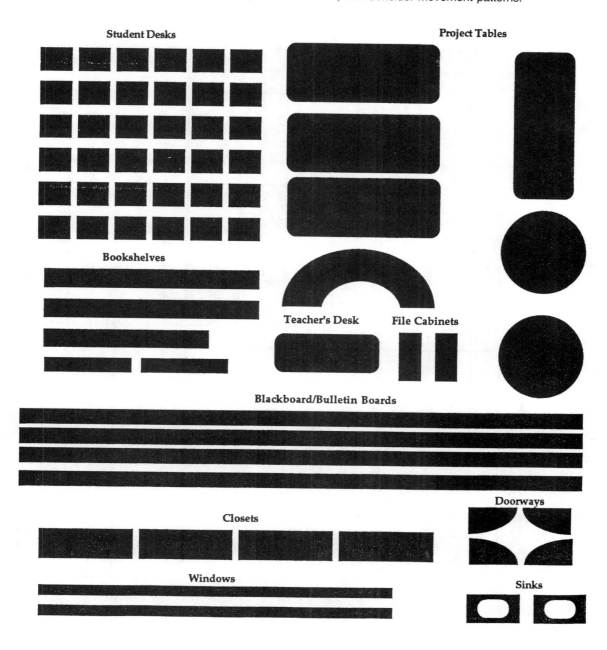

FIGURE 2.8 Creating a Classroom Model *(Continued)*

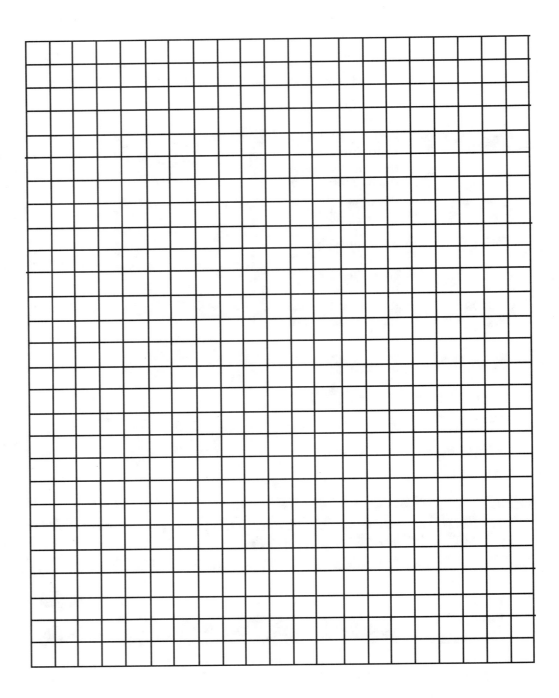

CHAPTER 3

INSTRUCTION

OVERVIEW

In the previous chapters, you have learned how proactive classroom changes that affect all students can be beneficial to those students who experience problems in their relationships with others. Having dealt with the factors related to the teacher—expectations and styles—and the environment—rules, time, and space—in encouraging positive behavior and productive interactions, we can now turn our attention to how instruction can be arranged to foster both academic and social competence.

We tend to think of instruction mostly in terms of academic goals and objectives while, in fact, it can be designed to provide many excellent opportunities for students to interact and practice social skills while simultaneously accomplishing academic tasks. Because classroom instruction is a controlled situation, teachers can use it as a way to guide students directly into interactions and relationships that will enable them to practice, maintain, and refine their social skills and enhance positive perceptions of themselves.

In this chapter, you will become familiar with three ways in which instructional goals can be structured, with an emphasis on using cooperative goal structures and the components of interactive learning in which students use social skills to achieve both academic and cooperative outcomes. Then, techniques for designing, implementing, and evaluating instruction will be discussed. Finally, an overview of the types of classrooms in which instruction takes place in elementary schools is provided.

GOAL STRUCTURES

To deal with the diversity of instructional needs present in most classrooms, teachers can structure goals in three ways—*individually, competitively,* or *cooperatively.* When an *individual* goal structure is used, students work toward a criterion that is individually determined, based on their own levels of ability or performance. In writing a short story, one student might be evaluated on spelling and punctuation, while another would be evaluated on the use of descriptive adjectives, in addition to spelling and punctuation. Another way to structure goals individually is to use mastery levels that differ such as, 80%, 90%, or 100%, according to a student's individual needs. Individual goal structures enable teachers to set success levels for all students regardless of their place on the learning continuum. However, individual goal structures do not necessarily encourage interactions with peers nor provide opportunities to practice the social skills needed to get along with one another.

When instructional goals are structured *competitively,* students compete either with their peers or their own past performance to achieve a goal. They may quiz one another on math facts, use the computer for timed drill and practice activities, participate in a spelling bee, or take a test that is graded on a curve reflecting the range of class scores. Competitive goal structures are very effective in the mastery of facts and information that must be rapidly retrieved.

However, one student's success is often achieved at the expense of another's. Therefore, the social skills needed for competitive activities differ markedly from those needed in cooperative activities. Further, the use of competitive goal structures is sometimes a problem for students from cultures that emphasize communal and cooperative rather than competitive endeavors (Baruth & Manning, 1992).

Cooperative goal structures teach students to work with their peers cooperatively in order to achieve a goal. They work in small groups to maximize not only their own but also one another's learning. The way in which the task is structured forces them to depend on one another in order to be successful. They may share materials or resources, earn points for their group by being helpful and cooperative, be responsible for the success of everyone in the group, or tutor one another. In these activities, cooperative skills needed to get along in a group are an integral part of the learning outcomes.

Each goal structure has its place in the classroom. Individual goal structures are very effective in guiding any student, regardless of ability, toward mastery of very diverse individual goals. Competitive goal structures can effectively encourage students to move toward greater accuracy and proficiency in a variety of learning tasks. Cooperative goal structures teach students how to work together to achieve instructional goals so that everyone is successful.

While each goal structure is effective in promoting achievement, no one should be used exclusively. Unfortunately, in recent years, both individual and competitive goals have been overused, often to the exclusion of cooperative goal structures. Sometimes, during individual and competitive activities, it may appear that students are working cooperatively because they are sitting near one another or focused on the same task. However, neither the goal structure nor the physical arrangements may *require* students to cooperate.

In addition, groups are often homogeneous so that students do not have the opportunity to learn to respect diversity and utilize one another's strengths for the good of the group. Leadership is not shared. In competitively or individually structured activities, students are more likely to learn to be responsible only for themselves, an approach that will not serve them well in today's workplace—where workers need to know how to collaborate, problem-solve, and cooperate.

On the other hand, a lesson that is structured cooperatively requires students to collaborate, problem-solve, and cooperate. Students must use the same behaviors and thinking skills needed to become more socially skilled. In the course of a cooperative lesson, specific behaviors that are needed to achieve both academic and cooperative learning outcomes are described, modeled, monitored, and evaluated. A cooperative approach can help students learn behaviors and thinking skills they will need not only to become socially more competent but also a more successful learner and employee. Therefore, it would seem useful for teachers to know how to transform competitively or individually structured lessons into cooperative lessons and also how to integrate various combinations of the structures within a single lesson or activity.

Figure 3.1 illustrates that the structure of the goal does not necessarily correspond nor depend on the physical arrangement. Within any of the three goal structures, students may work alone, in a small group, or within the context of the whole class. Students seated together in a small group completing a writing assignment may be working toward individual or competitive goals, while students in a large group might be evaluated competitively or cooperatively for their contributions to an ongoing discussion. It is

FIGURE 3.1 Physical Arrangements and Goal Structures

Physical Arrangements

Independent
(by myself)

Small Group
(with you)

Large Group
(with you)

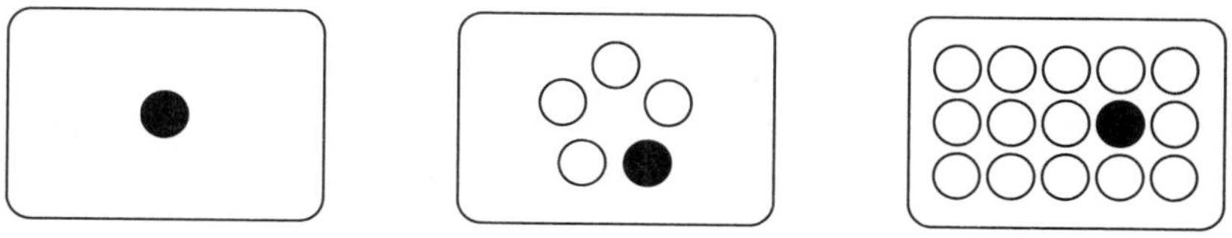

**Goal
Structures**

Independent
(for me)

Independent	Small Group	Large Group
Writing a report	Writing a report	Writing a report
Drilling and practicing	Drilling and practicing	Listening to a lecture
Using a computer	Modeling	Taking a mastery-based
Correcting	Coaching	test
Swinging	Tutoring	Taking notes
Reading a book	Reading a book	

Cooperative
(for us)

Writing a report	Brainstorming	Working on a project
Making a puzzle	Discussing	Listening to a lecture
Staying on task	Playing a role	Taking a mastery-based
Following directions	Drawing a mural	test
Correcting papers	Tutoring peers	Taking notes
Jumping rope	Jumping rope	Singing a song

Competitive
(vs. you)

Taking a test	Spelling in a bee	Playing volleyball
Studying	Playing basketball	Taking a test
Writing a report	Reading group	Discussing issues
Solving a problem	Playing a board game	Reviewing for a test
Reading a book	Using the computer	Understanding directions
Memorizing facts	Discussing issues	

important to note that, while students may observe and model their peers during a small or large group activity, physical proximity alone does not guarantee that students will use cooperative social skills.

In a cooperatively structured task, a small group of students might be assigned to produce a report on the foods of American colonists. Two students visit the library to find research materials, two plan and outline the presentation, and two others begin illustrations.

A large group such as a class, may decide to produce a play for the entire school. Although the students learn their parts individually and work in small groups to create scenery, write invitations, and rehearse, the culmination of all the activity is the large group presentation in which each student contributes to the achievement of a cooperative group goal.

Figure 3.1 also shows that it is possible to structure the same task according to any of the three goal structures and to use any physical arrangement in accomplishing the task. Students who are writing a report may be evaluated according to individually unique criteria, in comparison to peer products, or on the basis of the one product as part of a larger cooperative collection. They may write the report when they are alone or sitting with peers in a small or large group.

It is possible to transform individual or competitive instructional goals into cooperative goals. For example, students might work alone to fulfill individual objectives, with each student's work contributing to the achievement of a group goal. Once students complete the individual goal of writing an autobiography, they might work together to design a class book containing every student's autobiography. Individual students might paint different sections of a mural for the whole class to present at an open house for their parents. Similarly, while students compete to improve their own speed in reciting math facts, their individual achievement or improvement scores could be transformed to a composite score for the entire team or class. This allows students to work at their own level while earning improvement points for their team.

By using Figure 3.2 you can determine how much of your current instruction is truly cooperative. You may also wish to think about how activities you traditionally structure according to competitive or individual goal structures might be redesigned as activities with cooperative goal structures.

Of the three goal structures, cooperatively structured activities offer students the best opportunity to learn and practice cooperative social skills and become valued members of a group. Both social and academic competence can improve. Students can learn how to take the perspective of others, take greater responsibility for their own learning, increase their sense of self-esteem and self-efficacy, and consequently have greater expectations for future success. Academic success becomes the norm among peers, and attitudes toward school, subject areas, and peers become more positive. Students are more motivated, stay on-task longer, and learn to use critical thinking and problem-solving skills across instructional areas.

COMPONENTS OF COOPERATIVE LEARNING

In recent years, several authors have translated the notion of cooperative goal structures into the concept of cooperative learning. Aronson, Sharon and Sharon, as well as Slavin and his colleagues have developed strategies and curricula for teachers to use in planning cooperative learning lessons. These programs span both student ages and curricular areas (math, language arts, social studies, reading, and writing). Many are also adaptable across curricula. Figure 3.3 provides an overview of each of these models.

FIGURE 3.2 Assessing Your Use of Physical Arrangements and Goal Structures

PURPOSE:
To identify your use of the different types of physical arrangements and goal structures.

DIRECTIONS:
Select a typical day in your classroom. List the lesson or activity in the first column. Then record in columns 2 and 3 the physical arrangement and goal structure for each lesson activity. Examples are given.

Lesson Content	Physical Arrangement	Goal Structure
Handwriting	Individual	Individual
Reading	Small Group	Individual
Spelling Test	Large Group	Competitive
Science	Pairs	Cooperative

Count and fill in your totals in each category:

	Individual	Competitive	Cooperative
Individual			
Small Group			
Large Group			

INTERPRETATION:

Look over your results. Doing this exercise may point out that you are using some physical or goal structures more frequently and not taking advantage of others. If you want to increase your use of cooperative goal structures information about Cooperative Learning (Chapter 3) and Peer Tutoring (Appendix C) may be helpful.

FIGURE 3.3 Cooperative Learning Models

Model	Grade	Topic	Group Composition	Instructional Sequence	Authors
STAD Student Teams and Achievement Division	2–MA	Math Language Arts Social Studies Adaptable across the curriculum	Heterogeneous 4 members Individual quizzes 4–5 class periods	T: Present lesson S: Practice in teams	Slavin (1978)
TAI Team-Assisted Individualization	3–6+	Math	Heterogeneous 4 members	T: Present individual/ small group lesson S: Peer tutor, Check work Unit tests (individual)	Slavin, Leavey, and Madden (1984)
TGT Teams Games Tournaments	Adaptable	Adaptable	Heterogeneous 4 members	T: Present lesson S: Practice in teams, Weekly tournament with matched teams	DeVries and Slavin (1978)
CIRC Cooperative Integrated Reading Composition	3–5	Reading Writing	Heterogeneous teams of homogeneous pairs	T: Teach S: Practice with peers Quiz	Madden, Slavin, and Stevens (1986)
Jigsaw I	Adaptable	Adaptable	6 members	S: Study Teach one another own sections of material	Aronson, Blaney, Stephan, Sikes, and Snapp (1978)
Jigsaw II	Adaptable	Adaptable	6 members	S: Study Topic experts teach one another Individual quizzes	Slavin (1986)
Group Investigation	Adaptable	Social Studies	2–6 members	T: Advisor S: Select groups Select topics Complete individual tasks Report to group Group reports/products	Sharan and Sharan (1976)
Learning Together	Adaptable	Adaptable	4–5 members	T: Sets up discussions and activities S: Discuss, collaborate to solve problems, produce product	Johnson and Johnson (1986)

T = Teacher
S = Student

While all these models and programs have similar features, Johnson and Johnson's model incorporates five critically important components to ensure that learning activities are cooperative and students are successful. These components are positive interdependence, individual accountability, face-to-face interaction, cooperative skills, and group processing. Unless each component is included, there is no guarantee that students will be working cooperatively. We suggest that when these five components are integrated, students have more opportunities to interact productively and practice social skills. In the following sections, each component will be described and a framework provided to plan, implement, and evaluate cooperative activities.

POSITIVE INTERDEPENDENCE

Positive interdependence is the most important component because it forces students to rely on one another and requires interactions, thereby giving students actual opportunities to practice social skills. Teachers can ensure positive interdependence by structuring learning outcomes, rewards, resources, roles, group identity, and the environment so that students have to learn from and with one another.

Learning outcomes are structured in two ways—academic outcomes and cooperative outcomes. Students can be evaluated on the basis of one culminating product, individual academic products, or a combination of the two. Students can also be evaluated (during and following a lesson) on their use of specific cooperative skills or behaviors.

When structuring rewards, consider both their basis and their structures. Rewards can be based on academic and/or cooperative outcomes. In each case, either achievement and/or improvement can be rewarded. For example, each member of a group may be expected to demonstrate individual improvement on a spelling post-test. In addition, however, the group may earn points for its demonstration of specific cooperative behaviors during practice activities. Structure is the second consideration in planning rewards. There are many grading options: group score, individual score, total individual scores, average individual scores, random selection, lowest score, and/or bonus points. These may be used in isolation or combination to ensure that all members of the group are responsible in part for the group grade, as well as their own individual grade.

Some teachers prefer to use the points earned by groups as the basis for special activities such as pizza party, extra time with the computers, a special project, or a class auction. Others incorporate these points into a grading system where cooperation comprises a portion of the academic grade. If you decide to use this approach, documenting student behaviors is even more essential. It may be wise to discuss your rationale and policies with your administrators and students' parents.

By rationing resources, students have to use cooperative social skills such as sharing, taking turns, and assuming responsibility in order to complete a cooperative task. Giving a group only one pair of scissors, one copy of the paragraph to be reorganized, one page of the chapter, or one segment of an assignment necessitates that students interact with and rely on one another.

Roles within groups can also be structured to facilitate positive interdependence. Roles will depend on the requirements of the task. In some lessons a reader is needed and in others, a recorder. Other roles to consider are leader, encourager, monitor, help-getter, noise-controller, and resource/material supplier.

There are some additional considerations when planning to ensure positive interdependence. It may help groups to come together as a unit more quickly if they select a group name, motto, song, or flag. Rewarding groups for inter-group cooperation can encourage group interdependence. Finally, the ways in which the environment is arranged and activities are monitored can facilitate positive interdependence. The topics addressed in Chapter 2 on the use of rules, time, and space suggest arrangements to facilitate cooperative activities. Figure 3.4 can be used to determine whether you already use any of these features in your instructional activities.

INDIVIDUAL ACCOUNTABILITY

Cooperative learning activities emphasize group interactions and, in some cases, group projects, but they do not excuse students from being individually accountable for their learning outcomes. These learning outcomes may be social as well as academic. While rewards may be based in part on group achievement or improvement, they may also be based on individual achievement or improvement. For example, by telling a group that one student will be randomly selected to define vocabulary words, each student can feel responsible for learning the material and will work to ensure that each group member knows the material as well. Individual accountability can also be assured by telling a group that each individual component, as well as the final product, will be graded. While groups may study and practice together during the week, the test on Friday can determine the *individual* grade. Figure 3.4 can also be used to review your present methods for ensuring individual accountability through consideration of learning outcomes and rewards. As you plan cooperative learning activities, you can easily infuse grading practices you already use into group grading methods.

FACE-TO-FACE INTERACTION

To practice cooperation and social skills, students must be able to have face-to-face interactions. They need opportunities to look at one another, carry on conversations, share materials, and move about with some measure of freedom. (See Chapter 2 for the benefits of certain types of room arrangements and use Figure 2.7 to assess the use of space in your classroom.)

COOPERATIVE SKILLS

Students need to use many cooperative skills, also known as social skills, to learn cooperatively. For example, to complete a science project with academic goals, they might need to use the following social (cooperative) skills: participating in discussions, working cooperatively, and asking for help. To complete an activity with the cooperative goal of respecting the rights of others, students might need to use the following specific social skills or behaviors: sharing materials, taking turns, and listening when another person is speaking. In other words, regardless of the instructional goal, students need to use social (cooperative) skills and behaviors to succeed. Therefore, it is especially important to discuss not only the cooperative outcomes with students, but also the specific cooperative (social) skills they need during the activity. It is often useful to practice the skills and behaviors beforehand.

GROUP PROCESSING

Group processing is an integral component of successful cooperative learning. Students learn which skills and behaviors are expected, and their

FIGURE 3.4 Interdependence Checklist

PURPOSE:
To identify aspects of positive interdependence and ensure that you include as many as possible in planning cooperative learning activities.

DIRECTIONS:
Use this checklist to review current practices or plan cooperative activities. Review each item and check those that apply.

_____ Learning Outcome
Academic (written, discussion, presentation, report, play, etc.)
_____ One product _____ All products _____ Combined products
Cooperative (cooperating, discussing, completing tasks, sharing)
_____ During lesson _____ During summative discussion

_____ Rewards
Basis

Academic (mastery/criterion)
_____ Group achievement _____ Individual achievement
_____ Group improvement _____ Individual improvement

Group Process (mastery/criterion)
_____ Group achievement _____ Individual achievement
_____ Group improvement _____ Individual improvement

Structure
_____ Group score _____ Individual score _____ Bonus points
_____ Total individual scores _____ Average individual scores
_____ Random Selection _____ Lowest Score

Resources
_____ Supplies _____ Materials _____ Segmented Assignments

Roles
_____ Reader _____ Recorder
_____ Leader _____ Encourager
_____ Noise controller _____ Monitor
_____ Supplier _____ Ask for Help
_____ _____
_____ _____

Identity
_____ Name _____ Motto
_____ Flag _____ Song
_____ Intergroup _____

Environment
_____ Room Arrangement _____ Noise monitoring
_____ Activity monitoring _____ Movement monitoring

use of those skills during the activity is monitored. The teacher evaluates the overall functioning of the group. Teachers may initially assume responsibility for monitoring and evaluating the processing of the group, but students should be encouraged to take note of successes and failures during an activity, honestly evaluate their behavior, and plan for subsequent behavior during future cooperative learning activities. While some members of a group may exaggerate their successes and minimize their difficulties, other members will often state what actually happened. In this case, a teacher might make improvement on the following day an opportunity for bonus points.

At this time, it might be helpful to think back over a typical day to determine whether discussions of group process are part of what you already do. Although initially time consuming, taking the time to process group activity ultimately saves time and minimizes disruptive activity as peers learn to constructively manage peer behavior.

If each of these five components is carefully infused into lessons, students will learn cooperatively. Planning cooperative lessons takes time, and it can take years of practice to implement them successfully. In the next part of this chapter, you will learn how to plan, implement, and evaluate cooperative learning lessons, so that instruction will encourage more productive interactions and develop social competence.

PLANNING COOPERATIVE LEARNING

Cooperative learning activities involve expanding and restructuring many things that you already do when you teach. Therefore, it might be useful to review Figure 3.5. It lists commonly used peer or group activities that can provide a starting point for more structured cooperative learning activities.

Use the following guidelines to translate these activities into lessons that are structured cooperatively.

GUIDELINES
FOR USING
COOPERATIVE
LEARNING

- *Select One.* Select one subject area, one time of day, one class, or class period. One strategy is to use a peer or group activity identified in Figure 3.5.

- *Begin Immediately.* It is much easier to begin cooperative learning activities in the fall with a new class and a fresh start, so that they become the norm for the year.

- *Clarify Expectations.* Explain what will be happening when students begin cooperative learning activities. Chapter 1 describes how to set expectations that are realistic and appropriate.

- *Move Slowly.* When cooperative learning activities are going well in one area of curriculum, one time of day, one class or class period, gradually expand to another.

- *Build Peer Support.* Find ways to observe colleagues who use cooperative learning. Volunteer to demonstrate a cooperative lesson. Support one another. Share resources. Build a library of lessons. Take the time to analyze and reflect on your successes and failures together.

As we move through the following discussion, it may be useful to begin to plan a cooperative lesson. Figure 3.6 can serve as a record of your choices. This figure will help you select a subject area, determine learning outcomes, select materials, set a time frame, organize the classroom, organize groups, organize the task, implement the activity, monitor the group, evaluate student performance, and conduct a discussion.

FIGURE 3.5 Getting Started: Using What You Know

PURPOSE:
To identify activities you already use with your students that can be easily translated into cooperative learning activities.

DIRECTIONS:
Read each item. Place a checkmark beside those you already use. Think about other partner or group activities you already use. Add those in the spaces at the end of the list.

_____ Turn to Your Neighbor:
After you have talked for a few moments, students take a moment to review what they think you said with a partner.

_____ Reading Groups:
After group instruction, students complete reading assignments in groups of 2–3.

_____ Jigsaw:
Each student is the expert in one portion of the material and teaches the content to peers.

_____ Drill Partners:
Students drill and practice with each other using their individual sets of flashcards.

_____ Reading Buddies:
Students partner read aloud to a partner or a tape; partners then listen, critique, and praise.

_____ Worksheet Checkmates:
Students check one another's work. This is easily done with or without an answer sheet.

_____ Homework Checkers:
Students check one another's homework. This is easily done with or without an answer sheet.

_____ Test Reviewers:
Students help one another review for test.

_____ Composition Pairs:
Students write compositions and share responsibilities for proofreading, editing, and production.

_____ Computer Groups:
Students share computers to produce writing products or complete drill and practice activities.

_____ Book Report Pairs:
Students develop book reports together assuming different responsibilities.

_____ _____
       _____
       _____

_____ _____
       _____
       _____

INTERPRETATION:
These activities can be used as a starting point and can be expanded into cooperative learning activities.

FIGURE 3.6 Lesson Plan

PURPOSE:
Use this activity to plan cooperative lessons.

DIRECTIONS:
After reading the corresponding explanation and suggestions in the text, fill in each area.

SELECT A SUBJECT AREA:

DETERMINE LEARNING OUTCOMES:

	Expected Behaviors	Success Criteria
Academic Outcomes:		
Cooperative Outcomes:		

SELECT MATERIALS: (write quantity to be provided on line)
____ scissors ____ paste ____ glue ____ computers ____ textbooks
____ workbooks ____ worksheets ____ overhead transparencies
____ tapes _____ _____
_____ _____ _____

SET A TIME FRAME:
   Overall Project:
      How much time is required? _____
      Scheduled for: Date: _____
      Start Time: _____   Finish Time _____

   Completing Specific Task:
      How much time is required? _____
      Scheduled for: Date: _____
      Start Time: _____   Finish Time _____

   Evaluating Group Functioning:
      How much time is required? _____
      Scheduled for: Date: _____
      Start Time: _____   Finish Time _____

ORGANIZE THE CLASSROOM:
   Move furniture: _____
   Change seating: _____
   Equipment: _____
   Resources: _____

ORGANIZE GROUPS:
   Number of Groups: _____
   Size of Groups: _____
   Assign students to groups and roles to students:

Role	Group	1	2	3	4	5

Figure 3.6 Lesson Plan *(Continued)*

ORGANIZE THE TASK:
Positive Interdependence to be promoted by: _____
Delineation of roles: _____
_____
Selection and distribution of materials: _____
_____
Determination of Products: _____
_____
Individual Accountability to be promoted by:
Group grading procedure: _____
_____
Individual grading procedure: _____
_____

PROCEDURES:
How will you explain to students what you expect them to do?

How will you teach or model expected behaviors if necessary?

How will you explain the monitoring procedure?

Specify the time frame.

Provide a written evaluation form, if desired.

Check to be sure that students understand the task and their roles.

MONITOR THE GROUPS:
By: Teacher _____   Students _____
Focus: Whole Class _____   Individual Groups _____   Individuals _____
Intervention only for:
      Task assistance _____   Monitoring behavior _____
      Modeling collaborative skills _____   Other _____

EVALUATE GROUP PROCESS:
Academic Outcomes:
      Questions to ask:

      Feedback:

      Evaluation:

Cooperative Outcomes:
      Questions to ask:

      Feedback:

      Evaluation:

INTERPRETATION:
If there are gaps in your planning, this form will help you find and fill them.

SELECT A SUBJECT AREA

Begin with an instructional area in which you are comfortable and one you think is appropriate for group activities. For some teachers, this may be mathematics; for others, it may be social studies. Cooperative activities may comprise only one portion of the total lesson in a given instructional area. For example, during a math lesson you may present a problem or concept to the whole group; then have students problem-solve or practice in groups for a short period of time; and, finally, report their results and activities to the large group.

DETERMINE LEARNING OUTCOMES

Next, determine both the academic and cooperative learning outcomes—what you expect your students to accomplish during the lesson. An academic outcome might be (1) *The students will compare two historical figures,* (2) *perform long division,* (3) *read a poem aloud,* or (4) *correct misspelled words.* A cooperative outcome might be (1) *The students will demonstrate respect for the opinions of others,* (2) *share information, ideas, or materials,* or (3) *help other students learn.* (Use Figure 5.1 in Chapter 5 to identify social skills that can serve as cooperative outcomes for a lesson.)

Once academic and cooperative learning outcomes have been determined, identify the *expected behaviors* associated with each outcome and set the *criteria for success.* The behaviors associated with academic outcomes may include the completion of a worksheet, productive discussion, or a book report. The behaviors associated with a cooperative outcome may be more difficult to identify. (Use Figure 5.2 in Chapter 5 to identify social behaviors that students might use to achieve a cooperative outcome.)

You could also base your selection on your own observations of the dilemmas that students encounter, the unsuccessful behaviors they use, and the behaviors you would like to see instead. You might post two to three expected behaviors and evaluate students based on their demonstration of those behaviors during a lesson. Criteria for success may be based on factors such as how many times the behavior is performed, the duration of the behavior, or any other measure that provides useful feedback. Both academic and cooperative outcomes, their respective behaviors, and the criteria for success should be outlined and discussed with students before the cooperative portion of the lesson is begun. When students are unsure of behaviors, model and practice those behaviors for them. Students should know that both their academic and cooperative behavior will be monitored during the activity and evaluated afterwards. How the evaluation will affect their individual grade should also be explained.

SELECT MATERIALS

Determine what materials and resources will be needed for each group. Materials and resources might include such items as scissors, paste, glue, computers, textbooks, worksheets, and overhead transparencies. How these materials and resources will be organized to foster positive interdependence will be decided shortly.

SET A TIME FRAME

Cooperative activities can be as brief as ten minutes and as lengthy as an hour or more. Some projects are completed in one lesson; others span several days or weeks overall but are divided into many smaller tasks. As you plan your cooperative lesson, think about the time needed to complete the task and evaluate group functioning. Allow sufficient time so that students will not be frustrated by interruptions during the task.

ORGANIZE THE CLASSROOM

At this point, it is important to reconsider the physical arrangement of the classroom—the location of furniture, as well as equipment, resources, and materials needed. It may be helpful to refer back to Chapter 2 for ideas on how to use classroom furniture and space to facilitate face-to-face interactions.

ORGANIZE GROUPS

The structure of the groups will determine their success. Therefore, deciding on the number of groups, the size and composition of each group, and the roles that members will play are critical decisions. The size of the groups must be decided first. While the task itself may dictate the number of students needed in each group, keep in mind that it is much easier to interact in smaller groups where it is easier to be heard. This may give some students the advantage they need to practice social skills with their peers. Therefore, unless the task requires larger groups, begin with 2–3 students in a group. Then, decide on the number of groups. The number of groups in your class obviously depends on the number of students in your class and the size of the individual groups. It is best to keep groups even in number so that responsibilities are shared equally.

After the size and number of groups have been decided, roles within each group can be determined. When deciding on the roles for a cooperative activity, first consider the demands of the task. Do students need to read material, write responses, create a project, discuss information, or solve a problem? Will there be greater physical movement and noise levels? Obviously, when students are in the process of interacting, movement and noise levels are concerns. The use of noise-monitors within each group will allow several groups to function simultaneously within a limited area. The list of possible roles in Figure 3.7 may suggest some potential student roles.

Each role should be defined in simple operational terms. For example, the reader reads the paragraph to be rearranged to the group. The noise-monitor watches the (teacher controlled) noise gauge on the wall. If it approaches the red zone, monitors raise their fingers to their lips to signal other group members. Silent signals that do not create more noise work best.

For students to fulfill their roles, the responsibilities of each role must be clearly defined and, in some cases, practiced so they are understood by the students. To save time and later explanations, some teachers find it helpful to post roles and definitions on the wall or chalkboard so that students can refer to them throughout the activity and later, in group processing.

Finally, determine the composition of the groups and the role assignments within each group. Carefully assigned roles that take advantage of student strengths or promote individual social goals can provide students with opportunities to look competent among, as well as practice in the safety of, their peer group. The ability of groups to attain academic and cooperative outcomes depends on their reliance on the academic and social skills and abilities of one another. It is the heterogeneity of the groups— the mixture of abilities—that leads to interdependence; interdependence leads to interactions.

To organize students into groups that represent the academic and social diversity of your class, you may use either informal or formal methods. Informal methods include your best judgment, drawing names from a hat,

FIGURE 3.7 Student Roles

PURPOSE:
To select and define roles for a cooperative learning activity.

DIRECTIONS:
Review your lesson plan and select the roles that are appropriate. Write clear, concise definitions for each role—definitions that your students will understand and be able to fulfill.

Recorder: _____
_____

Reader: _____
_____

Encourager: _____
_____

Materials-Organizer: _____
_____

Checker: _____
_____

Runner: _____
_____

Noise-Monitor: _____
_____

Observer: _____
_____

Time-Monitor: _____
_____

Task-Monitor: _____
_____

Help-Getter: _____
_____

_____: _____
_____

_____: _____
_____

_____: _____
_____

_____: _____
_____

having students count off, using a matching game, or random selection. One teacher had a unique approach with groups of three. First she placed a high ability student in each group, then she placed a low ability student in each group. She then made sure that the third member was someone no one in the group liked. She then forced students to depend on one another positive interdependence by giving the peer who was disliked a major responsibility or key piece of information. In other words, the other students needed the third (disliked) member of the group, so they had to get along with one another. It worked beautifully.

You may also use more formal methods such as test scores, observations, or permanent products such as worksheets, or journal entries to construct groups. Preferred learning styles are another alternative in teaching students to respect differences and rely on one another to achieve a common goal. Many teachers rely on peer assessment to identify existing peer relationships and social categories.

PEER ASSESSMENT

While teachers may think they know the many aspects of students' relationships, they are frequently surprised by the results of peer assessment. The data obtained often contradict teacher assessment and student self-report. This is because students' opinions of their peers may be based on more frequent and long-standing contact. Students may also understand the demands of peer social situations better than their teachers do.

Peer assessment is a highly valid and reliable way to measure patterns of interaction that remain relatively stable over time, especially in upper elementary classrooms. While individual friendships and peer group composition may change, social categories such as rejected, isolated, and popular, are generally stable and tend to be filled by the same students throughout the year.

In peer assessment, students are asked to name or select classmates according to predetermined criteria. Students might be asked to name their best friend (a measure of friendship), rate how much they like to work or play with each classmate (a measure of acceptance), assign roles to classmates (a measure to associate behaviors with the social categories of students), or name the important persons in their lives (a measure of a student's social network).

Peer assessment can help teachers identify patterns of student interaction from the students' perspectives. Friendships and acquaintances that are reciprocal can be identified; those that are not are also revealed. Peer assessment can be used to categorize students according to their social abilities—whether they are perceived by their peers as popular, accepted, controversial, rejected, or neglected. (See Figure 3.8) This information can be used to ensure heterogeneity that is based on social competence in cooperative groups.

There are different methods of peer assessment, and teachers can choose the type most appropriate for their purpose. With some methods, students are given a list of names or a group of pictures of their classmates and are asked to rate their relationships to or categorize the role of each peer on the list. This approach enables teachers to identify popular; accepted; controversial; rejected and intentionally isolated or neglected students. However, because the name of every peer is presented, this approach does not identify the unintentionally isolated student. To identify the isolated/neglected student, students are not given a list of names but are asked to spontaneously nominate or name peers who fit certain categories such as *Who is your best friend?* or *Who do you like to work with?* The forgotten students are those not named for any category by their peers.

FIGURE 3.8 Social Categories

POPULAR:
Popular students are viewed by most of their peers as having many positive attributes. A large number of classmates consider them friends.

ACCEPTED:
Accepted students are viewed by many of their peers as having positive attributes. Many of their classmates like them.

CONTROVERSIAL:
Controversial students are viewed by most of their peers as having either many positive or many negative attributes. They evoke strong feelings. Many classmates like them and many do not. They are both accepted and rejected.

REJECTED:
Rejected students are viewed by most of their peers as having negative attributes. Many classmates do not like them.

ISOLATED/NEGLECTED;
Isolated/Neglected students are not considered by most of their peers to have either positive or negative attributes. They may be rarely mentioned, unknown, forgotten, or left out—sometimes intentionally.

Figure 3.9 is an example of peer assessment in which students are asked to rate peers as friend (F), others (O), nonfriends (N), or not known (D). With this information, teachers can determine student's social categories and see whether relationships are reciprocal.

Two additional peer assessments, the *Revised Class Play-Revised (RCP-R)* and *Social Networks* are included in Appendix C. In the RCP-R, students rate their peers according to predetermined hypothetical roles. This method enables teachers not only to categorize students and determine the reciprocity of relationships, but also associate specific behaviors with those students according to their roles. With Social Networks, students are asked to nominate peers according to varying criteria without a list of names. This method enables teachers to gain a sense of an individual student's network of friendships and a sense of relationships that may exist beyond the classroom. Sometimes these networks are much larger than teachers suspect. For example, a student with special needs may have friends in other classrooms, grades, or schools in the community. This will be especially true of students from certain cultural groups in which extended communal and multigenerational relationships are common.

Each of these peer assessment tools is designed to obtain specific information, but, do not hesitate to adapt them to meet your own needs or to answer your individual questions. For example, you might change the questions and ask students to rate peers with whom they like to work and play. You might also change the format from rating to nomination. You might also present the FOND or RCP-R in an open-ended format without a list of names. Ask students, "Who are your friends or who would fulfill the role of . . . ?"

Peer assessment may also indicate whether students with special needs or new students are being integrated into the existing social relationships and structure. It may also be used to identify and select peers with social status (popular or accepted), as viewed by their peers, who can help the isolated, controversial, or rejected student develop peer relationships.

Bear in mind however, that change takes time. The social history that students share is often more powerful than more recent (and incremental)

FIGURE 3.9 FOND

FOND:

The FOND is a method of measuring friendship designed to gain insight into the relationships of students through the ratings both given and received. Students are asked to rate classmates as F (Friend); O (Classmate is known to the student but s/he has no opinion about him or her); N (Not a friend); D (Don't know the classmate).

Teachers may choose from two forms of the FOND according to the ability of the students. Form 1 is best suited for administering to older students grades (3–6). Form 2 is more appropriate for younger students (grades K–2) or those with special needs. Administering the FOND to smaller groups of four to six students may result in more reliable and valid results.

Before teachers administer the FOND, a general script is first read to the students to introduce them to the concept of surveys. Then the teacher reads the specific script designed to accompany the FOND. Students then write their responses directly on the form.

DIRECTIONS:

For grades 4–6, use FOND: Form 1 and administer to the whole class. For younger students in grades 1–3 or for those with special needs, use FOND: Form 2 with smaller groups of four to six students. List the names of all girls on one copy of the appropriate form and the names of all boys on a second copy of the same form. Then, make a copy of the appropriate same-gender form for each student. Read the general introductory script for peer assessment before distributing the forms to students.

FORM 1: GRADES 4–6:

Introductory Script:

> *Have you ever heard of a survey? (Pause for student responses.) What do you know about surveys? (Pause for responses.) A survey usually consists of a list of questions that is used to ask people what they think or feel about something. For example, someone might telephone you to ask you to take part in a survey about the supermarkets in your community. The caller might ask you at which markets your family shops, and which one is your favorite and why. Your answers and the answers of other people may be used to improve a supermarket or to plan a new one.*

> *Today I am going to give you a survey that will ask you to think about how you get along with your classmates. The survey will take you about _____ minutes to finish. The information from the survey will help me organize groups of students that will work well together on class projects (or other activities).*

> *There are several important things you should know about surveys: one is that your answers are private or secret; another is that there are no right or wrong answers. So, you can express your honest feelings and know they will not be shared with anyone except me.*

Instructions:

> *The survey I would like you to fill out is about you and the other students in this class. The survey may be different from others you have done. Look at me and listen carefully to my directions so that you will understand what you are to do. At the top of the survey, you will find a space for your name and the date. When I give you your survey, write your name and today's date in the correct spaces as it is written on the board. If you are a boy, you will see the names of all the boys in this class on your survey. If you are a girl, you will see the names of all the girls in this class.*

> *Near the top of the survey, find the four letters-F,O,N,D.*

> *The ""F" stands for the students on the list who are your friends.*

> *The ""O" stands for others—the students whom you know, but don't feel strongly about. You may know their names, but you don't like or dislike them.*

> *The ""N" stands for those students who are not your friends.*

FIGURE 3.9 FOND *(Continued)*

The ""D" stands for those students whose names you don't recognize at all. You have no idea whose these students are.

Now look at the left–hand column. Read the question at the top of the list of names. The question asks, ""How do you feel about this person?" Notice that the names of all the girls or all the boys are listed in this column. Next to each boy's or girl's name, place a check mark under the letter that best explains the way you feel about that person. (Demonstrate how this task should be done.) If you do not want to answer, you do not have to. Be honest about how you feel. Remember that your answers are private.

When you have finished, turn your paper over and take out your . . . (independent reading book).

Allow students 15-20 minutes to complete their selections. Monitor students as they record their responses and praise those who are working appropriately. Collect forms when all students have finished. Check papers to be sure they are properly identified and completed. Begin a structured whole–class activity immediately to prevent students from sharing their responses.

FORM 2: GRADES 1–3:

Introductory Script:

Today I am going to give you a survey. Do you know what a survey is? (Pause for student responses.) A survey is a list of questions to ask people what they think or feel about something. For example, a person might ask someone in your family to take part in a survey about the supermarkets near your home. This person might ask where your family shops. He or she also might ask which market is your family's favorite and why. These answers and the answers of other people might be used to make better markets.

Today I am going to give you a survey that will ask you to think about how you get along with the students in this class. The survey will take you about _____ minutes to finish. The information from the survey will help me decide which students will work well together.

There are two important things you should know about surveys. First, your answers are private or secret. They will not be shared with anyone except me. Second, there are no right or wrong answers, so you can tell me your honest feelings.

Instructions:

The survey I am going to give you is about you and the other students in this class. This survey may be different from anything you have done before. Look at me and listen carefully to my directions. Then you will understand what you are to do. Do not write anything on the survey until I tell you to do so. (Distribute the appropriate same gender surveys to the students.)

Look at your survey. If you are a girl, do you see the names of the girls in this class on your paper? (Pause.) If you are a boy, do you see the names of the boys in this class/ (Pause.) Now look at the top of the survey. There you will see a space for your name and a space for the date. Write your name in the name space now. (Pause, allowing time for students to write their names.) Find today's date on the chalkboard. Write the date in the date space just as I have written it. (Pause. Observe students to see if they are doing this task correctly.)

Look again at the top of the survey. There you will see four faces: a face with a smile, a face with a straight mouth, a face with a frown, and a face with a question mark. Put your finger on each face as I name it: a face with a smile (Pause and monitor.) a face with a straight mouth (Pause and monitor.) a face with a frown (Pause and monitor.) and a face with a question mark (Pause and monitor.)

The face with a smile means the classmates on your list who are your friends. The face with a straight mouth means that you know these class-mates, but you don't really like them or you don't really dislike them. The

FIGURE 3.9 FOND *(Continued)*

face with a frown means those classmates who are not your friends. The face with a question mark means the classmates whose names you don't know at all. You have no idea who these classmates are. Do you have any questions about what these faces mean? (Pause, and answer questions asked.)

Now look at the left–hand side of your paper. Read the question at the top of the list of names. The question asks, ""How do you feel about this person?" If you are a girl, look at the list of girls' names; If you are a boy, look at the list of boys' names. Next to each name, make a checkmark under the face that best explains how you feel about that student. (Demonstrate for students on the chalkboard or on a transparency how this task should be done.) *For each name on your list, make a checkmark under the face that tells how you feel about him or her. Be honest about how you feel about each person on your list. Remember, your answers are private. Does anyone have any questions about what they are to do?* (Pause.) *When you have finished your survey, turn your paper face down on your desk. Then take out your . . . (independent reading book).*

SCORING:

1. Reproduce two FOND Recording Sheets (Form 3) one for the boys' forms and one for the girls'. Separate completed FOND forms by gender. In the left–hand column of each grid, list boys' or girls' names alphabetically on the appropriate grid. In the horizontal column at the top of the grid, list the names again. (Refer to the completed grid on page xxx.)
2. For one gender, record the FOND nominations given by the first student across the first row of the grid. Place an F in any box in the first row that corresponds to the name of a student selected as Friend. Since students should not nominate themselves, the first box in the first row will be blank, as well as the second box in the second row, and so on.
3. Following the same procedure described in Step 2, record Other nominations using the letter O, Not-a-Friend nominations using the letter N, and Do Not Know nominations by writing D in the appropriate boxes.
4. Repeat steps 1 & 2 for each student.
5. To determine the number of nominations each student *assigned to other classmates,* add the number of FOND nominations across the row opposite each student's name. Record these data in the far right-hand column entitled **GIVEN.**
6. To find the number of nominations each student *received from classmates,* add the number of FOND nominations down the rows. Record this information in the **RECEIVED** row at the bottom of the grid.
7. Repeat Steps 2–6 for the remaining students of this gender.
8. Repeat Steps 1–7 for the students of the other gender.

INTERPRETATION:

Data obtained from administering the FOND may help teachers understand the nature of their students' friendships. By comparing the number and type of FOND nominations received with the five Social Categories (See Figure 3.8), teachers may begin to relate FOND results to students' social functioning within the classroom.

- POPULAR students receive mostly F and some O ratings.
- ACCEPTED students receive mostly O ratings with one to two F ratings.
- CONTROVERSIAL students receive approximately equal numbers of F and N ratings.
- REJECTED students receive mostly N ratings. They may receive one or two O ratings or even an F.
- ISOLATED students may be those who receive mostly D ratings and very few, if any, F, O, or N ratings. However, because the names of these students were provided, they are not the truly forgotten/neglected students. They may be those who are beyond rejection.

A completed grid displays FOND results from a hypothetical class (female student only). Each grid contains two identical class lists: one listed vertically in the left-hand column, and the other listed horizontally across the top of the grid. The total number of nominations each student *assigned to other classmates* is

Figure 3.9 FOND *(Continued)*

apparent on the right-hand side of the recording sheet while the number of nominations each student *received from classmates* is located at the bottom of the corresponding column. Using this information, it is possible to see that Laura gave the following nominations F-2, O-8, N-1, D-0. The data reveal the number of girl classmates Laura judged as her friends (2), the number about whom she was opinionless (8), the number who were not considered friends (1), and the number of classmates whom she did not know (O). The set of numbers at the bottom of the grid reveal that she received the following nominations: F-1, O-9, N-1, D-0. These data indicate how her *classmates felt about her.* One student considered her a friend; nine were opinionless; one did not consider her a friend; and no one indicated that she was unknown. In other words, she was known by all her female classmates.

From the FOND results, one also may determine how each student felt about each classmate. By locating Student A's name in the far left-hand column and reading the grid from left to right, the nomination Student A gave to Student B can be determined. On the sample provided, notice that Laura A. indicated that Megan K. was her friend (F) although Megan K. was opinionless (O) about Laura A. This might indicate that Laura would be willing to share activities and model approriate social behavior for Megan.

The following interpretations may be made about the hypothetical class as a whole. By and large, the girls in this sample class appear to accept each other and feel friendly toward one another because there are many F and O ratings and relatively few N ratings. F ratings generally indicate some degree of closeness while the O ratings may refer to relationships that are less close, but are not unfriendly relationships.

In this class, there are a large number of girls who are well liked by their peers. The following girls may be categorized as "popular" in the class, as each received F ratings for over half the possible ratings awarded.

	F	O	N	D
Jennifer C.	6	2	0	3
Carol J.	6	4	0	1
Debbie F.	6	3	1	1
Jean R.	7	3	0	1

Two other girls, Suzanne L. (5-5-0-1) and Lisa R. (5-5-1-0) are also well-liked by their peers, even though they are not as popular as the four girls previously mentioned.

Laura A. may be categorized as an "accepted" student. Her score (1-9-1-0) indicates that almost no one has a strong opinion about her, but they all view her as a part of the class. Since Laura is only considered a "friend" by one girl (Elizabeth Q.) and is only viewed negatively by one classmate Laura is probably regarded by her peers as "O.K".

Mary E. and Diane L. each received scores of 3-5-1-2. These scores indicate that they are "accepted" among their female peers. They have a few friendships and are accepted by nearly half of their peers.

Megan K. is clearly the rejected student in this group of girls. Her rating of 1-1-8-1 indicates that she has few friends. She did not give any F ratings and had no opinion about ten of her eleven classmates. Of those ten girls, seven of them considered Megan Not-a-Friend. Megan's responses may indicate that she is not aware of her rejected status in the class. She would benefit from social skills training that would first teach her the skills she does not know, and then give her opportunities to practice those skills in the context of her peer group.

Nominations as a Friend or Not-a-Friend may be mutual; that is, one student who nominates another as a friend is in turn nominated by that peer as a frien. This reciprocity indicates that students have realistic views of their

FIGURE 3.9 FOND *(Continued)*

individual relationships. For example, the FOND data indicate that Jennifer C. and Debbie F. as well as Carol J. and Suzanne L. are mutual friends, while Laura A. and Mary E. are not. Laura A. selected Mary E. as a friend although Mary E. had no opinion of Laura A. This is an important clue to each student's functioning and indicates what his or her needs might be, especially if such reciprocity is not evidenced.

With the exception of Megan and Elizabeth, the girls in this sample class are socially well-integrated and fairly congenial. They were known by most of their classmates.

The FOND provides information regarding the friendships that exist in the classroom. Teachers may use this form of peer assessment to identify students who have friends and those who do not. As making and maintaining friendships may foster social competence, this information may help teachers ascertain how to organize social skills instruction in their classroom.

FIGURE 3.9 FOND *(Continued)*

Form 1

Name: _____   Date: _____

How do you feel about this person?   (F)   (O)   (N)   (D)

_____   _____ _____ _____ _____

_____   _____ _____ _____ _____

_____   _____ _____ _____ _____

_____   _____ _____ _____ _____

_____   _____ _____ _____ _____

_____   _____ _____ _____ _____

_____   _____ _____ _____ _____

_____   _____ _____ _____ _____

_____   _____ _____ _____ _____

_____   _____ _____ _____ _____

_____   _____ _____ _____ _____

_____   _____ _____ _____ _____

_____   _____ _____ _____ _____

_____   _____ _____ _____ _____

_____   _____ _____ _____ _____

_____   _____ _____ _____ _____

FIGURE 3.9 FOND *(Continued)*

Form 2

Name: _____   Date: _____

How do you feel about this person?   ☺   😐   ☹   ?

_____   _____ _____ _____ _____

_____   _____ _____ _____ _____

_____   _____ _____ _____ _____

_____   _____ _____ _____ _____

_____   _____ _____ _____ _____

_____   _____ _____ _____ _____

_____   _____ _____ _____ _____

_____   _____ _____ _____ _____

_____   _____ _____ _____ _____

_____   _____ _____ _____ _____

_____   _____ _____ _____ _____

_____   _____ _____ _____ _____

_____   _____ _____ _____ _____

_____   _____ _____ _____ _____

_____   _____ _____ _____ _____

_____   _____ _____ _____ _____

_____   _____ _____ _____ _____

FIGURE 3.9 FOND *(Continued)*

Form 3

FOND

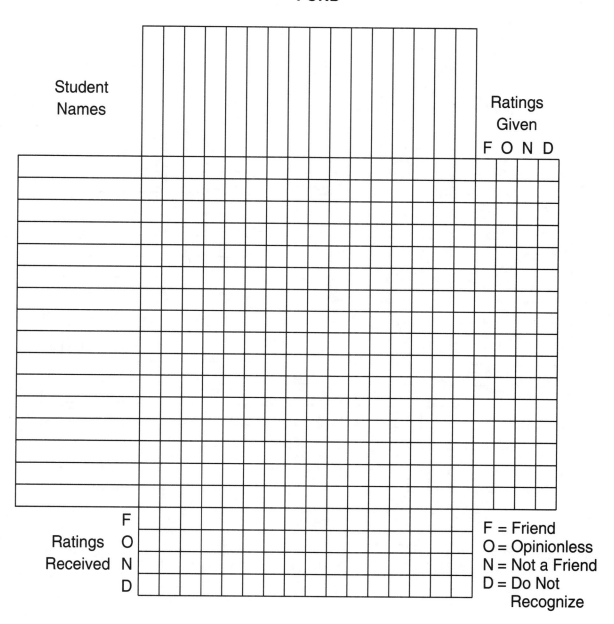

Student Names

Ratings Given

F O N D

Ratings Received

F O N D

F = Friend
O = Opinionless
N = Not a Friend
D = Do Not Recognize

FIGURE 3.9 FOND *(Continued)*

Completed FOND Grid

FOND

Student Names	Laura A.	Jennifer C.	Mary E.	Debbie F.	Carol J.	Megan K.	Suzanne L.	Diane L.	Sally O.	Elizabeth	Lisa R.	Jean R.					Ratings Given F	O	N	D
Laura A.	–	O	F	O	O	F	O	O	O	O	N	O					2	8	1	0
Jennifer C.	O	–	O	F	F	N	F	O	O	O	F	F					5	5	1	0
Mary E.	O	D	–	N	D	D	D	D	O	O	F	D					1	3	1	6
Debbie F.	O	F	O	–	F	N	F	O	O	O	F	F					5	5	1	0
Carol J.	O	F	N	F	–	N	F	O	F	O	O	F					5	4	2	0
Megan K.	O	O	O	O	O	–	O	O	O	N	O	O					0	10	1	0
Suzanne L.	O	F	O	F	F	N	–	F	F	N	O	F					6	3	2	0
Diane L.	O	F	D	F	F	O	F	–	F	D	O	F					6	3	0	2
Sally O.	O	D	O	O	F	N	O	F	–	N	F	F					4	4	2	1
Elizabeth	F.	D	F	D	O	N	O	D	O	–	F	O					3	4	1	3
Lisa R.	O	F	F	F	O	N	O	N	O	N	–	F					4	4	3	0
Jean R.	N	F	D	F	F	N	F	F	O	D	O	–					5	2	2	2
Ratings Received F	1	6	3	6	6	1	5	3	3	0	5	7								
O	9	2	5	3	4	1	5	5	8	5	5	3								
N	1	0	1	1	0	8	0	1	0	4	1	0								
D	0	3	2	1	1	1	1	2	0	2	0	1								

F = Friend
O = Opinionless
N = Not a Friend
D = Do Not Recognize

improvements in social skills. It may take a long while for peers to recognize change, forgive past behaviors, and accept students who have been unkind or unfriendly in the past; social categories tend to be fairly constant. It may also be more difficult for students in classrooms with fewer students to change categories since there is less variability with smaller numbers of peers.

It is also not clear how social status in one room relates to social status in another classroom. Chapter 4 examines other classrooms in which students spend time. You may want to conduct a peer assessment in another classroom to determine the consistency of a student's relationship or social category across settings. A student who is withdrawn in the mainstream classroom may be popular in the resource room; and as a result, may simply need encouragement rather than training to maintain and transfer social skills from one setting to another. Section 2 of this book deals with this issue in greater depth.

Information from peer assessment can be used to form cooperative learning groups. Once you recognize the friendship and acquaintance patterns and social categories in your classroom, you can create heterogeneous groups for cooperative activities to promote interaction, utilize and challenge established social categories, and foster the acceptance of diversity among your students. As an example, you might pair an isolated or rejected student with a popular or accepted student.

LEARNING STYLES

Another way to assign students to groups is to determine their learning styles, or how they prefer to approach learning tasks. Some learners prefer visual information in books, on worksheets, on a screen, or through the observation of others. Others prefer auditory input through a lecture or a taped presentation. Some need to take notes while receiving information.

Learners then process information in different ways. Some prefer to organize information from specific details toward a general idea, while others prefer to examine the whole idea or body of information before considering details. While thinking, some learners repeat (subvocalize) information to themselves. Others may close their eyes while they think. Most students develop their own strategies for organizing information. Others need to be taught.

Students can respond to information very differently; some respond impulsively while others respond reflectively. Impulsive learners dive into tasks, working quickly without focusing on accuracy. They generate many ideas in response to brainstorming activities. Reflective learners prefer to process information slowly, carefully weighing all input before responding. These learners tend to value a highly accurate performance.

Learners can express information by writing, speaking, demonstrating, or a combination of these actions. If a variety of ways to express information can be incorporated into cooperative lessons, then all students have the opportunity to demonstrate knowledge, participate, and be accurately evaluated.

Figure 3.10 may be used to identify students' preferred learning styles. This information may prove helpful in assigning group roles that take advantage of the way students prefer to learn. Activities may be arranged so that students with different styles work together according to their assigned roles. This also provides an opportunity to build interdependence by giving students key roles that will emphasize their strengths, enable their participation, stress their importance to the group, and promote an active role.

Teachers often ask how long groups should remain intact. This is an individual decision. Some teachers like to use groups that remain intact for

FIGURE 3.10 Learning Style Inventory

PURPOSE:
To identify preferred student (and teacher) learning styles.

DIRECTIONS:
Administer the inventory to students to determine your students' preferred learning styles. You may also complete this assessment yourself to increase your awareness of a learning style that influences the way you teach.

Rank each statement according to whether it matches you:
(3) most of the time . . . , (2) some of the time . . . , (1) hardly ever.
Circle the corresponding numeral.

1. I enjoy reading.	3 2 1
2. I prefer working alone on projects.	3 2 1
3. I enjoy working with my hands.	3 2 1
4. I like to work carefully and slowly.	3 2 1
5. I enjoy listen to stories.	3 2 1
6. I enjoy debates and class discussions.	3 2 1
7. I enjoy expressing myself in writing.	3 2 1
8. I'd rather get things done quickly.	3 2 1
9. I am able to get lots of information from looking at pictures.	3 2 1
10. I learn best when I am alone.	3 2 1
11. I like to participate in class discussions.	3 2 1
12. I don't really care if I make mistakes.	
13. I like to look at maps and graphs.	3 2 1
14. I enjoy studying with others.	3 2 1
15. I'd rather complete a diorama or poster than write a book report.	3 2 1
16. If I had to choose, I'd work quickly instead of accurately.	3 2 1
17. Sometimes pictures confuse me.	3 2 1
18. I seem to learn more when I work with a group.	3 2 1
19. I express myself better with words than with pictures or other graphics.	3 2 1
20. I think before I decide.	3 2 1
21. I remember what I hear.	3 2 1
22. I can concentrate better when I'm alone.	3 2 1
23. I'd rather solve math problems than discuss how they are solved.	3 2 1
24. I'd rather do the work correctly the first time than have to do it over.	3 2 1
25. I'm able to remember messages without writing them down.	3 2 1
26. I remember material best when I've studied alone.	3 2 1
27. I enjoy making things and working with my hands.	3 2 1
28. I like to complete each task correctly no matter how long it takes.	3 2 1
29. I like looking at things when I am listening.	3 2 1
30. It's harder for me to organize a big project by myself.	3 2 1
31. I enjoy talking in class.	3 2 1
32. I usually act before I think.	3 2 1

SCORING:
Write the score for each item next to its item number. Find the totals for each learning style. For each learning style, you may consider totals of 9 points or more to indicate a preferred style and totals of 5 points or less to indicate a non-preferred style.

Auditory	Visual	Social	Individual	Verbal	Nonverbal	Impulsive	Reflective
5__	1__	6__	2__	7__	3__	8__	4__
17__	9__	14__	10__	11__	15__	12__	20__
21__	13__	18__	22__	19__	23__	16__	24__
25__	29__	30__	26__	31__	27__	32__	28__
Totals							
—	—	—	—	—	—	—	—

Figure 3.10 Learning Style Inventory *(Continued)*

Plot points on the Learning Style Inventory Profile below:

4	5	6	7	8	9	10	11	12

Auditory

Social

Individual

Verbal

Nonverbal

Impulsive

Reflective

INTERPRETATION:

The above profile should reflect a preferred learning style. It may be helpful to compare your profile with those of your students, especially students who concern you. Differences may be reflected in learning problems they experience. Changing in the way you teach may help students learn more successfully.

an entire year. Others change groups according to academic areas and changing student needs (academic and social). With younger students, friendships change more rapidly; therefore, groups may need to shift more frequently. Some teachers believe that every student should have an opportunity to work with every other student. The choice depends on the purpose of a group, the ages and abilities of your students, and your own best judgment.

You can use social relationships and learning styles, as well as academic ability, gender, and ethnicity to create heterogeneous groups. Consider your overall academic and cooperative outcomes for this activity. Does a particular student need practice in a leadership role or does another student need to be included in a group? You may assign students to roles you have already determined, or if students need to take more responsibility for themselves, allow them to select roles within their own group.

ORGANIZE THE TASK

The next step is to organize the task to ensure positive interdependence, individual accountability, and clearly delineated procedures. This is possible through the specification of student roles, the selection and distribution of materials, and the determination of products and grading procedures. (Refer to Figure 3.4 for specific ideas to use in your lesson plan). Positive interdependence can be managed through the assignment of roles with specific task responsibilities. Each person might be responsible for a specific part of the assignment or for teaching specific content to peers. Decide whether to make tasks sequential or simultaneous. The initiation of one person's task might depend on the completion of another's. If some tasks are sequential, consider what students will be doing while they are waiting for their turn.

Interdependence can also be ensured by limiting the materials provided to students. You may decide to give a different portion of a chapter to each student with the responsibility of becoming an expert and teaching his or her peers. You might provide only one pair of scissors, one pencil, or one ruler so that students will need to take turns, wait, and share materials.

Individual accountability can be arranged either through the product/s of the activity or through grading policies. Students may be graded on one group product or their own individual product, or a combination of the two. These products provide evidence of both academic and cooperative outcomes. Group grades provide only a portion of a student's final grade in an academic area. Individual accountability is ensured through individual tests or products and provides individual grades. Grading options might include an individual score plus bonus points for all members meeting criterion, the lowest score, a group average, improvement scores, the total of individual scores, the average of individual scores plus bonus points for cooperation, dual academic/cooperative scores, a group score on single product, and random product selection. Once you have selected a subject area, determined academic and cooperative outcomes, scheduled time, selected materials, organized groups, the classroom, and the task, you are ready to implement your cooperative learning activity.

IMPLEMENT THE ACTIVITY

As you begin the lesson, outline and discuss academic and cooperative outcomes, expected behaviors, and criteria for success. Use the Procedures section of the lesson plan as a guide to explain the cooperative activity. Tell your students what you expect them to do. If they do not seem to know what showing respect for one another looks and sounds like, take the time to teach it. Specify the criteria you have set for success—both individual and group, academic and cooperative—and inform students as to monitoring procedures. List specific behaviors you expect to see on an evaluation form. Figure 3.11 can be used either by the teacher or students to record the occurrence of expected behaviors within groups.

Clarify the structure of the task (materials, resources, responsibilities, and roles). It is important for students to understand that they will be discussing and evaluating how well they demonstrate the expected behaviors. You may want to have a practice or simulation session. Give students a time frame for the activity and check for understanding. If you are confident that they are ready, tell them to begin.

MONITOR THE GROUPS

Once groups are in action, your role is to monitor group process. Simply placing students together does not ensure that cooperation will take place or that it will be worthwhile. Move around and observe the groups. Intervene or teach only when necessary.

Look for and record expected behaviors when they occur. Ensure that group members are fulfilling their roles and that the group is on-task. Watch for students who do not understand the task and their responsibilities. As groups become more skilled, encourage students to monitor group process and record instances of expected cooperative behaviors.

Deciding when to intervene is your individual decision and should be based on your knowledge of your students and your tolerance level. Sometimes, it is more important to allow the group to resolve its problem without your intervention. You may decide that students need assistance with the task, reminders to stay on task, or specific instruction in collaborative skills. As an intermediate step, you might ask the *encourager* or the *task manager* whether the group is on task or getting along and what suggestions he or she might have to resolve the difficulty. Moving groups toward finding their own solutions to problems encourages students to rely on themselves and on one another.

EVALUATE GROUP PROCESS

Teachers have always evaluated students to determine whether they have met instructional objectives. This evaluation is typically based on a product or demonstration that is then translated into a score or grade. Traditionally, evaluation has been the teacher's responsibility and has focused on academic outcomes.

Evaluating cooperative learning lessons may certainly include these traditional methods. However, a discussion of group process is an additional and critically important component of evaluation. During this discussion, teachers and students *share* responsibility for evaluating *both* cooperative and academic outcomes. Discussing outcomes together provides *closure* to a cooperative activity and helps teachers and students determine outcomes for future lessons. Group discussions also provide excellent opportunities for practicing and modeling appropriate responding and listening behaviors such as eye contact, listening, taking turns, and maintaining a conversation. Finally, students learn that everyone has problems at some time and that finding solutions are possible and highly probable when they are members of a group.

This discussion is conducted immediately following the cooperative learning activity because students are more likely to remember issues and

FIGURE 3.11 Observation Record

PURPOSE:
Use this observation sheet to record data during cooperative group activities.

DIRECTIONS:
In the left-hand column, enter the expected behaviors for the lesson. To monitor group behavior, enter the group names or numbers in the top row. To monitor individual behavior, enter the student names in the top row. Tally the occurrence of each behavior.

Group or Individual Names

Expected Behavior						

INTERPRETATION:
Use this information during processing discussion for evaluation or grading. Encourage students to monitor and evaluate their own behavior and that of the group.

specific examples of behaviors that occurred. During the discussion, focus on both the learning outcomes and how the groups functioned. Students should be able to evaluate both in order to plan the next cooperative learning activity. Use Figure 3.12 to develop an outline for your discussion. It includes examples of lower- and higher-order questions that also use student names in various ways.

Review academic and cooperative outcomes separately. Ask students whether their group achieved their outcomes and ask them for examples to justify their answers. Review the expected behaviors associated with each outcome. Ask students whether they saw expected behaviors in their groups and, again, ask for specific examples. At this point, you may wish to show your Observation Record (Figure 3.11). If students have collected data, ask them to share their information with the class. Discuss how many times students were observed demonstrating expected behaviors. Encourage students to talk about not only how much they did, but how well they did it. Finally, reward achievement and/or improvement according to your original plan for positive interdependence. Reward group points, privileges, or grades for demonstrating expected behaviors.

The coaching procedures outlined in Chapter 4 include questioning as a strategy within the Action phase of each coaching activity to help students think about their actions and how they can change their behavior. This framework can be adapted for processing cooperative learning activities. Teachers ask groups whether they attained any of the academic and cooperative outcomes and what it was about the group's functioning that contributed to the outcomes.

The expected behaviors discussed during the presentation/initiation phase of the lesson can then be used as part of evaluation. The following guidelines may be useful as you plan the evaluation discussion that follows a cooperative learning activity.

GUIDELINES
FOR EVALUATING
COOPERATIVE
LEARNING
ACTIVITIES

- *Take Time to Process.* It may only take two to three minutes at the end of a lesson or day. It is well worth the time and essential to the success of future cooperative learning activities.

- *Include as Many Students as Possible.* When students are included in the discussion, they learn they are valued members of the group and what they have to say has value and importance. For students who need to practice social skills, the experience of responding competently and having their responses accepted exposes them to feelings of accomplishment, helps develop their sense of self-efficacy, and also improves their self-confidence in social situations.

- *Adapt Questions to Individual Students.* Vary the level and type of questions so that all students, regardless of ability, can respond appropriately. Use lower-order or convergent questions to promote the participation of students who usually do not participate. Use higher-order or divergent questions to promote thinking skills, and consider consequences, justifications, or explanations.

- *Provide Time for Students to Think.* Give students time to think about their responses. This helps students learn to answer less impulsively, think more critically, and respond more meaningfully. Wait time is especially beneficial for students who need additional processing time or encouragement to use information they know.

- *Use Student Names.* Carefully infusing students' names before, during, and following questions can reduce inattention and interruptions,

FIGURE 3.12 Conducting a Group Discussion

	Lower-Order Convergent Questions *(did, do, is, can, which, will, what, would, should?)*	**Higher-Order Divergent Questions** *(how, why, if, what if, what could, why do you think, why should?)*
Evaluate Learning	What were the academic learning outcomes, Sam? What were the cooperative learning outcomes? Did your group achieve the academic/learning outcomes?	How do you know your group achieved . . . ? Why do you think your group achieved . . . ? How could you tell that Michael was being cooperative?
Evaluate Expected Behaviors	Which person in the group used *listening*? Did everyone in the group share materials?	How did *listening* enable your group to reach its learning outcome? Why was sharing materials so important in this activity?
Evaluate Roles	Did Susan monitor the noise? Did she do a good job?	Why do you think she did a good/poor job/ How do you think you could fulfill your role better next time?
Evaluate Group Process	Did your group work well together? Jeannie, give me an example to support his answer. Was Jackie in your group? Did she know all the members of the group? What happened?	Why was your group successful? What if your group had been on-task? Why did you decide to do it that way? Could you think of another way for your group to resolve that problem? How do you think she felt, John, when the other members of the group ignored her during the activity?

communicate the expectation that everyone participates, maintains the focus of instruction, and let students know that their responses are appropriate and appreciated.

- *Listen to Student Responses.* While students are speaking, model effective listening and respect for each student's opinion. Also, listen to language skills, pinpoint areas of strength and weakness, and note feelings and attitudes.

- *Be Supportive When Students Discuss Problems.* Remind students that experiencing problems is OK as long as we learn from our mistakes. Help them focus on behaviors, not personalities.

One way to introduce cooperative learning to both yourself and your class is through peer tutoring. Using this technique, students teach each other academic and social skills by working in pairs. One acts as the tutor, and the other is the tutee. Most of the planning, implementation, and evaluation methods you have learned about cooperative learning can be used for peer tutoring. Appendix C provides more specific information about how to use peer tutoring to promote and practice cooperative learning.

As you have learned in this chapter, instruction in any subject area can be designed to promote interactions that provide opportunities to practice social skills. In Chapter 4 you will learn more about how to create a productive and friendly classroom climate in which interactive instruction can flourish. In this and the two preceding chapters, we have focused mostly on your classroom, as if it were the only place in which your students spend time during the school day. In the following chapter, you will also learn to examine the other environments that your students experience in school, and to work towards coordinating the changes you make in your classroom with the rest of the school community.

The content of this chapter is based primarily on the work of Johnson and Johnson (See References). See Additional Resources for an extensive list of articles and books on the topic of cooperative learning.

CHAPTER 4

THE CLASSROOM

OVERVIEW

In the course of a typical schoolday, students move through many academic and nonacademic settings. These settings may include other classrooms, the lunchroom, playground, gymnasium, as well as areas for art, music, science, and specialized instructional support. As they move from one setting to another, students must cope with different expectations for behavior and interact with different individuals and groups of peers. As you learned in previous chapters, teacher expectations, rules, space, time, and instruction vary.

These factors also combine in unique ways to create a classroom climate. When the climate is positive, students expect each other to do well, they support one another and, at the same time, respect individual feelings and differences.

Chapter 4 considers the value of a positive classroom climate in promoting productive peer relationships. You can use this chapter to assess the climate in your classroom and consider changes aimed at creating and maintaining a positive climate. Then, because students change settings throughout their school day, you can consider the characteristics of other areas in which students must function in order to identify the specific features of those settings that may enable students to function more successfully.

CLASSROOM CLIMATE

A positive classroom climate is characterized by cooperation, achievement, efficiency, inclusion, involvement, responsibility, and harmony among all its members. Supportive classrooms in which appropriate social interactions are structured and encouraged are conducive to learning and inappropriate and disruptive interactions are reduced and prevented. Teachers can spend more time teaching and less time managing behavior, while students can spend more time learning and feeling good about themselves.

When students have positive and productive interactions, they also learn to develop and maintain peer relationships. Some students who lack social skills or self-confidence need opportunities to practice interacting with their peers. In some instances, they may become more competent simply by watching and modeling more competent peers. Correspondingly, more socially competent students gain additional confidence by serving as role models.

Positive classroom climates encourage students to use social skills confidently while also accomplishing academic tasks. In positive climates, students expect each other to do their best, support one another, and respect individual differences. They also believe their views are heard by their teachers and peers and, in turn, value their classmates as competent contributors. Students are more likely to have confidence in themselves and feel positive about school. Because students who are socially competent do not need to act inappropriately, productive interactions are more likely to occur and potential behavior problems are avoided. Students learn that cooperating and using social skills help them achieve academic tasks and gain acceptance from their peers.

In contrast, negative classroom climates hinder student growth and development. In these classroom, students are less likely to be socially or academically competent. They have fewer opportunities to interact and, when they do, their interactions tend to be inappropriate or negative. Students are frequently off-task and learn inappropriate behavior from one another. When students and their teachers do not value or respect each other as contributors, the management of inappropriate behavior becomes a primary concern. Feelings are easily hurt, self-confidence is consistently undermined, and the general mood is not conducive to learning and feeling comfortable in school. Without mutual support, members of classrooms with negative climates are less able to learn and achieve, either academically or socially.

Creating and maintaining a positive classroom climate is a constantly evolving and changing process. It takes time and perseverance, especially now that classrooms are becoming increasingly diverse. As greater numbers of students with special instructional needs are being included in general education classrooms for greater periods of time, clearly, there is a need to understand and accept differences. For some, these changes in attitude may take time to develop or change. Focusing on the classroom and the creation of a positive climate may encourage students to get along with one another and reduce the need to intervene with students on an individual basis. Ultimately, considering the classroom first, as suggested in these first four chapters, may be the most effective and efficient way to help most students improve their social competence.

Figure 4.1 can be used to assess the climate in your own classroom by observing student interactions, interviewing students, or reflecting on one's own personal experiences. The content of this activity highlights student behaviors that reflect positive or negative classroom climates. By identifying areas of strength or concern, and making appropriate modifications, you can foster a positive classroom climate in which all students will be more likely to engage in productive social interactions. Results from this activity may reveal factors present in your classroom that contribute to the climate. You may use the items in the checklist together with Figure 4.2 to design activities that promote a more positive classroom climate.

For more individualized interventions, consider changes in the ways students are paired and grouped. See Chapter 3 to facilitate productive interactions and reduce those that may be disruptive. You might change seating arrangements or make partner and group assignments that pair up contributors with those who are excluded. This is only a general rule. By experimenting with different ways to pair students, you may find some unlikely combinations that work. You can also give excluded students more specific classroom responsibilities. Students who are included in group activities develop feelings of belonging to the group and attempt to meet the group's expectations. As groups stabilize, a sense of cohesiveness—a supportive learning environment—develops as well. For additional ideas related to the classroom climate as a whole, you may find it helpful to review specific sections of Chapters 1 through 3 that relate to items you have identified.

It is also important to consider all classrooms, not only the general education classroom, that provide opportunities for students in elementary schools to learn. How these classrooms are organized and how well students are able to make transitions and function successfully within and across these settings directly affects not only their individual success but also the overall climates in those classrooms.

FIGURE 4.1 Assessing the Classroom Climate

PURPOSE:
Use this activity to get a general sense of the climate in a classroom.

DIRECTIONS:
Ask yourself the following questions to begin to identify areas of concern, as well as areas of strength.

Do students generally feel happy and want to learn?   Yes _____   No _____
If they don't feel happy, there may be several contributing factors.

YES	NO	
_____	_____	Do students feel free to ask each other questions?
_____	_____	Do students have opportunities to make choices?
_____	_____	Do students seem to care about each other?
_____	_____	Do students help each other?
_____	_____	Do students share materials?
_____	_____	Do students share ideas?
_____	_____	Do students work together?
_____	_____	Do students have freedom to move about the classroom?
_____	_____	Do students move about without distracting others?
_____	_____	Do students feel comfortable attempting new activities?
_____	_____	Can students deal with making mistakes?
_____	_____	Do you make it possible for students to achieve academic and behavioral goals?
_____	_____	Do all students feel responsible for maintaining classroom order?

INTERPRETATIONS:
"YES" answers identify areas of strengths.
"NO" answers may identify areas of concern. To address these areas refer to the appropriate chapter in SECTION I.

FIGURE 4.2 Improving Classroom Climate

PURPOSE;
To look at the activities and behaviors that may improve the climate of your classroom.

DIRECTIONS:
Review the following list of items. Select those that may be most appropriate in your classroom.

_____ Have more partner and small group activities.

_____ Have activities, both curriculum tasks and games, that require students students to help each other.

_____ Before, during, and after group work, have students talk about their process for working together and how well it is working.

_____ Have class discussions on the topics of how to:

   _____ Give feedback to others.
   _____ Accept feedback from others.
   _____ Deal with making mistakes.
   _____ Help others.
   _____ Receive help from others.
   _____ Ask for help from others.
   _____ Help one another look competent.

_____ Allow more movement in the room.

_____ Emphasize themes of caring for and helping others found in reading and social studies curriculum materials.

_____ Model caring and acceptance. Talk about what you do.

_____ Have a class project such as community service or an entertainment event that will bring the class together.

_____ Have _Show and Tell_ sessions so that students can get to know more about one another.

_____ Try to help students resolve interpersonal conflicts that may be adversely affecting the class atmosphere.

INTERPRETATION:
The items you have selected will likely be those that will help your students and yourself meet the goals and expectations that you have established for effective, productive functioning of the class.

CLASSROOMS IN ELEMENTARY SCHOOLS

While for many, the term *classroom* brings to mind a setting in which students spend most of their day and in which one teacher presents instruction to a homogeneous group of students, this picture does not truly reflect today's typical elementary classrooms. Not only is the traditional general education classroom itself changing, but most elementary students function in several different classroom settings during a typical school day. There are classrooms where instruction in other academic subjects—music, physical education, art, language, and remedial reading—takes place. Students may also spend part of their day in the cafeteria, playground, library, auditorium, and the hallways between classes. While not usually considered as classrooms, these areas are laboratories for students to extend, maintain, and generalize academic and social learning. To succeed in these diverse settings, students must work with many different teachers and with many different peer groups.

General education classrooms have traditionally been comprised of a fixed group of 20–30 students of approximately the same age whose individual ability levels may differ significantly. Most general education teachers have been prepared to teach content areas such as reading, mathematics, social studies, and science within a specified grade range. In other words, a fourth grade elementary teacher has been the expert in fourth grade reading, mathematics, social studies, and science. Most instruction has been designed to meet the needs of students who are generally able to succeed without individualized attention. Accordingly, the environment, the teacher, and instruction have focused on large or small groups of students, rather than individuals. Now, in order to meet the needs of an increasingly diverse student population, many general education teachers are considering new ways to deliver instruction to all students, regardless of need or category of disability. Many general education teachers are collaborating and sharing instructional responsibility with one another, as well as with their special education colleagues. They are learning to teach together, to take risks, and continue to learn from one another.

Instruction has traditionally been organized according to topics within the scope and sequence of a single grade. The school day has been divided into instructional periods that correspond to instructional areas such as reading, spelling, and science. An alternative is to provide instruction that is more holistic and based on the language needs and interests of the students. All instruction—reading, spelling, science—is designed with language as the focus. In either case, instruction is delivered in large or small groups or independently and focuses on *academic* goals and objectives. Most transitions are from one subject to another and from one area of the classroom to another.

There are other classrooms within an elementary school to which whole classes of students travel as a normal part of their school day. There they receive specialized instruction in physical education, art, or music. While the composition of the student group may remain somewhat stable, the teachers, the environment, and the instruction that takes place there may differ significantly. Teachers in these specialized settings have traditionally been prepared as experts in physical education, art, or music. These areas differ not only from the general education classroom, but also from one another. Instruction may take place in groups or teams and focus on an instructional topic requiring very different behaviors, such as physical actions, than those used in the home classroom. Physical space is used very differently in the gymnasium, an art room, or a library. Systems for managing behavior may also differ. The lack of consistency across these settings may cause problems for students who are less skilled in making the transition from one type of classroom to another either because they are less able to perceive the differences or change their behavior accordingly.

There are other classrooms in an elementary school that are available to a limited number of students. Students may travel to these classrooms either as members of a small group or by themselves. Resource rooms are designed to accommodate 10–20 students at a time with mild to moderate special needs whose age and grade range may span up to four years. The teacher, environment, and instruction usually differ significantly from the mainstream classroom.

Teachers in resource rooms are usually prepared to teach students with mild to moderate learning disabilities, mental retardation, and behavior disorders across a wide range of ages and abilities. Resource room teachers establish rules and expectations that vary according to the needs of individual students. Instructional groups tend to be smaller and more individualized as a function of both scheduling and specific student needs. Individual programs of instruction are common and may focus on both academic and social goals and objectives.

The environment is designed to accommodate an ongoing influx and departure of students as individual students spend varying amounts of time in the room. Consequently, both teacher and student schedules may vary daily and students must make transitions both within as well as between general and special education classrooms throughout their schoolday.

Self-contained special education classrooms also accommodate students with individual needs. These classrooms are for students who experience more serious problems in mainstream settings or the less restrictive resource rooms. Because these students have special needs that are more severe than those of students in resource rooms, the classes sizes tend to be smaller and the group more fixed over time.

Teachers in self-contained special education classrooms are typically prepared to teach students with moderate to severe special needs. Teachers establish general classroom rules and expectations as well as standards designed to meet the individual student's needs. Usually, instruction is individualized and focuses more on social/behavioral than academic goals and objectives. While these students may spend a small portion of the day in a general education classroom, they typically move as a group across settings that may include the cafeteria, the playground, art, music, and physical education. Most independent transitions are within the special education classroom.

Students with limited English proficiency (LEP) receive either bilingual instruction of English as a Second Language (ESL) programs, in self-contained bilingual classrooms with instruction in the students' native language to pullout programs in which students are provided additional instruction and assistance with subject matter in their native language (Padilla, 1990). Students may receive instruction in Spanish in one general education classroom in the morning and then move to a different general education classroom in the afternoon for instruction in English in other academic areas. Other programs provide total instruction in one language in a self-contained setting during the first year of school with a gradual infusion of a second language during the subsequent academic years. Students who lack competence in a language, a critical component in social interactions, are moving from classroom to classroom in the early elementary years.

As students move between classrooms, they have many opportunities to become skilled at coping with diverse situations. They learn to recognize the differences between different classroom environments, teachers, and instruction; and to adjust their behavior accordingly. Within the elementary school, students can learn to expect diversity across settings and to accept responsibility for monitoring the appropriateness of their responses.

Most students are able to learn from these experiences. However, students with special needs or those who are not native English speakers are particularly vulnerable. Their instruction is supposed to take place in settings that enable them to be most successful. For some, this may mean spending most of their school day in one classroom. For others, it may mean dividing their time and making several transitions between classrooms. Students are frequently included in non-academic activities such as music, art, physical education, recess, or lunch to give them opportunities to interact with their peers.

Unfortunately, these students are often simply expected to know what to do in these settings. A good teacher would never expect a student to participate in academic activities without considering student abilities and task difficulty. However, for many students, the expectation to deal successfully with both academic and social demands in different settings remains. It seems that those with greater need are asked to cope more frequently with different classroom settings. Thoughtful planning and preparation are needed. It is inappropriate to assume that students can succeed socially without planning and monitoring, just as it is inappropriate to assume they can function academically without guidance. To give students the greatest opportunity for success, it is especially important to consider the differences and similarities between mainstream classrooms and specialized settings with regard to environment, teacher, and instructional factors. Students' achievement and self-esteem are at-risk when they are placed in settings without consideration of and preparation for differences that may exist.

Figure 4.3 can be used to compare two (or more) classrooms in which students must function in order to examine the differences that may exist with respect to the environment, teachers, instruction, and other factors. With the information gathered in Figure 4.3, you can consider ways to deal with the differences between classrooms that may be causing problems. You can also identify the features in other classrooms that enable students to succeed. You may decide to make changes in the other classrooms, modifications in your own classroom, or teach students how to function more successfully in classrooms that differ from yours. Use the following guidelines to decide what to do.

GUIDELINES
FOR DEALING
WITH CLASSROOM
DIFFERENCES

- *Collaborate.* Talk with other teachers about classroom differences in teacher expectations, the environment, and instruction. Brainstorm ways to make classrooms more similar for students who are experiencing difficulty with functioning in environments that vary. Share features of your classroom that seem to work for your students.

- *Modify.* Identify those features of your classroom that might be modified to make your classroom more similar to other classrooms for students who are experiencing difficulty.

- *Teach.* Point out the salient features in other classrooms. Provide students with opportunities to discuss areas of potential difficulty and plan a course of action before the student moves to the other setting.

- *Monitor.* Monitor student behavior in other classrooms. Provide opportunities for students to discuss their functioning in other classrooms.

FIGURE 4.3 Classroom Comparison

PURPOSE:
To compare two different classroom environments on a variety of factors in order to determine differences that either cause problems or are beneficial to individual students of the whole class.

DIRECTIONS:
Choose two classrooms to compare. In most cases, you will want to compare your classroom to another one your students are in. Use the term "classroom" broadly. It may include environments such as the gym, lunchroom, playground, resource room, ESL classroom, or music room. Use the form that follows: fill in the blanks for every factor that you can. You may have to do some observation or interviewing to find out more about classrooms unfamiliar to you. This research can include interviewing students who may have very different ideas of the rules and expectations.

Classroom _____   Classroom _____

Teacher Expectations	Teacher Expectations
1.	1.
2.	2.
3.	3.
Teaching Style/s	Teaching Style/s
Rules	Rules
1.	1.
2.	2.
3.	3.
Use of Time/Schedules	Use of Time/Schedules
Transitions	Transitions
Organization of Space	Organization of Space

Goal Structures   Goal Structures
_____ Independent   _____ Independent
_____ Cooperative   _____ Cooperative
_____ Competitive   _____ Competitive

Organization of Instruction   Organization of Instruction

_____ 1-1 Adult/Student   _____ 1-1 Adult/Student
_____ Small Group   _____ Small Group
    _____ heterogeneous   _____ heterogeneous
    _____ homogeneous   _____ homogeneous
_____ Large Group   _____ Large Group
    _____ heterogeneous   _____ heterogeneous
    _____ homogeneous   _____ homogeneous
_____ Peer Tutoring   _____ Peer Tutoring
_____ Independent   _____ Independent
_____ Cooperative Learning   _____ Cooperative Learning

Assignments   Assignments

_____ Worksheets   _____ Worksheets
_____ Written Papers   _____ Written Papers
_____ Projects   _____ Projects
_____ Demonstration   _____ Demonstration
_____ Group Discussion   _____ Group Discussion
_____ Other   _____ Other

INTERPRETATION:
Looking down the two lists, circle any areas of disagreement. When you have done this for the whole list, look over the circled areas and answer the following question:

For which students does this disagreement cause a problem?
List their names. What type of problem(s): (academic, social, other)?

When the features of all classrooms in which students spend their time are considered, it is more likely that learning experiences will be successful. Students will then believe they can succeed in every classroom. These will be classrooms in which productive peer interactions are possible as a result of a positive classroom climate.

In this chapter you have had the opportunity to examine the overall climate of your own classroom and the features of your own and other areas in the school that contribute to that climate. You have also had the opportunity to plan changes that can enhance the social competence of students in your class.

In this first section, you have also had the opportunity to examine the specific aspects of yourself, the classroom itself, and the instruction that takes place there. What you have accomplished so far will reduce the need for individualized help and benefit all the students in your classroom. However, despite your best efforts, some students may need more individualized instruction.

At this point if you feel there is nothing more you can do to improve the systemic factors discussed in Section 1, which focused on the classroom, and if you still have concerns about the social competence of individual students, you can move Section 2, which focuses on the student. There you will find teaching, assessment, and intervention techniques for improving social skills and increasing social self-confidence.

FOCUSING ON THE STUDENT

While all students benefit from a structured classroom designed to improve social competence, some students may require more direct and specific interventions. Even though they have opportunities to interact with their peers, even though models of appropriate social interaction are available to them, and even though their teachers support and encourage them; some students still fail to interact appropriately and successfully with their peers.

Students who act aggressively toward others, those who hit, kick, push, fight, or throw objects come to mind immediately. Those who tease, name call, swear, interrupt, tattle, and yell at others are also targeted by their teachers. These students stand out quickly because their actions disrupt classrooms.

Other students who lack social competence behave differently. They fail to interact with their peers. They often avoid or withdraw from social situations. They play or work alone, select individual activities, or avoid sitting where they may have to interact with others; sometimes they even cry. The physical and verbal behaviors of both aggressive and withdrawn students suggest a lack of concern for others when, in fact, they may behave in these ways because they lack social skills or the self-confidence to use the skills they do know.

People who lack social competence are less able to get along in their world and are typically rejected or avoided by others. Others simply do not like them or want to be with them. Their behavior, regardless of the reason, precludes productive interactions with others—interactions that would teach them how to develop meaningful social relationships. These students will continue to fail in the social arena with their peers. They will also remain at a disadvantage to acquire the social skills they need—a situation that becomes even more disparate as they mature.

Social competence is critical for a student's overall development. It has an impact on every aspect of an individual's life—at home, in school, and in the community. Those who fail to acquire basic social skills needed in simpler social situations in first grade will lack the skills and confidence needed to interact in more demanding and complex social situations in fifth or sixth grade. Without intervention, these students are at risk for academic problems, referral for special needs, problems in later adjustment, delinquency, dropping out of school, and a poor self-concept.

Several reasons can explain why these students continue to have difficulty getting along with others despite many opportunities. First, they may not know basic social behaviors such as establishing or maintaining eye contact. Second, they may know a social behavior, but not know when to use it; they do not establish eye contact when greeting others (even though they know how). Third, they may know the behavior and when to use it, yet lack the self-confidence to do so in actual peer interactions. For example, they know how to make friends and have demonstrated they can use the appropriate behaviors yet they still fail to do so in real life situations. These students either lack social skills or the confidence needed to use the skills in ways to become more socially competent. In sum, *social incompetence* can be the consequence of inexperience, learning or cultural differences, negative self-perceptions, or current setting. For these students, simply providing opportunities is not enough; direct teacher intervention is needed.

Direct teacher intervention benefits many students. First, students learn a specific behavior that has many applications; knowing how to establish eye contact is a social behavior students will use in many situations. Second, students learn problem-solving strategies appropriate for academic and social situations; deciding which strategy to use and evaluating its effectiveness is a valuable process when joining a group or solving a mathematical problem. Third, knowing what to do and when to do it helps students feel more self-confident and consequently, they may begin to view themselves as more competent individuals.

Social competence is relevant and important throughout a student's life, and teachers play an important role. With direct intervention and well-planned activities, teachers can teach social behaviors and develop social knowledge and self-confidence. Without teacher intervention, students continue their unproductive behavior. By the time they reach the upper elementary grades, they often join others who reinforce their behavior. For some students, instruction in the classroom may be their only hope in learning how to become more socially confident and get along in their world.

CHAPTER 5

SOCIAL SKILLS

OVERVIEW

Some students continue to experience problems with social competence even when their teachers have organized their classrooms to encourage productive social interactions as described in Section 1. Despite consideration of teacher expectations, the environment, instruction, and the classroom, these students are still unable to get along with others.

These problems persist because these students may not be socially skilled. They may lack social behaviors and simply not know what to do. They may also lack the social knowledge to know when and how to use the social behaviors they do know. Teachers can play a pivotal role by recognizing and respecting diversity among their students and setting the tone for the acceptance of differences in their classrooms. However, it is necessary for these students to, themselves, develop the social skills by which they can gain acceptance within the culture of their classroom and school. Their teachers can intervene directly to provide instruction in these social skills so that these students can begin to interact more appropriately with their peers.

This chapter will deal with helping students become more socially skilled. It defines these social skills and then describes how and when to use two tested techniques—modeling and coaching—to teach them. The social skills addressed within this chapter are those that are important for students in the typical elementary classroom.

SOCIAL SKILLS

Social skills consist of social behaviors and social knowledge—knowing what to do and when to do it. Participating in group discussions, asking for help, and dealing with peer provocations are examples of culture–specific social skills. Figure 5.1 lists social skills that are typically needed by most students in American elementary schools.

Students who have social skills are able to correctly perform the actions that make up appropriate social behavior and choose the appropriate social behavior to perform in a given social situation. In order to teach social skills to students who lack competence, both abilities must be considered.

The term social behaviors refers to specific, observable actions such as smiling, maintaining eye contact, or respecting another's space. Specific social behaviors are frequently linked together to form strategies. The term social knowledge refers to the problem–solving process necessary to perform these behaviors appropriately; that is, correctly *perceive* the social situation, *decide* what to *do,* and *act* on that decision. Perception includes understanding the social situation in an appropriate cultural context. Decision making invokes the finer steps of identifying one's social goal (such as *wanting to play with the group,* and selecting a strategy to use to reach that goal like *going up to the group and asking to join in.*) Action involves not only using a strategy, but also evaluating the actual consequences of its application. This thoughtful selection of social goals, strategies, and behaviors is based on recollection and evaluation of prior experiences or instruction. Overall,

FIGURE 5.1 Social Skills

Accepting help	Entering a group in the classroom
Interrupting an activity (play)	Participating in group discussions
Making conversation	Joining an ongoing conversation
Asking for help	Interrupting an activity (academic)
Joining a group (lunchroom)	Joining a group (playground)
Maintaining friendships	Dealing with loneliness
Dealing with peer pressure	Dealing with disappointment
Dealing with overt rejection	Dealing with covert rejection
Responding to teasing	Making friends
Working cooperatively	Playing with one other person
Leaving a group	Avoiding conflict
Working in a large group	Playing cooperatively
Dealing with embarrassment	Accepting a new group member
Working in small groups	Playing in a large group
Working independently	Working with one other person

students with social skills have a repertoire of culturally appropriate social behaviors and are able to use a three step problem–solving process to apply those behaviors.

To remain socially skilled, students must not only continually learn new social skills, they must also know how to adapt the skills they already know to new situations. *Making a friend, asking for help,* and *sharing* are social skills that are needed throughout one's life but differ in ways they are implemented. Being friends in kindergarten may mean sharing a toy, while being a friend in sixth grade may depend on sharing values. These skills may also be manifested differently in different cultural contexts and settings.

Some students grow up in situations different from those that are commonplace in the dominant culture. These cultural differences may result in different understandings of what behaviors are appropriate and when to use them. Cultural differences can also limit a student's understanding of abstract social concepts or interfere with a student's ability to attend and respond appropriately in certain situations. Consequently, these students may be excluded from social activities and opportunities to learn new skills or use the skills they already know.

Those who are socially skilled are more likely to be socially competent if they have the confidence to use their skills. (See Chapter 6.) Those who become more skilled are also more likely to become more academically competent. This improvement may occur because many of the same skills needed for productive social interactions are also needed for academic tasks. For example, getting along with peers, participating in discussions, and staying on-task enable students to learn, regardless of whether the focus is primarily adademic or social. Furthermore, the problem-solving process that underlies social knowledge can also aid students as they confront academic challenges.

SOCIAL BEHAVIORS

Social behaviors are the behaviors used in situations that others can see or hear. The gestures or actions that individuals make or the words they speak are observable/audible social behaviors. Some behaviors, such as smiling, may occur in isolation, while others might consist of a sequence of behaviors. For example, initiating a conversation might involve establishing eye contact, waiting, saying something appropriate, and accepting feedback from other participants. The number and sequence of behaviors that are appropriate depends on many factors, such as the age of the participants and the setting in which the interaction occurs. In some cultures, for example, it is not appropriate to establish eye contact. If teachers recognize these differences, they may understand that what appears to be a lack of skill may simply be a difference in experience and expectations. Figure 5.2 provides a list of behaviors that are common to a wide range of social situations in American elementary schools. Again, keep in mind that social behaviors are culture–specific and will vary from one group to another.

Individual social behaviors are often used as part of a string of actions that constitutes a social strategy. For example, in one situation, where students need help to complete an assignment, they might select any of the following strategies: *ask the teacher, ask a peer,* or *wait.* Each of these strategies would involve a different combination and sequence of social behaviors such as *hand–raising, moving to the teacher's desk, establishing eye contact,* or *calling out across the classroom.* Strategies, in other words, are collections of behaviors that will vary according to the situation and the social goal.

Some students are unable to quickly execute a sequence of behaviors that require discrete and smoothly performed motor skills such as *establishing eye contact, waiting, nodding,* or *saying 'hi'* at exactly the right moment. The students may be able to execute each motor skill (behavior) in isolation, but unable to perform a sequence of behaviors smoothly and accurately under pressure in a real situation. For example, they may execute the sequence too slowly or leave out one behavior critical to the success of the interchange. Others may simply not know all of the behaviors or be unclear of the proper order. The selection of which social strategy to use and when to use it is a process that is part of a student's *social knowledge,* which will be described in the following section.

SOCIAL KNOWLEDGE

Social knowledge consists of the problem–solving process that individuals use to carry out the appropriate social behaviors. This process includes three

FIGURE 5.2 Social Behaviors

Smiling	Establishing eye contact
Maintaining eye contact	Greeting others
Initiating conversation	Maintaining conversation
Ending conversation	Introducing oneself
Listening	Asking for help
Accepting help	Offering help
Leaving others	Nodding
Accepting praise	Giving compliments
Interrupting appropriately	Asking permission
Forming lines	Walking in line
Giving praise	Saying nice things
Negotiating	Sharing materials
Taking turns	Accepting criticism
Telling the truth	Keeping secrets
Making an apology	Asking for a favor
Ignoring unkind remarks	Waiting one's turn
Taking care of belongings	Being assertive
Respecting another's space	Leaving others
Keeping hands and feet to oneself	Making a suggestion

aspects—perception, decision making, and action. Students must select and apply social strategies (comprised of one or more social behaviors) to effectively achieve a goal. For example, a teacher might tell a student entering the classroom to join an existing group (social goal). A student who is socially skilled would rapidly perceive the situation, decide what to do, act on that decision, and evaluate the effectiveness of that action. Figure 5.3 outlines the three aspects of this process, which are described in detail in the following sections.

PERCEPTION

In a given social situation, socially skilled students first take a moment to perceive and understand the present situation by identifying the overall goal of a group they must join, the participants, the strategies and behaviors of the group, and any concepts relevant to the situation. The overall goal of the group might be to *play competitively* or to *work cooperatively*—goals that, incidentally, may call for very different responses (strategies and behaviors) in situations that may appear similar. For example, a group might include three classmates who are friendly acquaintances. Knowing about the group's membership might help a new member decide which strategy to use and with whom that strategy might be more effective. Strategies that might be effective include *listening when another person speaks, sharing ideas, taking turns,* and *praising*; observable behaviors that might be incorporated into several of these strategies include *nodding, maintaining eye contact,* or *making conversation.* In a different group, where the new member perceives that

---

FIGURE 5.3 Social Knowledge

PERCEPTION:
Identify Present Situation:
    group goal, participants, strategies/behaviors, and relevant concepts
Interpret Present Situation:
    participant roles, motives, attitudes, feelings, and relationships
    consequences of strategies/behaviors

DECISION MAKING:
Select Personal Goal
Recall Previous Situations:
    group goals, participants, strategies/behaviors
    consequences and relevant concepts
    participant roles, motives, attitudes, feelings, and relationships
Evaluate Possible Responses:
    consequences associated with known strategies/behaviors
    comparison of possible responses
Review Response Repertoire:
    known strategies
    known behaviors
Select Response

ACTION:
Implement Response
Monitor and Evaluate Response Effectiveness:
    participant feedback (words, actions, gestures, etc.)
    personal feedback (words, actions, gestures, feelings, etc.)
    goal achievement
Consider Need for Recycling

---

members are unfriendly, different strategies and behaviors would be appropriate.

Students learn not only to *identify* the components of a situation, but also *interpret* the culturally appropriate social roles involved. They learn to see the different roles played by participants; to understand the motives, attitudes, feelings, and relationships; and to anticipate the consequences of the strategies being used in the group. Some participants assume the role of leader while others become onlookers. Some participants want to achieve the goal while others interfere with the process. For example, one member of the group might be monopolizing the conversation, so that the group is having difficulty finishing a project. Other members of the group might be feeling angry and frustrated. Knowing how the group members relate to one another and how they feel helps students interpret the situation accurately.

Recognizing that certain social concepts such as sharing, friendship, and cooperation may be relevant to a situation and having some notion of those concepts can help students identify appropriate strategies. The strategies and behaviors that students associate with social concepts are dependent on their age and stage of cognitive development. For example, younger students may view *sharing* as sharing objects, while older students consider sharing of ideas more important.

Not all students can interpret social situations successfully enough and recognize the perspectives of others. Many students have difficulty perceiving situations due to inattention, information processing disabilities, cognitive deficits, impulsivity, or unfamiliarity with the situation. Consequently, they misunderstand the goal of the group and are unable to identify the strategies and behaviors being used by members. There are others who remain egocentric in their thinking long after it is age-appropriate. They are not able to identify the participants and interpret the interrelationships that exist among them. Further, cultural differences have an impact on the ways students understand and make sense of the culture of the school, and expectations about appropriate social behaviors. Consequently, these students may not have accurate and realistic perceptions when they make decisions about what to do.

DECISION MAKING

Socially skilled students then use their perceptions to make decisions about possible strategies to use. To make an appropriate decision, they select a personal goal, recall previous situations, evaluate possible responses, review their own repertoires, and select a response.

First, socially skilled students select a personal goal—what they hope to achieve. On the basis of their perceptions, students might decide to set *joining a group* as a personal social goal. This determination then influences their subsequent series of decisions.

Next, where possible, students recall previous situations that were similar in terms of goals, participants, strategies and behaviors, consequences, and relevant social concepts. This situation might have been one that the students remember observing, hearing about, or actually experiencing. They might remember, for example, joining a group working cooperatively. These recollections help them realize that a certain strategy, such as *focusing on the group leader,* was effective. Students might also remember that certain social behaviors, such as *waiting, establishing eye contact,* and *smiling at the group leader* resulted in being asked to join the group. This positive result helps the students make future decisions in similar situations.

Students can evaluate these potential strategies by comparing the potential consequences of their implementation. They might remember a situation where a student barged in and interrupted a group and consequently was told to leave. They might also remember another situation when a student waited patiently and eventually was asked to join the group. With this knowledge, students can decide which responses might be the best or worst to use in the present situation.

After evaluating and comparing possible responses, students would review their own repertoires to see which strategies and behaviors they already know. With this knowledge, they could decide what to do. This process of review and comparison enables students to make choices with greater potential for success.

Some students experience difficulty with this part of the decision–making process either because they do not have a repertoire, fail to use the strategies they do know or use those strategies appropriately, or simply do not take the time to evaluate their repertoire. Others lack a history of social interactions and therefore lack the resources from which to select possible actions. Still others have problems remembering previous situations and strategies that were effective or ineffective. The process of recalling past experiences is particularly difficult for students who act impulsively and lack the self-control to think reflectively. Many students with learning and behavioral problems also have difficulty evaluating and prioritizing possible strategies and behaviors. This makes the next step, *Action*, less likely to be successful.

ACTION

In the final step of the problem–solving process, socially skilled students act on their decisions. They implement the strategy they have selected and then monitor and evaluate its effectiveness in achieving their personal goals. For example, they might select strategy of focusing on the group leader and of waiting, establishing eye contact with the group leader or a group member, and smiling.

The evaluation process is ongoing, beginning with the implementation of the selected strategy. This means monitoring feedback from other group participants: their words, actions, gestures, and feelings. Students should also monitor their own words, actions, gestures, and feelings. Both participant and personal feedback helps students decide whether they are achieving their personal goals or whether they should reexamine their perceptions or decisions to select more effective responses and try again. If focusing on the group leader to enter the group was an effective strategy, and, if waiting, establishing eye contact, and smiling at the group leader were effective social behaviors, the students might decide to keep those strategies and behaviors in their repertoire to use in similar situations.

Effectiveness means that personal goals are achieved and students can add this experience to their personal histories of successful interactions. They can use this information to make decisions in the future. If, on the other hand, the response was unsuccessful, if they were ignored or asked to leave, students might wish to repeat the perception, decision making, and/ or action steps.

Evaluation is difficult because it requires reflection and taking responsibility for one's actions. Thinking about something that was not successful may evoke difficult feelings for some students. Some simply never take the time to consider the impact of their actions. Some do not accept responsibility for the role their behavior played in the situation. They may continue to blame others for their bad luck. Even when actions are successful, these students typically attribute the success to factors unrelated to their own actions. When this happens, these students can not enjoy the positive feelings associated with the selection and implementation of appropriate and effective strategies and behaviors. This hinders the learning and feedback process, becomes part of their ongoing social history, and influences subsequent interactions in negative ways.

PREPARING TO TEACH SOCIAL SKILLS

Most children acquire social behaviors and develop social knowledge through their experience in a particular cultural context. By watching their peers, problem–solving, trying new responses, being successful, and then applying these experiences in new social situations, they become socially skilled. Behaviors are relatively easy to acquire because students can see or hear behaviors and then simply copy the actions or imitate the words.

Developing social knowledge, however, is more complex. It depends on both cognitive development and experience. Some students have learning disabilities that interfere with their ability to perceive, make decisions, or take action effectively. Others are not able to transfer social skills from one setting to another or think carefully before acting due to behavioral or attention problems. Still others have grown up in different or experientially impoverished cultural situations and have simply not had the benefit of social opportunities to learn how to act in ways that are acceptable in the dominant culture.

For all of these students, simply providing an environment rich in social opportunities and support is not enough. Without an awareness that these differences exist and direct intervention and instruction from their teachers, these students will continue to have problems with their social relationships and remain at-risk for social competence. Their inappropriate interactions will continue to interfere with their academic achievement as well.

As teachers, we are comfortable and competent in addressing academic issues. We would never simply tell students who have reading difficulties to simply *read better*; we teach them. However, we have been guilty of telling students who are disruptive, off–task, or inattentive to simply *behave*. We say such things as "Get busy," "You know what to do," or "Go join that group over there." These statements assume that students *know what* to do and *when* and *how* to do it—that they know the behaviors and have the knowledge to implement them effectively.

Just as we teach students to read, we must teach some students social behaviors and improve their social knowledge. To prepare to teach social skills, it is easiest and most logical to select the students and determine learning outcomes (social behaviors and/or social knowledge) for those students first; and then, based on those decisions, teach social skills either by using modeling to teach social behaviors or coaching to develop social knowledge.

SELECT STUDENTS

There are several sources of information to use in selecting students who would benefit from social skills instruction. Teacher judgment, whether based on formal or informal assessment, is a highly reliable source. Information based on peer assessment is a second valuable resource. The students themselves can provide a third, and often overlooked, perspective.

TEACHER JUDGMENT

Teachers are fairly skilled at informally identifying students who would benefit from social skills instruction without the benefit of formal methods. It is easy to pick out students who interrupt, argue, fight, swear, tattle, tease, hit, lie, talk incessantly, show off, act without thinking, and so forth. These are the students who bother other people and, as a result, tend to interfere with instruction and learning. They are often labeled as *aggressive* or *outward acting*.

Teachers can also identify students who do not volunteer for activities, who play alone, who do not seem to have friends, and so forth. These are the quiet students who do not seem to interact with others and whom teachers frequently label as *withdrawn* or *inward acting*.

These selections are typically based on a general sense of prior experiences and informal observations of these students. While this type of information is accurate, it fails to provide specific data that can be used to make thoughtful decisions about what to teach and how to evaluate the effectiveness of that instruction. More structured measures enable teachers to determine whether behaviors exist at all or simply exist inconsistently. This information would then direct whether a student needed instruction in a specific social behavior or simply supportive or corrective feedback when a behavior did occur. Examples of more formal teacher assessments are provided in the subsequent section of this chapter that deals with *determining learning outcomes*. Descriptions and forms for conducting observations are provided in Appendix C.

PEER ASSESSMENT

Peer assessment provides information about students who are rejected by, isolated from, or neglected by their peers. While this information can be determined by observation, peer assessment can also point out the interpersonal relationships that exist among students that often escape a teacher's notice. While teachers perceive many aspects of students' relationships, students' opinions of their peers are based on more frequent and long-standing contact. Students also understand the demands of peer social situations better than their teachers. This source of information also identifies socially competent students who could serve as models and peer support during social skills instruction. Peer assessment was discussed in Chapter 3 and additional instruments are provided in Appendix C.

STUDENT SELF-ASSESSMENT

Students who are candidates for social skills instruction are often overlooked as sources of information. Yet their feelings, beliefs, or sense of personal competence provide an important third perspective—one that may substantiate or clarify findings obtained from teacher and peer assessments. For example, teacher and peer assessments may have indicated that an individual student does not enter ongoing groups and, therefore, has limited interactions with peers. Student self-report may contradict the natural assumption that the student does not know what to do and reveal that the student does, in fact, know several behaviors or strategies for joining a group, but fails to carry them out in the classroom. This student does not need to learn how to join a group, as the teacher and peer assessments might seem to indicate; rather, the student might benefit from coaching activities or peer support to encourage the student to employ social behaviors and strategies already known.

Student perspectives also make it possible to investigate the reasons why certain behaviors or strategies may be present, absent, or occur infrequently. Some students do not perceive their social skills realistically or in quite the same way that others do. For example, a student may believe that he or she has many friends and the skills to maintain those friendships when, in fact, this student may be rejected by or isolated from peers and never demonstrates the skills needed to make and maintain friendships. In this instance, listening to the student's perspective may explain, both to teachers and the student, why the student behaves in certain ways.

Teachers who take the time to ask students what they think communicate interest and a readiness to listen. With this type of support, students are encouraged to recognize their own strengths and weaknesses, monitor their behavior and evaluate themselves, and begin to assume greater responsibility for themselves and their actions.

There are several ways to obtain a student's perspective. First, the rating scales provided in the following section can be adapted for use in student self-assessment. Student versions of the *Social Skills Rating Scale* (for teacher's version, see Figure 5.4) and the *Social Behavior Rating Scale* (for teacher's version, see Figure 5.5) are included in Appendix C. The instrument *What You Do When . . . ?* (see Figure 5.6 in this chapter) is an example of an open-ended interview technique by which students can describe their use of social knowledge in a variety of social situations. Other sources that provide information about the student perspective include journal entries, role playing, and illustrations.

Despite the many benefits of student self-report, the information obtained may be limited or influenced by a student's cognitive, physical, or emotional status, as well as by cultural and linguistic differences not correctly understood by the teacher. Some students do not understand particular questions or cannot respond to written tasks. Others respond impulsively and provide answers that are not truly indicative of their actual thoughts or opinions. Student responses are not always truly representative of what a student might know or actually be able to do in a social interaction. Or students can demonstrate the appropriate social behaviors and social knowledge in hypothetical situations but not exhibit the social skills in actual interpersonal situations. Therefore, as with other measures of student behavior, student self-report should be supplemented with other types of assessments conducted by other individuals (including parents), in more than one setting, and at more than one time.

Although this discussion has been fairly extensive, the process of selecting students for social skills intervention is relatively easy. The students themselves are usually easily identified and the techniques used to validate their selection are simple to use. Taking time to document the need for intervention at this point will not only enable you to monitor changes in behavior and social status as they occur but also make appropriate instructional decisions quickly and accurately.

DETERMINE LEARNING OUTCOMES

Having selected students who are candidates for social skills instruction, the next step is to determine the learning outcomes that are most appropriate for these students. You need to decide whether these students lack social behaviors, social knowledge, or both. At this point, all you know is that your own data and opinion, as supported by those of peers, colleagues, and students themselves, suggest that direct intervention is needed and appropriate. The task now is to pinpoint the specific social behaviors and aspects of social knowledge that are troublesome for these students. With this information it will be possible to select an intervention strategy. There are three approaches for determining learning outcomes. Select the one that seems most logical to you.

The first option is to work from the broad social *skills* perspective—one that incorporates both social behaviors and social knowledge. This involves looking at social skills that are typically needed by students in elementary schools; these may also be the skills that you have already identified as troublesome in your classroom. They may include skills such as *asking for help, joining a group,* or *working cooperatively.* The more lengthy list of skills listed in Figure 5.1 has been incorporated into Figure 5.4 which can be used to evaluate whether students exhibit these skills *usually, sometimes,* or *never.* This instrument will delineate skills that are troublesome for students and enable you to select them as learning outcomes for specific students.

While this first approach provides an easy entry point, it does not tell you what to do about the skills identified as lacking. To know how to help students acquire these skills, you first need to determine the specific behaviors needed and whether the students have the social knowledge to use them effectively. To do this, we need to look at either the second or third approach.

The second approach is to consider discrete social behaviors. You may decide to begin with this approach because it is clear that the lack or inconsistency of very specific social behaviors, such as those listed in Figure 5.2, are a problem for certain students. This second approach may also be the logical next step if you have already identified social skills that are problematic and want to identify the specific social behaviors. In either case, Figure 5.5 contains social behaviors in a simple instrument that indicates whether specific behaviors are *usually, sometimes,* or *never* used by a student. The observation instruments provided in Appendix C can also be used to identify and substantiate the information obtained from the rating scale. With these data, you can then set these behaviors as learning outcomes, choose *modeling* as the instructional approach to use, and also monitor the effectiveness of that intervention.

A third alternative to determine learning outcomes is to approach the task from the perspective of social knowledge. In other words, consider a student's ability to perceive situations, make decisions, and take effective action. You may decide to begin with this approach if your experience with a student's academic learning suggests similar difficulties with social tasks. For example, memory problems might affect a student's ability to recall names of acquaintances as well as names of numerals. Figure 5.6 can be used to clarify whether a student can use social knowledge to make appropriate decisions and apply social behaviors effectively. The individual coaching questions described in a subsequent section can be used to interview students. An additional measure, *What is a Friend?*, is provided in Appendix C. They can be used and adapted to determine whether a student understands concepts such as friendship, truth, honesty, sharing. With the information gathered from these exercises, you can set aspects of social knowledge as learning outcomes, choose *coaching* as the instructional approach to use, and also monitor the effectiveness of that intervention.

The following guidelines may also be helpful in determining learning outcomes.

FIGURE 5.4 Social Skills Rating Scale (Teacher Version)

Student _____ Grade _____ Age _____

Rater _____

PURPOSE:

Drawing on the social skills listed in Figure 5.1, this list can be used to evaluate whether students exhibit these skills *usually, sometimes,* or *never.* Use this instrument to select skills as learning outcomes for specific students.

DIRECTIONS;

Determine whether the student demonstrates each skill:

NEVER: You have seen the student *never* or *hardly ever* exhibit the skill.

SOMETIMES: You have seen the student exhibit the skill *at one time and not another.*

USUALLY: You have seen the student exhibit the skill *consistently* and *appropriately in different situations.*

Place a checkmark under the appropriate column. If a skill is targeted for intervention, enter the date under the TARGETED column. To measure change and evaluate the effectiveness of interventions, administer the *Social Skills Rating Scale–T* at a later time. Use different colors to record ratings completed at different times on the same form.

The Student:	Never	Sometimes	Usually	Targeted
joins a group in the classroom	_____	_____	_____	_____
interrupts an ongoing activity	_____	_____	_____	_____
participates in group discussions	_____	_____	_____	_____
joins ongoing conversations	_____	_____	_____	_____
makes conversation	_____	_____	_____	_____
asks for help	_____	_____	_____	_____
accepts help	_____	_____	_____	_____
joins a group in the lunchroom	_____	_____	_____	_____
joins a group on the playground	_____	_____	_____	_____
maintains friendships	_____	_____	_____	_____
deals with loneliness	_____	_____	_____	_____
deals with peer pressure	_____	_____	_____	_____
deals with disappointment	_____	_____	_____	_____
deals with covert rejection	_____	_____	_____	_____
deals with overt rejection	_____	_____	_____	_____
responds to teasing	_____	_____	_____	_____
makes friends	_____	_____	_____	_____
is on-task in a group	_____	_____	_____	_____
works cooperatively	_____	_____	_____	_____
leaves a group	_____	_____	_____	_____
avoids conflict	_____	_____	_____	_____
participates in discussions	_____	_____	_____	_____
plays cooperatively	_____	_____	_____	_____
responds to being left-out	_____	_____	_____	_____
deals with embarrassment	_____	_____	_____	_____
accepts a new group member	_____	_____	_____	_____
works in a large group	_____	_____	_____	_____
works in a small group	_____	_____	_____	_____
works with one other person	_____	_____	_____	_____

INTERPRETATION:

Whether the student performs a necessary skill *sometimes* or *never* can make a substantial difference in how the teacher can help the student. The text of Chapter 5 has suggestions for dealing with the students.

FIGURE 5.4 Social Behavior Rating Scale (Teacher Version)

Student _____ Grade _____ Age _____

Rater _____

PURPOSE:

Drawing on the social behaviors listed in Figure 5.2, this list can be used to evaluate whether students exhibit these behaviors *usually, sometimes,* or *never.* Use this instrument to select behaviors as learning outcomes for specific students.

DIRECTIONS;

Determine whether the student demonstrates each behavior:

NEVER: You have seen the student *never* or *hardly ever* exhibit the behavior.

SOMETIMES: You have seen the student exhibit the behavior *at one time and not another.*

USUALLY: You have seen the student exhibit the behavior *consistently* and *appropriately in different situations.*

Place a checkmark under the appropriate column. If a behavior is targeted for intervention, enter the date under the TARGETED column. To measure change and evaluate the effectiveness of interventions, administer the *Social Behavior Rating Scale–T* at a later time. Use different colors to record ratings completed at different times on the same form.

The Student:	Never	Sometimes	Usually	Targeted
smiles	_____	_____	_____	_____
establishes eye contact	_____	_____	_____	_____
maintains eye contact	_____	_____	_____	_____
greets others	_____	_____	_____	_____
initiates a conversation	_____	_____	_____	_____
ends a conversation	_____	_____	_____	_____
introduces self	_____	_____	_____	_____
listens	_____	_____	_____	_____
asks for help	_____	_____	_____	_____
accepts help	_____	_____	_____	_____
offers help	_____	_____	_____	_____
accepts praise	_____	_____	_____	_____
respects another's space	_____	_____	_____	_____
gives compliments	_____	_____	_____	_____
interrupts appropriately	_____	_____	_____	_____
asks for permission	_____	_____	_____	_____
forms a line	_____	_____	_____	_____
walks in line	_____	_____	_____	_____
leaves others appropriately	_____	_____	_____	_____
gives praise	_____	_____	_____	_____
says nice things	_____	_____	_____	_____
negotiates	_____	_____	_____	_____
shares materials	_____	_____	_____	_____
takes turns	_____	_____	_____	_____
shares ideas	_____	_____	_____	_____
gives criticism	_____	_____	_____	_____
accepts criticism	_____	_____	_____	_____

INTERPRETATION:

The observation instruments provided in Appendix C can also be used to identify and substantiate the information obtained from this rating scale. Use these data to set learning outcomes. Chapter 5 gives suggestions for the different approaches to use depending on whether a student *sometimes* or *never* uses a behavior.

FIGURE 5.6 What Do You Do When . . . ?

PURPOSE:
Use this exercise to clarify whether a student can use social knowledge to problem-solve in social situations and to apply social behaviors effectively.

DIRECTIONS:
From the list below, select questions that seem typical of the social situations that students in your classroom and elementary school face on a daily basis. Consider, as well, the social and academic competence of the student when selecting questions.

Tell the student that you are going to ask what s/he would do in certain situation.

Ask the student: *What do you do when you . . . ?*

Probe for additional information by asking if there is anything more.

Audiotape responses and then, on the Response Form below, fill in the questions asked, enter the student's words *verbatim,* and note whether the topic addresses *Perception, Decision Making,* or *Action (Evaluation).*

Questions
What do you do when you . . .

1. hear two of your friends arguing?
2. brush your teeth?
3. want to use the swing and someone else has had it for a long time?
4. see a classmate all alone during recess?
5. see two classmates fighting?
6. see someone cheat on a test?
7. need to get the teacher's attention?
8. know the correct answer during a class discussion?
9. are tutoring a classmate?
10. meet the principal?
11. see someone crying?
12. disagree with someone?
13. come into the classroom and everyone is busy in a group?
14. need help?
15. finish a task?
16. answer the telephone?
17. bump into someone?
18. feel like crying?
19. are playing a game with a friend?
20. meet a friend in the hallway?
21. have to deliver a message to a teacher and the classroom door is closed?
22. feel lonely?
23. are disappointed?
24. lose a game?
25. win a game?
26. are given something by someone?
27. know that someone needs your crayons?
28. are afraid?
29. go to recess?
30. ride the school bus?
31. see the teacher at the post office?
32. are embarrassed?
33. see someone in trouble?
34. are angry?

FIGURE 5.6 What Do You Do When . . . ? *(Continued)*

35. want a sticker that a classmate has?
36. can't figure out the right answer?
37. are given a compliment by someone?
38. fail?
39. want a classmate to do something with you?
40. make a mistake?
41. think the teacher doesn't like you?
42. have to do something you don't like to do?
43. are frustrated?
44. know that someone else has done something wonderful?
45. have to do something new?
46. feel left out?
47. have forgotten the directions?
48. finish your work early?
49. think your teacher is wrong?
50. think a classmate is telling lies about you to your classmates or teachers?

Response Form

A. What do you do when you _____ :
   Response:

   _____ Perception _____ Decision Making _____ Action (Evaluation)

B. What do you do when you _____ :
   Response:

   _____ Perception _____ Decision Making _____ Action (Evaluation)

C. What do you do when you _____ :
   Response:

   _____ Perception _____ Decision Making _____ Action (Evaluation)

INTERPRETATION:
Notice if the student is having difficulty with perceiving, decision making, and/or suggesting actions. Chapter 5 suggests many techniques for dealing with these types of situations and developing the three aspects of social knowledge.

- *Identify What is Most Important to Learn.* While it may be tempting to focus only on what you wish to have happen in your classroom, it is also important to identify what might be most important for students to learn.

- *Focus on Possibilities.* Determine what students might be doing if inappropriate or bothersome behaviors were reduced or eliminated. If students do not interrupt, they might be listening or thinking about possible responses—things you can teach. Observe socially skilled students for ideas.

- *Involve Students in the Process.* Ask students what they want to learn. You are more likely to gain their interest and cooperation. Your interventions are more likely to succeed because students tend to learn when they are motivated. Observations of socially skilled students might also suggest social skills that have value to individual students and their peers.

- *Select Outcomes with Natural Reinforcers.* Social behaviors that result in immediate natural feedback from peers (a smile, a thank you, or a pat on the back) or decision-making skills that can also be used in academic tasks may be highly motivating to students.

- *Make it Real.* Use real problems and realistic solutions. Students will view the learning as worthwhile and useful to them if it is part of their daily experience. They are also more likely to apply social skills if they see the similarity between instruction and real life settings. Observe students and their peers in many situations throughout the school to make instruction and real life settings more similar and increase the likelihood that students will actually apply social skills.

- *Provide Students with a Rationale.* Discuss learning outcomes with students. Talk about how these new skills will help them feel better about themselves. Help them understand how being more socially skilled will allow them to take greater control and responsibility for all their learning.

There are no absolutely correct answers when determining learning outcomes; the choice depends on the situations that students face. For some students, it will be more helpful to learn specific behaviors needed in specific situations such as how to enter a classroom or the lunchroom. For others, it will be more useful to learn one social behavior such as establishing eye contact, that could be used in many different situations. Still for others, it might be more important to learn how to use social knowledge to cope with problematic social situations. If joining a group in the classroom is particularly difficult for a student, teaching how to select from many behaviors might be more useful than teaching a specific behavior.

Sometimes the best choice is that which is the easiest to teach or the easiest to learn. A small immediate success might have the greater positive social consequences overall. Teachers should not hesitate to rely on their own judgment because they have the best knowledge of the needs of their individual students and their class as a whole.

Once learning outcomes have been determined, they can be easily incorporated as social goals, objectives, and instructional techniques into the individual educational plans of students with special needs. If instructional time is an issue, social skills instruction can be included in the *additional information* or *individual learning profile* sections of an Educational Plan. Appendix D: *Goals and Objectives for Individualized Educational Plans (IEPs)* provides examples of social goals and objectives that can be incorporated into educational plans. These same goals and objectives might serve as models for addressing the individual instructional needs of other students in your classroom as well.

TEACHING SOCIAL SKILLS

Once students have been identified and learning outcomes determined, it is natural for teachers to start teaching social skills immediately. However, there are two points to consider first. The first point is simple, usually overlooked, and frequently an effective action that should always be taken before teaching. Find out not only what students know but also what they will and will not do. You might be pleasantly surprised if you simply ask the student to stop behaving in a certain way—"Could please talk less?" or to start behaving in an appropriate way—"Will you stand farther away from me?" For those unaware of the effect their actions have on others, a simple request might work. "I'm sorry; I guess I could get up and get a tissue."

The second tactic is less simple but can be very effective in changing behavior. Develop a plan. Identify meaningful contingencies—rewards that students will work to achieve and consequences they will work to avoid. Carefully measure the frequency or duration of inappropriate behaviors and implement rewards or punishments according to a schedule. An appropriate plan can help students reduce or eliminate behaviors that interfere with productive social interactions.

Two techniques to teach social behaviors and improve social knowledge are described in the following sections. These techniques incorporate strategies designed to ensure accuracy and proficiency, as well as opportunities for practice and transfer to other situations. To use these techniques most appropriately, you should know whether students *always* have problems with certain social behaviors or aspects of social knowledge, or whether these problems are *inconsistent*. The assessment data you have already gathered should indicate where to begin. *Always* suggests beginning with instruction. *Inconsistency* (sometimes) suggests beginning with practice and praise. Practice and praise help students become more proficient and perform with greater accuracy, speed, and consistency. If you provide opportunities for students to practice social skills with their peers, students are more likely to maintain social behaviors and use this knowledge without ongoing teacher-directed drill and reinforcement. Transferring social behaviors and using social knowledge in other situations is the final measure of successful social skills instruction.

In the following sections, the modeling and coaching procedures to teach social behaviors and to improve social knowledge are described. A sample activity is included for both modeling and coaching within the following sections. Additional activities are provided in Appendices A and B.

USING MODELING TO TEACH SOCIAL BEHAVIORS

Students who have difficulty with social behaviors may not demonstrate the behaviors at all or do so without accuracy and/or fluency. They either fail to perform the behavior or they perform the behavior incorrectly and inefficiently. Modeling is the best way for teachers to help students acquire, practice, and begin to apply specific social behaviors both accurately and fluently.

To model, teachers or peers demonstrate (model) the behavior; then the student imitates the behavior. If the student imitates the behavior correctly, the model provides praise. If the student imitates the skill incorrectly, the model provides corrective feedback and repeats the modeling sequence.

To use modeling effectively, teachers select social behaviors that are either visually or audibly observable and easily imitated. Nodding, smiling at others, standing an acceptable distance away from others, saying hello, or establishing and maintaining eye contact, are examples of social behaviors that can be seen or heard. Each of these behaviors also may be easily demonstrated by models. Modeling is especially helpful to teach behaviors that are new to a student, are rarely exhibited, or are being performed incorrectly. For example, if students never greet friends or do so infrequently or incorrectly, modeling will enable students to acquire or refine their performance of this behavior.

Social behaviors learned in isolation may be linked to other social and cultural behaviors to form the longer sequences of social behaviors that may be used as social strategies. Picking up the telephone receiver, saying hello, listening to the speaker's message, responding appropriately, saying goodbye, and replacing the receiver, are individual behaviors that may be learned in isolation by modeling, and then linked together to enable students to perform the strategy of answering the telephone. Linking individual behaviors together to form strategies is an appropriate way for students to learn how individual social behaviors can be used in different ways that are socially appropriate. Linking also helps them develop the flexibility they need to deal with different social situations effectively.

Modeling has several advantages. First, it may be used to help students manage many common everyday situations. For example, when students seek the teacher's attention inappropriately (calling out), teachers can intervene immediately and model the correct procedure (hand raising or silent eye contact). When modeling is used this way, errors are corrected immediately.

Second, teachers can give immediate supportive or corrective feedback to students because the behaviors are observable (waving hello) or audible (saying hello). This type of feedback reduces the chance that students will continue to practice errors and encourages them to use successful behaviors.

Third, it is easy to measure behavior change by tallying the number of correct responses during a modeling activity or the number of times a student uses the behavior in real situations. Peers and students themselves can learn to monitor their own behavior and begin the process of taking greater responsibility for their own actions.

Fourth, modeling is effective because it is familiar to students. Since infancy, children have learned by observing and imitating their parents, peers, and others. At home, children have learned by observing and imitating their parents, peers, and others. At home, children have learned to set the table, fold laundry, put dishes in the dishwasher, and pour milk from a carton without spilling because they observed and modeled their parents and siblings as they performed these tasks. On the playground they have mimicked their peers to learn how to play a new game. In the classroom, students have learned to line up, raise their hands, form the letters of the alphabet, and pledge allegiance to the flag by copying their peers or their teachers. Modeling social behaviors is a natural extension of a student's most common learning mode and is especially appropriate for teaching social behaviors.

While modeling is usually an effective way for most students to learn, some students have specific learning problems that interfere with their ability to acquire social behaviors. They have difficulty perceiving the many subtle behaviors, social cues, and words that others use in social interactions. For these students, providing distinct visual and auditory cues and a meaningful purpose for the activity helps.

Other students lack the motivation or self-control to participate in modeling activities successfully. For these students, using incentives, feedback, and reinforcement provides the external structure needed to model skills accurately.

To implement modeling to teach social behaviors, use the following eight-step sequence in Figure 5.7. Each step is keyed to the letters of the word M-O-D-E-L-I-N-G to help you remember how to use the modeling procedure.

1. *Make Choices.* First, choose the appropriate behavior to be modeled The behavior should be one that the student needs to learn or relearn. The behavior should also be meaningful to the particular student. Next, choose an individual to model the behavior. The model should be highly skilled in the behavior and respected. The model must also know how to act in a friendly and helpful manner and provide appropriate feedback. Teachers will find many models in a school setting; these models include peers, other teachers, paraprofessionals, and staff members. While adults may serve as effective models, students often prefer to copy models of the same sex, similar age, or social status. Characters from television, movies and stories also are appropriate and motivate students to imitate.

2. *Organize the Behavior.* After both the behavior and the model have been selected, organize the behavior by parts (or steps) and sequence the parts, either from simple to complex or in chronological order. For example, to listen effectively, an individual must:

   a. Establish and maintain eye contact.

   b. Keep a pleasant expression.

   c. Nod when understanding.

   d. Ask questions or make statements when not understanding, needing clarification, or when the other person pauses.

3. *Demonstrate the Behavior.* The person selected as a model demonstrates the behavior to the student. To teach *listening* the model might say the following:

   Watch me as I show you how to listen.

   Pretend that someone else is talking to me.

   First, I look at the other person's eyes.

   While I am looking, I keep a pleasant expression on my face (like this).

   If I understand what the other person is saying, I nod my head (like this.)

   I do not understand, I might say: "Excuse me, could you repeat that last sentence.

   The model then demonstrates the behavior.

4. *Encourage the Student to Imitate.* Review each step of the behavior and, if appropriate, emphasize the importance of a particular step. Then ask the student to imitate (model) the behavior. It is essential to give the student immediate feedback as s/he imitates the

FIGURE 5.7 Modeling

- **M**ake Choices
  Select a behavior and a model.

- **O**rganize the Behavior
  Divide by parts and sequence.

- **D**emonstrate the Behavior
  Use verbal and nonverbal cues at first.

- **E**ncourage the Student to Imitate
  Provide praise or corrective feedback.

- **L**ink the Behavior
  Connect behavior to other behaviors, situations, self-confidence.

- **I**ntegrate into Classroom Routine
  Provide opportunities to use new behaviors.

- **N**otice the Behavior
  Provide praise or corrective feedback.

- **G**eneralize the Behavior
  Practice in other situations, with other people, and at other times.

---

behavior. If the student imitates the behavior correctly, tell the student that it was performed correctly and praise that performance (supportive feedback). If the student has difficulty following the total sequence, tell the student why the imitation is incorrect (corrective feedback). Then, either demonstrate the entire behavior again or only that portion of the behavior that was imitated incorrectly. Then encourage the student to demonstrate the behavior again, proceed more slowly, and reward or praise each correct imitation. As each step is performed correctly, help the student link each correctly imitated step together until the total behavior sequence is complete. For example, if the student listens accurately with the exception of establishing eye contact, do the following:

a. Practice establishing eye contact until the student masters this behavior. Praise or provide corrective feedback.

b. Link *establishing eye contact* to *keep a pleasant expression*. Practice until the student masters these two behaviors in sequence. Praise or provide corrective feedback.

c. Continue to add skills to the sequence until the entire sequence has been modeled. Praise or provide corrective feedback.

d. Then repeat the sequence from the beginning. Reward or provide corrective feedback.

e. Repeat this process until the behavior is demonstrated correctly.

If someone other than the teacher is the model, it is important to reward that person as well. If models receive rewards for performing social behaviors appropriately, students learn that correct performances lead to pleasant consequences. This knowledge provides additional motivation for students to perform the behavior correctly and then serve as models for their peers.

5. *Link the Behavior.* After the student has successfully demonstrated the behavior, link the behavior to other behaviors and situations. For example, discuss how important listening is, the many opportunities for listening in the classroom, and the rationale for listening. Combine listening with other behaviors such as maintaining a conversation or participating in a discussion. Encourage students to use the listening behavior to help them feel more confident about their ability to get along with other people.

6. *Integrate into Classroom Routine.* Once students have begun to demonstrate a behavior with direct instruction and feedback, they need more opportunities to practice that behavior. Structure these practice times and cue students as to when to practice certain behaviors. You might tell a student that s/he will be giving directions for a reading assignment and that other students will need to listen carefully. Review the steps for listening and tell students to watch a particular student (who listens well) as a model. Giving students opportunities to practice social behaviors during academic tasks improves both social and academic achievement. Tell your students you expect them to listen and post listening as a classroom rule. This will reinforce and clarify this expectation.

7. *Notice the Behavior.* As students practice behaviors during the school day, notice their behavior and provide praise or corrective feedback. Encourage other students to provide praise or corrective feedback to their peers. In this way, the behavior is reinforced or corrected more frequently than if only you were noticing the behavior.

8. *Generalize the Behavior.* The final measure of the success of modeling is how well the student is able to use the behavior in other situations, with other individuals, and at other times. Encourage generalization by discussing opportunities for using the behavior outside the classroom, by asking peers and other adults to provide both opportunities and feedback to the student, and by requiring students to monitor their behavior and report their successes and efforts outside the classroom. The goal is for students to use behaviors spontaneously and appropriately without teacher guidance.

Figure 5.8 provides detailed instructions to guide a modeling activity. Additional modeling activities are outlined in Appendix A. The following guidelines may also be helpful as you use modeling to teach social behaviors.

GUIDELINES
FOR USING
MODELING

- *Use the Teachable Moment.* If a situation arises in which a student might benefit from learning a social behavior, teach it then and there. Social behaviors are very discrete actions that can be modeled and imitated quickly. They are most likely to be remembered and applied in the future effectively if you take advantage of real behaviors as they occur in the classrom.

- *Set Up Your Students.* Guarantee that situations will arise in which students will need to use the social behaviors they have learned. Not only will this give them opportunities for additional practice and refinement, it will also enable them to look competent in front of their peers.

FIGURE 5.8 Social Behavior: Listening

RATIONALE:

Knowing how to listen—a basic behavior needed to make and maintain friendships—makes other people think you are interested in what they are saying. If you do not listen, others will think you are not interested in them or that you do not care about them. As a result, they may think you do not want to be their friend, and they may not seek you out.

Make choices:

1. Select a behavior: listening
2. Select a model: a peer or a teacher

Organize the behavior:

1. Establish and maintain eye contact.
2. Keep a pleasant expression.
3. Nod when you understand.
4. Use verbal (ask questions or make statements) or nonverbal (puzzled expression or slight move ment away) responses when you do not understand or want clarification.

Demonstrate the behavior:

1. Demonstrate listening with another adult in a conversation with the goal being to listen for one full minute.

Encourage the student to imitate:

1. Review the steps for good listening. Use key words: eye contact, smile, nod, and ask questions.
2. Discuss with students that it is important to let the other person know that you understand what the person is saying by nodding and smiling.
3. Discuss with students that it is important to let the other person know, by using verbal or nonverbal responses, that you do not understand what the person is saying.
4. Ask the student to imitate listening.

Link the behavior:

1. Review the rationale for listening; discuss why listening is an important social behavior.
2. Discuss opportunities for listening the classroom.
3. Have students discuss how not listening could interfere with their ability to get along with others.
4. Provide students with a variety of role-plays for them to practice listening and responding in various ways, such as asking for clarification or repeating what a person has said.
5. Combine listening with other social behaviors such as making conversation or receiving praise.
6. Combine listening with other social skills such as participating in group discussions or working cooperatively.
7. Discuss feelings of increased social self-confidence when students are able to listen effectively.

Integrate into classroom routine:

1. Cue students when it is important for them to listen for directions, instructions, and clarifications.
2. Provide students with many opportunities to listen and follow directions to complete academic tasks. This practice may help students focus for longer periods in structured situations.
3. Discuss with students various ways by which they can ask for help when they do not understand instructions.
4. Periodically review with students good listening behaviors.
5. Expect students to listen.

Notice the behavior:

1. Praise and reinforce students when they listen and ask for clarifications.
2. Allow students to ask for clarifications, without being admonished for not listening. Students should feel comfortable saying they don't understand.
3. Teach students to praise one another when they listen.

Generalize the behavior:

1. Discuss various times during the school day outside of the classroom when it is important for students to listen.

- *Catch Your Students Using Social Behaviors.* Use your own antennae to monitor and reinforce students who take the time to model social behaviors for one another. Reward them for supporting one another. Again, use peers to help you in this effort.
- *Call Attention to Modeling in Other Areas.* Tell students when modeling happens at other times in the school day. Point out how they are copying you or one another to learn math algorithms, classroom transitions, a song, a dance, or a game.

USING COACHING TO TEACH SOCIAL KNOWLEDGE

Students who lack social knowledge do not apply behaviors they already know in appropriate and effective ways. They may not identify or interpret situations correctly or have the social experience to know what behaviors and strategies were effective in the past. They may not evaluate possible responses to determine consequences or select the best possible response. They may fail to monitor and evaluate the effectiveness of the actions they do take. Coaching is the most efficient, effective way to help students develop, practice, and implement the problem-solving abilities they need to apply social behaviors to resolve the social dilemmas they face in their daily lives.

The coaching procedure is familiar to most teachers, children, and parents. Teachers and parents often coach children on what to do should a stranger approach them, should they try to cross a busy street, or should they discover a fire in their home. In this informal coaching procedure, children discuss with an appropriate adult how a particular situation might evolve and how to solve the problem. If a child wants to cross a busy street, for example, s/he might ask for an adult's help, wait for the traffic light to change to a red and yellow light, or push the button to turn on the WALK signal. Through a problem-solving discussion with a parent or teacher, the child considers alternative responses and the consequences before selecting one that might be effective.

Coaching is an effective way for students to develop social knowledge. To coach students, teachers first present a hypothetical social problem in the form of a story or picture. Teachers then ask a series of coaching questions designed to help students learn a cognitive problem-solving process within a hypothetical situation to apply social behaviors in real social situations. These questions ask what the students have seen or heard and what they might do in this situation. Then, students are assigned roles and the situation is acted out with the suggested responses. Students then discuss whether their responses were effective in resolving the social problem and achieving the social goal.

To use coaching effectively, teachers should select hypothetical social situations that have relevance for students and require the use of more than one social behavior. For example, some students might need to learn how to respond to teasing while others would benefit from learning how to join an ongoing classroom activity. These situations are difficult for students who have problems accurately perceiving a situation, making a correct decision, and taking action; yet they are situations that students continue to face every day.

Coaching has several advantages. First coaching is flexible and it can be used alone or in combination with modeling. Used alone, coaching helps students learn how to problem–solve. Used in combination with modeling, coaching gives students additional opportunities to practice and refine newly acquired behaviors to resolve a real social dilemma in the relative safety of a hypothetical situation. Coaching sessions also enable teachers to identify behaviors that students do not demonstrate with accuracy or proficiency. In these cases, modeling might be combined with coaching to focus on those specific behaviors.

Second, coaching also enables students to practice combining social behaviors into strategies. For example, to join a group working cooperatively, a student might combine the behaviors of *smiling* and *establishing eye contact* to implement the strategy of *joining a group*. Coaching also gives students the opportunity to explore alternative strategies and combinations of behaviors in similar social situations. Therefore, students quickly learn how some behaviors may be applied to more than one social situation.

Third, coaching gives students the opportunity to practice their responses through a guided re-enactment. As students implement their strategies, the teacher, as coach, uses comments to guide the students' actions. A student learning to answer the telephone properly might hear cues such as, "First say hello. Then ask who's calling. Give your name only if you know who is calling. Remember to offer to take a message." Prior discussions followed by guided practice enable students to achieve greater mastery of social goals, strategies, and behaviors.

Fourth, coaching can motivate students to learn and use problem-solving as an effective strategy in a variety of learning tasks. Although coaching situations are hypothetical, students are more likely to consider and engage in behaviors that may be too difficult or sensitive for them to try out in real situations, without the support that coaching affords.

Fifth, coaching takes full advantage of peers. As students become involved in coaching situations, the teacher steps back and lets students learn to rely on one another and themselves. The course of action is prescribed by peers rather than by teachers, and interactions are practiced with and immediately reinforced by peers, not teachers.

Sixth, coaching facilitates the reciprocal relationship that exists between social and academic competence because the problem-solving process used in coaching can be applied to both types of tasks. Knowing how to perceive, make decisions, and act on those decisions are skills students can apply across the curriculum.

Finally, the fact that coaching situations are hypothetical enables teachers to help students develop strategies for situations that occur beyond the classroom environment. Teachers can deal with family issues, as well as issues from the playground, the bus, the lunchroom, or another classroom. Students can also be helped to develop strategies for dealing with other individuals in their lives: parents, bus drivers, specialists, lunch monitors, and other members of the school community. Teachers can also model the coaching procedure for colleagues and parents to apply in other school settings and at home.

While coaching is an effective way for students to develop social knowledge, some students still have difficulty using coaching effectively. Those with cognitive deficits, learning disabilities, or behavior problems may be less able to determine social goals, to remember previous social situations, to consider response consequences, or to evaluate the effectiveness of a response.

Still others tend to give up if their first attempt is not successful. For students who have a history of unsuccessful social interactions, one more failure during the coaching session may simply reinforce their perceptions of themselves as failures. Teachers and peers who encourage a second and third try that is ultimately successful help these students rethink their self-perceptions and also learn the value of persistence.

To implement coaching as a way to teach social knowledge, use the following eight-step sequence in Figure 5.9. Each step is keyed to the letters of the word C-O-A-C-H-I-N-G to help you remember the procedure.

1. *Construct a Hypothetical Social Problem.* Select situations that are real and have meaning to your students. These situations must contain a believable social problem or dilemma that presents itself often in their lives of your students. Observe or ask students for ideas, or use prepared situations found in the coaching activity that follows this outline, one of those provided in Appendix B, in the literature your students read, or in the television or videotapes they watch. Sources are innumerable and limited only by your imagination and persistence, but be sure to use fictitious characters, names, locations, and time frames.

2. *Organize a Discussion.* Once you have selected an appropriate situation, organize a group discussion among a heterogeneous group of students. Take special care to include students of varying academic and social abilities in the groups. This group may consist of as few as three or four students or the entire class. The greater the number of students, the greater the number of ideas and possible solutions that will be generated during discussion. However, it is easier for individual students to contribute in smaller groups. You might present a situation such as the following to your students in the form of a picture or story:

   Linda and Brian were assembling a new puzzle during indoor recess. Both Linda and Brian enjoy puzzles and usually play well together. When they were halfway through the puzzle, Karl approached them, sat down, and began to break apart the finished section of the puzzle. Linda and Brian shouted at Karl and began to push him away from the table.

   Consider the circumstances, the participants, the alternative actions or behaviors, and the possible outcomes.

3. *Ask the Coaching Questions.* Guide students through the coaching procedure by asking several questions about each of the three components of social knowledge: perception, decision making, and action. You can select from those suggested in Figures 5.10 and 5.11. Select one or two questions from each component to help students decide on specific strategies or behaviors that could be used to resolve the dilemma. Let the students decide what to do, even if you think there might be a better way. In regard to the situation presented before, you might ask:

   Perception

   > *What's going on here? What's happening in this story?*
   > *Who are the people in the story?*
   > *What are Linda and Brian trying to do?*
   > *How does Karl feel? How do Linda and Brian feel?*
   > *Are Linda and Brian friends?*

   Decision Making

   > *What is Karl trying to do?*
   > *Have you ever been in a situation like this?*
   > *What did you do? What did the other people do?*
   > *What happened when you tried _____ or _____ ?*
   > *What could Karl do in this situation? What might happen?*
   > *What else could he do?*
   > *What is the best idea to solve this problem?*

FIGURE 5.9 Coaching

- **C**onstruct a Hypothetical Social Problem
  Use a real problem in a make believe format.

- **O**rganize a Discussion
  Select a heterogeneous group of students.

- **A**sk the Coaching Questions
  Perceive situations.
  Make decisions.

- **C**hoose Students to Play Roles
  Match students to roles.
  Let students act out the situation.

- **H**elp Students Evaluate the Effectiveness of Responses
  Evaluate effectiveness of behaviors.

- **I**ntegrate into Classroom Routine
  Provide opportunities to use new knowledge.

- **N**otice Interactions
  Provide praise or corrective feedback.

- **G**eneralize Social Knowledge
  Practice in other situations, with other people, and at other times.

4. *Choose Students to Play Roles.* Once students have identified some possible solutions to the problem and perhaps selected the best strategy, choose students to play the roles of the participants in the social problem that was presented. Use your best judgment to provide every student with opportunities to either watch or act out new roles. Give typically passive students and onlookers active roles in which they can try out a new behavior within the safety of a make-believe situation. Reverse roles and give the class bully an opportunity to be bullied. For others, it may be more valuable to observe. If you have organized a large group for the discussion, you might assign several students roles as official observers who watch and perhaps record the actions of those who actually play roles.

5. *Help Students Evaluate.* After students play out the social problem with the solutions suggested, help students evaluate how successful their strategies were, what the positive and negative consequences were, and how each person felt. Conduct follow-up discussions in which everyone, both role players and observers alike, participates. Refer to Figure 5.12 for ideas. In reference to the situation presented above, you might ask:

Action

What happened? What did the others do?
What did you do? How did you feel?
Did you reach your goal?
Should you try again?

At this point, let students act out the situation again if they wish so they can try out alternative strategies. Emphasize that any problem can have more than one good solution.

FIGURE 5.10 Social Knowledge: Perception Questions

IDENTIFY PRESENT SITUATION:
Group Goal:

What's going on here?

What's happening in this story/picture/movie?

What are the members of the group trying to do?

What is their goal?

Is there anything else they are trying to accomplish?

Participants:

Who's in the group?

What are they doing to accomplish the goal?

What else are they doing?

Relevant concepts:

What is . . . (a friend, sharing, trust, etc.)?

Why is . . . (a friend, sharing, trust, etc.) important?

How do you . . . (make a friend, learn to share, trust, etc.)?

INTERPRET PRESENT SITUATION:
Roles:

Who is the leader?

Which members are participants/onlookers?

Motives:

Why is . . . acting that way?

What does s/he want?

Attitudes:

Which members have positive/negative attitudes?

How do you know?

Feelings:

How does she or he feel?

How do you know?

Relationships:

Which members are friends? How do you know?

Which members like/dislike each other? how do you know?

Consequences of Strategies and Behaviors:

What is happening as a result of the strategies and behaviors being used?

Are there any problems in this situation?

FIGURE 5.11 Social Knowledge: Decision-Making Questions

SELECT PERSONAL GOAL:
As a participant in this situation, what do you want?

What do you hope to have happen?

RECALL PREVIOUS SITUATIONS:
Group Goals:

Have you ever been in a situation like this?

What was going on?

What were the members of the group trying to do?

What else were they trying to do?

What were you trying to do?

Participants:

Who was in the group?

Who was there?

What were their roles? motives? attitudes? feelings? relationships?

Strategies and Behaviors:

What were the members of the group doing?

What were you doing?

What strategies and behaviors were being used to achieve the goal?

Consequences:

What happened as a result of the actions of participants?

What happened when you _____? or _____?

EVALUATE POSSIBLE RESPONSES:
Consequences of Responses:
What might happen if you . . . ? or if you . . . ?

Compare Responses:

What could you do in this situation?

What else could you do?

What is the best strategy or behavior?

What is the worst strategy or behavior?

What is the next best or next worst strategy or behavior?

Review Response Repertoire:

Which strategies do you know?

Which behaviors do you know?

SELECT RESPONSES:
Which strategy/behavior will you use? Why?

FIGURE 5.12 Social Knowledge: Action Questions

MONITOR AND EVALUATE RESPONSE EFFECTIVENESS:

Participant feedback:

What happened?

What did the others say or do?

How do you think they felt?

Personal feedback:

What happened?

What did you say or do?

How did you feel?

Goal Achievement:

Were your responses effective? Why? Why not?

Did you reach your personal goal?

Need for Recycling:

Do you think you might reach your goal if you tried again?

Were your perceptions of the situations accurate?

Were your decisions appropriate?

What might you do differently?

What will you do the next time?

6. *Integrate into Classroom Routine.* Integrate opportunities to practice problem-solving that includes action and evaluation at other times during the school day. Structure these practice times by setting up many opportunities for students to play and work together. Let students know that you expect them to use these problem-solving procedures to solve academic as well as social problems.

7. *Notice Interactions.* Provide praise or corrective feedback when students interact with one another and solve problems together. Encourage other students to provide praise or corrective feedback to their peers in these situations.

8. *Generalize Social Knowledge.* Encourage maintenance and generalization by discussing opportunities to use social knowledge in other situations, with other individuals, and at other times. Ask peers and other adults to provide both opportunities and feedback to your students. Require students to monitor their social skills and report their successes and efforts outside the classroom.

Figure 5.13 provides detailed instructions to guide you through a coaching activity. Additional coaching activities are outlined in detail in Appendix B.

The following guidelines may also be helpful as you use coaching to teach social knowledge.

GUIDELINES
FOR USING
COACHING

- *Select Believable Situations.* Be on the lookout for problem situations that your students face. Try to think of similar situations that occur in the stories they read or in the cartoons they watch. Use their *culture* as the basis for discussions.

- *Camouflage your Motives.* Use imaginary names for characters and locations. Change the ages and alter the motives. Your objective is to raise issues, not embarrass students.

- *Let Students Make Mistakes.* Try very hard to be quiet when students are coming up with possible solutions to the dilemma. Try to let the action take its course and the reactions come from peers.

- *Advertise the Process.* Post a simplified version of the coaching questions for students to use in other situations. List the questions on written activities that might involve problem-solving (word problems, comprehension questions that involve prediction, etc.).

- *Spread the Process.* Use the coaching process in other areas of instruction. Embed social issues into a lesson on punctuation by having students record and then punctuate the words spoken in a role play. The role play might involve a situation in which the skills needed to deal with loneliness or make a friend were an issue.

- *Take Advantage of the Socially Competent Whenever You Can.* Enlist the support (within reason) of those students who are socially competent and kind persons as well. They can serve as group leaders and role models in cooperative activities and supporters and encouragers of their peers at unexpected, yet important, moments.

DECIDING WHEN TO USE MODELING OR COACHING

You have many options to address the social needs of your students within a school day. You might (1) teach and/or model specific behaviors to

FIGURE 5.13 Social Knowledge: Asking for Help

RATIONALE:
Knowing how to ask for help will enable you to participate more fully in group activities. Everyone needs help at some time and generally understands when another person asks for help. Giving help to another person also makes the giver feel better. With help, you will become a more skillful participant in group activities—some other group members may then seek you out and ask you to join in other activities.

Construct a hypothetical social problem: (See page 120)
Everybody in Joe's class was working in a group. Joe's group was supposed to make one story and one graph about insects. Everybody in Joe's group knew how to do the work on the project except Joe. He didn't know how to do his part of the job. He didn't know whether to ask for help or sit quietly, hope no one noticed, and let the others do everything.
What should Joe do?

Organize a discussion:
1. Select a heterogeneous group of students to discuss the problem.
2. Include students who are socially competent as well as those who need to develop social knowledge and become more socially skilled.
3. Read the hypothetical social problem and/or show the picture to the students.

Ask the coaching questions:

Understand Concepts:	What is helpfulness?
	Why is helpfulness important?
Perceive Situations:	
Recognize the situation:	What's going on here?
	What's happening in this story?
Identify the participants:	Who are the people in the story?
Identify the goals:	What are the students in Joe's group trying to do?
Identify behaviors:	How are they doing this?
	What else are they doing?
Identify the social problem:	What's the problem in this situation?
	What is Joe trying to do?
Identify the perspective of others:	How does Joe feel?
Make Decisions:	
Recall past experiences:	Have you ever been in a situation like this?
Identify previous behaviors:	What did you do?
	What did other people do?
Identify consequences:	What happened when you _____ ? or _____ ?
Identify behaviors to use:	What could Joe do in this situation?
	What might happen?
	What else could he do?
	What could the others do?
	What might happen?
	What is the best idea to solve this problem?

Choose students to play roles:
1. Select students of varying social abilities to play key roles.
2. Give students opportunities to practice new ways of behaving.

Figure 5.13 Social Knowledge: Asking for Help *(Continued)*

3. Provide other students with the experience of being treated differently by their peers.
4. Allow students to role play the situation using the behaviors they have selected.
5. Provide students with as much direction as is needed.
6. Assign other students roles as observers.

Help students to evaluate the effectiveness of behaviors used:
1. Ask students the following questions:
    What happened? What did you do? What did the others do?
    Were the behaviors you selected effective? Why or why not?
    What else could you have done? Would that have been more effective?
    How did you feel? How do you think the others feel?
2. Permit students to reenact the situation using different behaviors or actors if they wish.
3. Ask evaluation questions again and compare results.

Integrate into classroom routine:
1. Provide many opportunities for students to practice asking for help in the classroom.
2. Expect students to use appropriate behaviors and problem-solving techniques to solve social problems.
3. Encourage students to help one another as they try to solve social and academic problems.

Notice successful interactions:
1. Praise and give other positive reinforcement to students when they use successful behaviors to ask for help.
2. Teach students to praise one another when they use effective behaviors.
3. Teach students to discuss why certain behaviors are not effective and encourage one another to try again.

Generalize social knowledge:
1. Work with other staff members to provide opportunities for students to ask for help in other classrooms and situations throughout the school.

Figure 5.13 Social Knowledge: Asking for Help *(Continued)*

ASKING FOR HELP

individual students, (2) use the teachable moment to focus on an issue of immediate concern, (3) incorporate social skills instruction into an academic lesson, (4) or set aside specific periods of time for students to practice and learn social knowledge through coaching activities.

Modeling and coaching activities can be infused into ongoing instruction or provided on a stand-alone basis. Infusion can heighten student interest and motivation and provide a clearer understanding of the application of the behaviors in meaningful situations. It might also seem to save time. On the other hand, it may not always be in the student's best interest to stop and model a behavior in the middle of an academic lesson. Despite your positive attitude and encouragement, some students might be embarrassed while others might not be able to learn the behavior as quickly as you hoped. Consequently, the cost in the student's self-esteem and the lost instructional time might outweigh the potential benefits of the immediate attention.

Setting aside a separate period for instruction has its advantages and drawbacks as well. The focus may be direct and seemingly appropriate in a lesson that focuses on social behaviors or social knowledge. However, you might not consider it worth the cost to reshuffle and possibly limit other areas of instruction.

So, when are you going to find the time to teach this additional subject area? It is at this point that you need to weigh the needs of your students, fully appreciate the advantages of teaching social skills to students, be confident in your ability to do so, and *take risks*. Know that it is possible to think of academic and social goals and objectives simultaneously, especially by recognizing that improved social problem solving skills will also enhance academic problem solving. Your knowledge of individual students and their classmates will help you make this important decision. Regardless of the choices you select, trust your instincts and believe that whatever you decide to do, your students will reap both social and academic benefits.

In this chapter, you have seen how coaching and modeling can be used to build students' repertoires of social behaviors and to develop their social knowledge. For many students, these activities will suffice to improve their social skills. However, for some of your students, knowing how to perform a behavior and when to use it will still not result in the performance of the behavior. These students may lack self-confidence to risk using a new behavior. In the next chapter, you will learn methods for helping students develop their self-confidence so that they can apply their new social behaviors and improved social knowledge.

CHAPTER 6

SOCIAL SELF-CONFIDENCE

OVERVIEW

Even though they may have social skills, some students continue to either avoid or ignore situations that provide opportunities to practice and develop their social skills. They may act this way because they do not have social self-confidence. They may have an unrealistic *self-concept* and not know who they are. They may have *low self-esteem* and do not feel very good about themselves. They may lack a sense of *self-efficacy* and not trust their own abilities. These three elements, alone or in combination, undermine self-confidence and result in the student's unwillingness to take risks in social situations.

Teachers can intervene to help students develop realistic self-concepts, to feel better about themselves, and to learn to trust their own skills. This chapter defines the elements of self-confidence and provides activities that teachers can use to identify students and select an approach to address self-concept, self-esteem, and self-efficacy.

SELF-CONFIDENCE

Self-confidence is the sense that students have about their ability to succeed in social situations. This confidence is based on their knowledge and feelings about themselves. Those who are self-confident have a realistic estimate of who they are (self-concept) and feel good about themselves (self-esteem). They believe that they can use their social skills effectively in a given situation (self-efficacy). They can act to resolve social conflicts because they believe that their behaviors will bring about a positive outcome. They believe that, regardless of how a situation is structured (goals, participants, activities), they can select and implement strategies and behaviors that will enable them to achieve their personal goals. Consequently, they tend to be successful in their interactions. These interactions result in positive feedback from others and provide information that then contributes to a view of themselves as competent participants in social situations. This view of themselves increases the likelihood that they will succeed in future interactions.

Students with poor self-confidence are easily recognizable. Their verbal and nonverbal behavior usually give clear indications that they lack competence in social situations. They appear sad and/or unhappy, they make negative statements about themselves and their abilities, and they often try to avoid tasks by being absent, off-task, or disruptive. These behaviors interfere with social and academic achievement and point to students who have a unrealistic self-concept, low self-esteem, or lack a sense of self-efficacy.

SELF-CONCEPT

Self-concept represents the way students describe themselves—their roles, beliefs, feelings, and personal characteristics. These descriptions evolve over time as children interact with people who are important or significant to them. Initially, mothers, fathers, and primary caretakers play predominant roles. When children enter school, their teachers and peers assume more significant roles. As children interact with and receive feedback from significant others, they form and reform their sense of self so that their own views of themselves reflect the views of others. This view becomes their present real self.

They may describe themselves in many ways: academically as a math student, artist, reader, or speaker; socially as a friend, group member, brother, etc.; emotionally as affectionate, kind, or unhappy; and/or physically as a skilled athlete, pretty, attractive, or short. How students describe themselves can depend on physical attributes, interests, roles, cognitive abilities, learning style, ethnicity, and temperament. They may describe themselves as *relatively* attractive, *avid* basketball fans, *terrible* spellers, *loyal* friends, *capable* students, *loners, Hispanic* adolescents, and *happy* persons.

At the same time students are defining themselves as they are (their real selves), they may be trying to define themselves as they would like to be (their ideal selves). When there is syncronicity between the real and ideal self, a good self-concept results. This may happen in two ways. The individual may view the real as the ideal *(I am a poor speller and will probably continue to have problems., but that's OK, and I can live with that.)* Or they believe that the ideal is attainable *(I am a poor speller, but that's OK because I am working on it.)*

To form a realistic self-concept, students need to incorporate the perceptions of others into their own views of themselves. They may incorporate the views of others to raise *(The teacher says I spell as well as most other students in the class)* or lower *(The teacher says not to be discouraged. Some people never spell well.)* their evaluation of their abilities to a realistic level.

There are several reasons why students have unrealistic self-concepts. They are often confused about who they are *(Who is my real self?)* because their views of themselves are not accurate and do not match the views of others. For example, they may deny disabilities *(I'm good at math; I know how to read)* or misinterpret feedback from peers *(I have lots of friends.)* They may be so overwhelmed by their negative perceptions of themselves that they give up. *(I can't do that. They'll never pick me.)* They may also focus on and exaggerate only one aspect of themselves. *(I'm a star in art. I don't care about reading.)* Finally, there may be a large discrepancy between their real and ideal selves. They may believe they can achieve unrealistic goals *(I'm going to be a doctor when I grow up)* while they are actually 14 years old, reading at a pre-primer level and are unable to think abstractly. The realization that the ideal self may not be attainable can lead to a poor self-concept. Students with unrealistic self-concepts have problems in their social interactions because their actions may not reflect the positive perceptions that others have of them or do reflect the negative perceptions that others have.

SELF-ESTEEM

Self-esteem represents a student's self-evaluation—the judgments made regarding the components of self-concept. Students look at how well they do in each component of their self-concept-academic, social, emotional, physical-*(I am good in school, less competent in large groups, a happy person, and a little clumsy.).* They then decide how important each component is. Being a good athlete may be extremely important to one student while success as a learner is essential to another.

These judgments are based on an individual student's growth and development, the value judgments of others, and social mores. The way students meet developmental challenges, such as shifting their source of approval from parents and teachers to peers, influences not only their own opinions of themselves but also the opinions of others. The opinions and value judgments of family members, neighbors, teachers, and school staff then influence the value systems of the individual. In the middle elementary grades, peer influences become more powerful. Social and cultural mores and norms also influence self-esteem and are communicated to students via television, music, newspapers, and personal communication.

The value that students place on the components of their self-concept determine whether their self-esteem is high or low. High self-esteem results when self-perceptions are in synchrony with those values. A student who is a skilled athlete and a poor reader may have high self-esteem because greater value is placed on athletic skill than on an academic skill. When students are content with their evaluation, self-esteem tends to be high. High self-esteem enables them take risks, accept greater challenges, and take responsibility for their own behavior. Consequently, those with high self-esteem tend to be more valued by peers because they make more positive and appropriate contributions to social interactions.

If, however, a skilled athlete is also a poor reader and academic skill has greater value, the student's self-esteem could be affected significantly. Students with low self-esteem do not feel good about who they are. They wish they could be different and believe they have failed because they are not. Students with low self-esteem often view themselves as unworthy and have difficulty accepting everyday challenges and positive statements from others. They may be overly dependent, critical of others, resistant to new ideas, and reluctant to try. They do not contribute effectively in social interactions, are less valued by peers, and their views of themselves as failures is reaffirmed. This view then reinforces their belief that, regardless of what they do, their behavior will not change the outcome. Consequently, social relationships are difficult to establish and maintain.

SELF-EFFICACY

Self-efficacy is the sense that students have about their ability to accomplish tasks or deal with situations. Students who have a sense of self-efficacy know social behaviors and believe they can use their knowledge to apply those behaviors to reach a desired goal such as *joining a group, resolving peer conflict,* or *initiating a friendship.* Students with a sense of self-efficacy have the expectancy that their behavior will bring about a desired outcome.

Self-efficacy represents how much students believe they can predict and control social situations. Accurate assessment of one's ability to accomplish tasks depends in part on how individuals perceive themselves (self-concept) and how they evaluate themselves in terms of their strengths and weaknesses (self-esteem). Students who feel capable and valued can develop high expectations for success. They are able to confront situations, set realistic goals, play out success scenarios in their minds, devote time and effort to attaining their goals, use efficient analytical thinking skills to solve problems, and persevere to complete tasks.

When students have a sense of self-efficacy, they are able to accomplish more in the classroom. They take on responsibilities and confront situations because they believe they can complete tasks successfully. Confronting and participating successfully in a variety of social and academic situations gives students opportunities to practice and refine the social behaviors and knowledge they need to be socially competent.

Students without a sense of self-efficacy tend to avoid or give up in difficult situations. Given time, these students may come to view themselves as social failures despite the fact that they have social skills. Once they adopt this view, they may attribute future failure to themselves. If they are successful, they do not attribute their success to their own efforts or ability. Similar to those with low self-esteem, they often lack a sense of their own skills and mistrust themselves in social situations. They may avoid similar situations in the future and continue to miss opportunities to interact with their peers and practice the very skills they need to acquire to become more socially skilled.

Many students who lack social self-confidence have a history of unsuccessful failed social interactions. They may not have had the opportunities to interact with others, they may not have received appropriate feedback, or they may simply not have been able to take advantage of the interactions they have experienced. Therefore, they have little sense of their potential for interacting successfully even though they know social behaviors, have used social knowledge appropriately in hypothetical situations. They remain hesitant to take risks in real interactions. They continue to miss opportunities for feedback—feedback that occurs naturally in interactions, that might support changes in behavior, and that could contribute to subsequent risk-taking.

Even if students with a history of social failure do garner the courage to take a risk and succeed, they may still fail to connect their behavior with the ultimate outcome of the interaction. Also, they often inaccurately assess their performance on social tasks. They may see themselves as failures all the time, regardless of the results.

DEVELOPING SOCIAL SELF-CONFIDENCE

Teachers can reverse this cycle. To help students become confident enough to use social skills in real situations, first identify students who lack self-confidence and then select an approach.

IDENTIFY STUDENTS

To get a true picture of the skills and self-confidence that your students possess, gather information from more than one source and setting. Some students learn to behave in certain ways according to the expectations of others or roles assigned to them in specific settings. They may be accepted in the resource room and rejected in the mainstream, so they have learned to behave in certain ways according to their surroundings. By assessing students' self-confidence in more than one setting, a more accurate picture is obtained.

There are several formal instruments to identify students who have a poor self-concept, low self-esteem, and lack a sense of self-efficacy in social situations. These include the *Inferred Self-Concept Scale, Piers-Harris Self-Concept Scale, Coopersmith Self-Esteem Inventory,* and the *Perceived Competence Scale for Children,* (See Appendix C for additional information.) These instruments typically ask students to rate self-descriptions in terms of how much they are *like* or *unlike* the student, or situations in terms of how *easy* or *hard* they are for the student.

While these are reliable and valid options for identifying students who lack social self-confidence, there are also simple, accurate, and less formal methods for identifying students that can be used immediately. Many of the techniques we used to identify social skills and social behaviors can be adapted to identify students who lack self-confidence. Figure 6.1 provides a list of observable behaviors discussed in previous sections that are indicators of a poor self-concept, low self-esteem, and/or a lack of self-efficacy. This activity can be easily utilized by many teachers.

You can also use the observation instruments provided in Appendix C to document the frequency or duration of any of the observable behaviors that are indicators of poor self-confidence, low self-esteem, or a lack of self-efficacy. For example, you might observe students to see if they look socially self-confident, listen to their conversations to see if they sound socially self-confident, and watch students as they interact with others to determine whether they fail to use skills they already know.

The methods considered so far depend on the opinion and judgment of individuals other than the student. To obtain the perspective of the student, use Figure 6.2, which asks the student how *easy* or *hard* he or she finds specific social situations to be.

Journals offer another alternative to obtain the student's perspective. Through journals you can engage in daily *conversations* with your students about their feelings and self-perceptions. Students can express their feelings without fear of judgment, know that their ideas will be accepted, and that you, as their teacher, will listen to them. Journals enable you to know your students as individuals with unique qualities, special interests, valid feelings, and important concerns. You can also support your students in their efforts to think more reflectively about what they do—why they do certain things, the consequences of their actions, and other alternatives they might consider. To use journals to identify students who lack social self-confidence, follow the guidelines provided below.

GUIDELINES
FOR USING
JOURNALS

- *Require Students to Make One Journal Entry per Day.* The amount is not important. What matters is the experience of learning to think about and share feelings and ideas with another person.

- *Tell Students They Can Write About Anything.* Topics might include how they feel, what is going on in their lives, or what they wish would happen.

- *Assure Students That Journals are Private.* The content of a journal is confidential unless students decide to share their entries with others besides you.

- *Provide Journal Starters.* Let students select a card with an idea. On some, list sentence starters such as *I hate it when . . . , I love to . . . , I wish I could . . . , The best thing that ever happened to me was. . . .* On others, you might attach pictures that stimulate thinking.

- *Assign a Specific Time for Journal Writing.* Journal writing can be an effective transition activity either at the start of the school day or when students have completed an activity and are about to start another.

- *Read, Never Correct Journals.* Use the content of journals to learn about how students feel and to plan instruction. If you respond, be empathetic and/or supportive. Do not write in journals except to make comments that reflect your understanding of what they are trying to say.

FIGURE 6.1 Social Self-Confidence Rating Scale

Student _____ Grade _____ Age _____

Rater/s _____ _____ _____ _____

PURPOSE:
Use this activity to identify students who lack social self-confidence.

DIRECTIONS:
Determine whether the student demonstrates the following behaviors. Use the blank spaces for additional behaviors that you notice and consider important in developing social self-confidence.

Never   You have never seen the student *never* or *hardly ever* exhibit the behavior.

Sometimes You have seen the student exhibit the behavior at one time and not another.

Usually   You have seen the student exhibit the skill consistently and appropriately in different situations.

Place a checkmark under the appropriate column. To measure change and evaluate the effectiveness of interventions, readminister the scale at a later time. Use different colors to record ratings completed at different times or by different raters.

The Student	Never	Sometimes	Usually
looks sad or unhappy	_____	_____	_____
makes negative self-statements	_____	_____	_____
avoids tasks	_____	_____	_____
is absent	_____	_____	_____
is disruptive	_____	_____	_____
gives up	_____	_____	_____
makes untrue self-statements	_____	_____	_____
criticizes others	_____	_____	_____
resists new ideas	_____	_____	_____
is reluctant to try	_____	_____	_____
is scapegoated by peers	_____	_____	_____
attributes success to luck	_____	_____	_____
attributes failure to self	_____	_____	_____
has an unrealistic self-view	_____	_____	_____
_____	_____	_____	_____
_____	_____	_____	_____
_____	_____	_____	_____
_____	_____	_____	_____
_____	_____	_____	_____
_____	_____	_____	_____

INTERPRETATION:
If a student has rated several checks in the *usually* or *sometimes* columns, ask teachers who have the student in other settings to confirm your impressions. If the student is consistently demonstrating these indicators of low self-confidence, consider using the interventions in Chapter 6.

FIGURE 6.2 Social Self-Efficacy Rating Scale

Student _____ Grade _____ Age _____

Rater/s _____ _____ _____ _____

PURPOSE:
Use this activity to identify students who lack social self-efficacy in social situations.

DIRECTIONS:
Review the list below and add other activities that may be appropriate. Say to the student: This is a list of things that kids do with each other. This is not a test. There are no right or wrong answers. Read each item and make your best guess about how you feel.

Joining a group in the classroom is	EASY	easy	hard	HARD
Interrupting an ongoing activity is	EASY	easy	hard	HARD
Participating in group discussions is	EASY	easy	hard	HARD
Joining ongoing conversations is	EASY	easy	hard	HARD
Asking for help is	EASY	easy	hard	HARD
Accepting help is	EASY	easy	hard	HARD
Joining a group on the playground is	EASY	easy	hard	HARD
Joining a group in the lunchroom is	EASY	eash	hard	HARD
Dealing with being teased is	EASY	easy	hard	HARD
Making a new friend is	EASY	easy	hard	HARD
Playing with friends is	EASY	easy	hard	HARD
Working with friends is	EASY	easy	hard	HARD
Working independently is	EASY	easy	hard	HARD
_____	EASY	easy	hard	HARD
_____	EASY	easy	hard	HARD
_____	EASY	easy	hard	HARD
_____	EASY	easy	hard	HARD
_____	EASY	easy	hard	HARD
_____	EASY	easy	hard	HARD
_____	EASY	easy	hard	HARD
_____	EASY	easy	hard	HARD
_____	EASY	easy	hard	HARD
_____	EASY	easy	hard	HARD
_____	EASY	easy	hard	HARD
_____	EASY	easy	hard	HARD

INTERPRETATION:
If a student has placed several checks in the *hard* or *HARD* columns, consider whether you agree with this student self-report, and ask a teacher who has the student in other settings for his or her impressions. If there is a discrepancy between the student's view and that of others, you might want to focus on developing self-concept. If the student's observable behavior parallels the self-report, consider using the appropriate interventions in Chapter 6.

- *Adapt Journal Formats.* Have younger students draw pictures, then dictate and trace sentences that describe the picture. Incorporate entries into an ongoing journal. With older students, staple composition paper together to make a book. Commercial products are also available that provide pictures or sentence starters.

Journals enable you to synthesize information about your students and contribute to your making appropriate selections. Once you have selected students, you can consider what action or approach to take to change their situation.

SELECT AN APPROACH

Select students who are experiencing problems in self-confidence is relatively easy. Helping them may prove more difficult. The reason that *the* correct approach may not be clear is that the aspects of social self-confidence (self-concept, self-esteem, and self-efficacy) are not mutually exclusive. They clearly overlap. When dealing with affect—how students feel—there may not be one correct, appropriate, and effective alternative. Improving self-confidence needs to permeate all aspects of classroom life and the most appropriate and effective action may not be clear or identifiable. However, there are two approaches to consider, and they should be used concurrently.

One approach is to create a supportive classroom climate in which students feel accepted as individuals—where they are encouraged to try and to learn from mistakes in an atmosphere of mutual respect. Classrooms with reasonable and positive expectations (See Chapter 1), a structured environment (See Chapter 2), and instruction that provides supportive feedback enhance the development of social self-confidence. Chapter 3 provides specific activities for structuring learning opportunities in which positive and supportive feedback from peers is expected and monitored. If you followed the suggestions provided in Chapters 1–3, then it is likely that a positive and supportive classroom will develop (See Chapter 4).

The second approach is to focus on the individual components of self-confidence: self-concept, self-esteem, and self-efficacy. Arrange activities that deal with each component and permeate everything you do with your students. It should not matter *when* you intervene, only that you *do*.

To help students develop realistic self-concepts, provide opportunities for students to think about themselves in depth. To make more accurate self-descriptions, encourage students to explore their own interests, ethnic backgrounds, and family history. Help them appreciate all the attributes they have and recognize the many things they can accomplish. Allow them to consider new dimensions to roles they already know, identify new roles, and associate behaviors, attributes, and responsibilities with specific roles. Give students opportunities to see themselves as others do or to observe others as models of particular roles. With this information, students may develop more realistic views of themselves. Select from the suggestions provided in Figure 6.3 to address this aspect of social self-confidence.

To help students develop high positive self-esteem, teach them how to identify and evaluate their own attitudes, beliefs, feelings, and values. Teach them how to make positive self-statements and encourage them to make these statements by teaching them self-evaluation. Select from the suggestions provided in Figure 6.4 to address this aspect of social self-confidence.

FIGURE 6.3 Fostering Realistic Self-Concepts

PURPOSE:
To help students make accurate self-descriptions, see themselves as others do, consider new role dimensions, identify other roles, match roles and behavior, identify/reflect on roles and attributes, associate responsibilities with roles, and observe others as models.

DIRECTIONS:
Select suggestions from the following list and integrate them into the daily life in your classroom. Some ideas may be more appropriate for younger or older students. Adapt these ideas to your own needs and those of your students.

_____ Have students draw self-portraits.

_____ Use the overhead projector to make silhouettes of the students.

_____ Trace the outline of younger students' bodies on large sheets of paper and have the students color themselves.

_____ Have students write mystery descriptions of themselves and ask their peers to identify them.

_____ Use murals as a cooperative activity. Select topics of interest to students: dinosaurs, the beach, their town, vacations, space, etc.

_____ Require students to keep journals.

_____ Compare self-portraits done at the beginning of the year with those done at the end of the year. Discuss changes/growth.

_____ Ensure that each student has a special day during the year. If you celebrate birthdays, be sure that acknowledging the day does not interfere with religious or cultural practices.

_____ Create maps of the classroom, the school, the neighborhood, and the community—areas that are important to students.

_____ Create collages that illustrate the things that students love or like.

_____ Let students write their autobiographies—from memory or by interviewing family members and people who have known them in the past.

_____ Tell/show students when they look neat or attractive.

_____ Tell/show students how they look: happy, afraid, nervous, etc.

_____ Let groups of students create bulletin boards about subjects that interest them.

_____ Keep a full-length mirror in the classroom.

_____ Let students create drawings of themselves by using the mirror.

_____ Let groups of students write and present plays on topics that interest them.

_____ Create a cookbook of favorite student recipes.

_____ Keep an activity timeline of events throughout the school year.

_____ Take pictures of your students throughout the year; create a slide show to share with parents.

_____ Let students write a _future_ autobiography about who they will be in one year, two, years, or 20 years; ask them to describe what happened to them in the interim.

_____ Measure students' height at the beginning and end of the school year. Graph/chart information and incorporate into academic instruction.

_____ Take photographs of your students and important events to incorporate into bulletin boards and a class scrapbook.

_____ Have the students write and share essays on topics such as A Friend, My Scariest Moment, or The Most Fun I Ever Had.

_____ Find something unique and special about each student to emphasize.

_____ Give students opportunities to have responsibilitiews in other classrooms or throughout the school.

_____ Let students role play real life roles: custodian, letter carrier, nurse, fire-fighter, parent, sister, brother, grandmother, etc.

_____ Take field trips to other classrooms and students. Have students observe different types of learners and teachers and different ways other class-rooms are organized.

_____ Let students interview one another about topics such as their favorite food, activities, and music. Help them identify peers with common interests/activities.

FIGURE 6.3 Fostering Realistic Self-Concepts *(Continued)*

_____ Ask students to interview adults in the school regarding their roles, responsibilities, etc.

_____ Have students write letters to individuals whom they admire.

_____ Help students research and create family trees.

_____ Conduct discussions about different types of families.

_____ Have students interview an older relative or friend.

_____ Invite parents of students to be guest speakers to talk about their work, demonstrate a craft, or tell a story about their family's history.

_____ Have students make a book in which they describe people they admire or friends they know.

_____ Help students identify and interpret mixed messages: body and verbal language that are not synchronized (a pleasant expression with a sarcastic remark).

_____ Point out admirable qualities in those whom students might model: movie stars, television and video personalities, cartoon characters, politicians, musicians, scout leaders, favorite teachers, etc.

_____ List the characteristics of a friend. Find pictures to match the characteristics.

_____ Create friendship collages.

_____ Help students define abstract terms: loyalty, empathy, honesty, courage, independence, self-confidence, persistence, flexibility, compassion, tolerance, etc.

_____ Conduct discussions of role similarities and differences.

_____ Talk about roles: how people have different roles (son, brother, friend, student, etc.) and how roles change.

_____ Adopt an elder citizen, either as a class or as individual students. Let students adopt a younger or less able student.

_____ Talk about disabilities and how they affect a student's ability to learn or make friends.

_____ Have a *Backwards Day* in which students and teachers exchange roles.

_____ Give students opportunities to wear braces, ride in a wheelchair, or use crutches to develop their understanding of handicapping conditions.

_____ Have students draw family portraits.

_____ Use children's stories to illustrate problems. Read the story; then have students retell the story in their own words. Discuss the characters, the problems, and the solutions. Talk about the students' feelings about the story.

_____ Let each student have individual personal space in the classroom. Expect students to be responsible for maintaining their spaces.

_____ Assign classroom responsibilities to students.

_____ Help students feel secure in the classroom by enforcing rules consistently and fairly.

_____ Teach students to accept responsibility for themselves, to follow schedules, and to take care of materials.

_____ Have students face a peer and mirror body movements.

_____ Use pictures and videotapes to evaluate body language.

_____ Invite the principal or other teachers to participate in activities in the class.

_____ Let students *follow* an adult in the school to observe his or her role and responsibilities. Have students report back to the class.

_____ Invite parents of students to volunteer in the classroom.

_____ Use those students who are socially self-confident as models for students who are less positive about themselves.

_____ Talk about how to become self-confident.

_____ Monitor communication with students to ensure equitable contact with each student (high/low achievers, girls/boys, etc.).

_____ Monitor feedback and waittime to all students to ensure fairness (high/low achievers, girls/boys, etc.).

_____ Let students know that you know what they are doing.

FIGURE 6.4 Fostering High Self-Esteem

PURPOSE:
To help students determine how much value they place on the different aspects of their self-concept, decide what makes them feel good, determine how well they accomplish certain tasks, recognize the influence of parents, peers, the media, their teachers, etc., learn to make changes, and accept that which they might not be able to change.

DIRECTIONS:
Select suggestions from the following list and integrate them into the daily life in your classroom. Some ideas may be more appropriate for younger or older students. Adapt these ideas to your own needs and those of your students.

_____ Encourage discussions of attitudes, beliefs, feelings, and values.

_____ Set aside at least one period of time each day/week in which students can talk about themselves and share their ideas and feelings. You may have rules for these special times such as: everyone has a chance to talk, but no one has to talk.

_____ Require students to keep journals to let them know that it is OK to share ideas, feelings, beliefs, and problems.

_____ Use problem situations in the classroom, on the playground, or in the news as opportunities for students to practice talking about their feelings.

_____ Help students reflect in order to better understand their feelings: *It sounds like . . . It seems like . . .*

_____ Initiate conversations with openers such as *I see, Really, Tell me . . . (about it, more . . . the whole story).*

_____ Use pantomime to learn how to express feelings without words.

_____ Set aside a joke time in which students can tell each other jokes. This time might be perfect to discuss why some jokes are funny and others are hurtful or prejudicial. Students might then develop guidelines for the types of jokes that are funny.

_____ Use pictures and videotapes to recognize the feelings of other people.

_____ Create masks with distinct expressions (anger, frustration, happiness, surprise, boredom). Practice making faces to match the masks and identify situations that would make students feel that way.

_____ Let students practice dealing with problem situations by telephone.

_____ Use the local newspaper to identify issues of concern in the community: the elderly, homeless children, unemployment, etc. Discuss how students feel about these problems and how they might take action.

_____ Give students the experience of being disabled: taking a blindwalk, walking with braces (rules taped to legs), or writing with their non-preferred hand. Talk about how it feels.

_____ Have students conduct surveys to determine the favorite food, book, television program, brand of sneakers, music group, etc. of the class/school. Have students collect, analyze, and publish data.

_____ Praise yourself (in front of your students) when you do something right.

_____ Teach students to praise you when you do something right.

_____ Teach students to praise themselves when they do something right.

_____ Think of the class as individuals, not a group.

_____ Move closer to students when they are feeling frustrated or unhappy.

_____ Use humor cautiously. Be sure that students understand why something is funny.

_____ As frequently as possible, speak to individual students at their eye level.

_____ Schedule transitions in the classroom to coincide with times individual students must get up and leave or return to the classroom.

_____ Monitor your body language; it should match your words.

_____ Treat your students as you would your best friend.

_____ Give each student a summer calendar with special events and individual activities marked. For example, send a postcard to the teacher, write a letter to a classmate, keep a diary of feelings, etc.

_____ Before school begins, write to each student to introduce yourself, describe the classroom, and share your enthusiasm for the coming school year.

FIGURE 6.4 Fostering High Self-Esteem *(Continued)*

_____ Schedule regular private conferences with each student.

_____ Help students find pen pals to correspond with throughout the year.

_____ Develop private signals for students to use to communicate with you.

_____ Tell students know how much you enjoy being their teacher.

_____ Give each student an older peer as a buddy or an adult confidante, someone to whom the student can go to with problems or in times of stress.

_____ Keep a question box in the classroom by which students can anonymously ask about troublesome situations or ideas. These questions might then be the topic of class meetings, coaching activities, or sharing time.

_____ Teach students to praise and encourage one another.

_____ Give each student an audiotape. Let other students use the tape to leave personal messages of encouragement or praise.

_____ Teach students how to be appropriate members of an audience—to appreciate and reward the efforts of their peers.

_____ Greet students at the door of the classroom each day.

_____ Praise models.

_____ Smile.

For students who need a sense of self-efficacy, apply basic effective teaching principles. Many of the strategies that you use to teach students to believe in their ability to succeed academically can also be applied to social tasks. You can teach your students to trust their social skills by praising their use through all phases of learning—when they are first learning their new skills, when they are becoming more proficient, as they maintain them over time, and as they generalize their skills to new settings and situations. Reward efforts, as well as accomplishments. teach your students to identify their personal strengths and weaknesses, monitor, evaluate, and reward performance and efforts. Use problem-solving abilities and develop and practice success scenarios (See Coaching Activities in Appendix B). Select from the suggestions provided in Figure 6.5 to address this aspect of social self-confidence.

The activities provided in Figures 6.3, 6.4, and 6.5 suggest specific actions that you can take to foster social self-confidence among your students. Appendix D provides suggestions for incorporating these activities into educational plans for students with special needs. Use the following guidelines when taking action to foster social self-confidence.

GUIDELINES
IN TAKING ACTION
TO FOSTER SOCIAL
SELF-CONFIDENCE

- *Do It Now.* While it may be reassuring to have assessment information or instructional confirmation, just do it. These aspects of social self-confidence are so abstract and interwoven that their separation and identification, while helpful, is not crucial.
- *Infuse.* The suggestions offered in Figures 6.4, 6.5, and 6.6 are not meant to be isolated opportunities. Infuse them whenever you can into who you are and what you are teaching.
- *Try Something Else.* Again, this is a very abstract area. If your efforts do not seem to be working, try something new. You never know for sure what makes students feel better about themselves, but keep monitoring, searching, and thinking as to what you might try next. Plan plans, not results.

By teaching social skills and focusing on the specific components of self-confidence, you would be justified in expecting some improvement in how students act and feel, their willingness to take risks, and a sense of how their new skills may help them. However, years of failure and negative social experiences take time to undo. This is why a supportive environment is so important. Your students need a place and time to become more confident. They need a place in which they themselves, their peers, and you, as their teacher, can recognize their efforts. They need time to practice and become more proficient with support that includes both praise for their successes and supportive feedback for their initial attempts. By focusing on the topics and activities described in this chapter, in the context of such a supportive classroom environment, you may be assured that your students will are more likely to become more confident and have successful and productive social interactions in the future.

Keep in mind that, while the exact nature of the link between social and academic achievement and competence may remain unclear, the connection does exist. Time spent in creating opportune environments and teaching social skills will be spent wisely. The improvements in social and academic achievements for your students will immediately benefit the students, their peers, their families, your colleagues, and yourself, and will continue to enhance their quality of life and increase their potential for success and happiness throughout their lives.

FIGURE 6.5 Fostering a Sense of Self-Efficacy

PURPOSE:
To help students learn to make predictions, assume control over outcomes, accurately assess their own abilities, rehearse success scenarios, set realistic goals, analyze situations, and reward their efforts and accomplishments.

DIRECTIONS:
Select suggestions from the following list and integrate them into daily life in your classroom. Some ideas may be more appropriate for younger or older students. Adapt these ideas to your own needs and those of your students.

_____Stop the class with your special signal and call attention to a wonderful event, regardless of how minute—*Sarah just offered to help Matt with his math. Time for a silent cheer.*

_____Use praise that is specific and describes what the student is doing correctly-*Putting your toy in your pocket will help you concentrate on your job.*

_____Use feedback that is informative and tells the student how a behavior will help the student—*Listening to the directions will help you do this activity correctly.*

_____Select or elect a *Star of the Week* for the classroom.

_____Give awards for the best or *most improved* reader or mathematician.

_____Give awards to students who are the kindest, most helpful, friendliest, etc.

_____Encourage efforts and accomplishments.

_____Focus on the number of correct responses: 19 correct or 19/25, not 6 incorrect.

_____Mark correct items, not incorrect items. Use a color other than RED.

_____Advertise successes in your classroom in a newsletter, on a bulletin board, or as school announcements.

_____Minimize the use of phases that include the words *I like—I like the way you said Charlie's name when you saw him this morning.* Try to describe the behavior and provide a rationale for continuing—*Saying the other person's name when greeting someone will help you remember their name in the future.*

_____Use an extra school phone line and an answering machine to leave messages for parents about their child's achievements during the week/day. Assign students a number or secret name to ensure confidentiality.

_____Call attention to positive events each day.

_____Avoid helping students too much; encourage them to try independently.

_____Divide the class into teams. Monitor helpful, kind, and friendly behavior. Give points to teams. Reward the team with the most points.

_____Reward effort, regardless of how small.

_____When speaking to students individually, get down to their eye level.

_____Give correction privately but give praise publicly.

_____Use stickers, stars, asterisks, check marks, smiley faces, exclamation points, plus signs, and words when correcting student work.

_____Post student work in the classroom and in the hallways.

_____Write a class newspaper to share with other classes and parents.

_____Have an end-of-the-year picnic with students and parents.

_____Hold a special open-house for parents of students in your class.

_____Send an end-of-the-year letter to your students.

_____Be an active listener: maintain eye contact, ask questions, rephrase, respond to feelings teach students how to listen to one another.

_____Spend time with students in unexpected ways: eat lunch or snack with students. Go to recess, art, music, or physical education with students.

_____Use encouragement to demonstrate acceptance, confidence, appreciation, trust, and recognition.

_____Talk about unpleasant chores (grading, meetings, etc.) and how you manage these tasks.

_____Write personal notes to students.

_____Group students heterogeneously.

_____Give each student an adult buddy, someone to whom the student can go with problems or in time of stress.

FIGURE 6.5 Fostering a Sense of Self-Efficacy *(Continued)*

_____ Include students with disabilities or cultural/language differences in as many classroom activities as possible.

_____ Send students without disabilities to the resource room or special classes to act as tutors or simply finish their work.

_____ Structure activities so that students must work cooperatively in order to complete the tasks successfully.

_____ Require students to keep journals.

_____ Talk about your own strengths/weaknesses/preferences.

_____ Develop individual contracts with students to improve behavior, develop skills, achieve important goals, etc.

_____ Let students read with a partner, tape-record, listen, and evaluate themselves and one another.

_____ Let students use their individual audiotapes to record their goals for the week or day and evaluate their achievements.

_____ Teach students to evaluate their own behavior: for example, they might rate (1-2-3) how well or how often they accomplished a task like saying thank you or offering to share materials).

_____ Show students how to correct their work and to analyze why certain responses were correct and others were incorrect. Look for patterns: random guessing, incorrect algorithms, not following directions, etc.

_____ Video- or audiotape record classroom activities/conversations to help students become more aware of how they sound and look to one another.

_____ Use body relaxation techniques to help students learn to become more reflective and better able to focus on themselves and their thoughts.

_____ Help students evaluate inappropriate behavior. What happened? Was it helpful? Why not? What could you have done instead? What will you do next time?

_____ Have students evaluate how well they followed their schedules and consider revisions that might help them do a better job.

_____ Let students use teacher guides to correct their work immediately.

_____ Use self-correcting materials

_____ Tell students the criteria for grading when tasks are assigned.

_____ At the beginning of each day, review rules and expectations. At the end of each day, let students evaluate their ability to follow rules and live up to expectations.

_____ Compare students to themselves, their own improvement, not that of others.

_____ Teach students to monitor their own behavior: for example, they might color in a circle on a chart if they walk into the room or remember to put their materials away or they might give themselves a checkmark if they are on-task by a pre-arranged signal (tape-recorded beep).

_____ Teach students to reinforce their own behavior: for example, when they have accumulated a certain number of checkmarks/tallies, they take a prearranged reward (a special activity, time with a friend, etc.)

_____ Encourage the students to share their successes with the principal and other teachers.

_____ Let students keep a folder of their best work.

_____ Provide alternative ways of accomplishing the same task. Give students choices about the best way for them to complete their work.

_____ Teach students to advocate for themselves—to speak up when they know how they can accomplish a task.

_____ Teach students how to compensate when the task cannot be altered by taking notes, prereading, mnemonic clues, or alphabetizing lists to be memorized.

_____ Permit students to share their strategies for learning spelling words, remembering rules, prioritizing jobs to be finished, etc.

_____ Let students make mistakes while they are learning to problem-solve.

_____ Help students set realistic goals for the week and for each day.

_____ Create a quiet spot in the classroom for students to use when they want to be alone or work independently.

_____ Role play stressful situations and think of alternatives.

_____ Use open-ended questions that allow many correct answers. Students have a greater opportunity to succeed and do so in front of their peers.

FIGURE 6.5 Fostering a Sense of Self-Efficacy *(Continued)*

_____ Let students develop their own schedules. Given a list of tasks, students decide the order. Be sure to include pleasant times (recess, lunch, freetime).

_____ Give instructions in more than one way: say it and show it.

_____ Assign a peer to update and orient students who return to the classroom in the midst of an activity.

_____ Make finger, ring, paperplate, or sock puppets with which students can role play various social situations.

_____ Give students individual schedules to follow.

_____ Teach peers to ignore unkind remarks or inappropriate behavior. Discuss why they should so so.

_____ Review the schedule for each day; note any unusual event before hand respond to high expectations.

_____ Set reasonable expectations for each student; articulate expectations to students.

_____ Expect the best from every student.

MODELING ACTIVITIES

ACTIVITY A-1

SMILING

Rationale: If you smile when you interact with other people, they will think that you are interested in them and may want to be their friend. Consequently, they are more apt to want to get to know you. If you don't smile, others may think you are unfriendly or unhappy and they may not want to extend friendship to you.

❑ **M**ake choices:

1. Select a behavior: smiling
2. Select a model: the teacher or a peer who is regarded as a friend.

❑ **O**rganize the behavior:

1. Look at the eyes of the other person.
2. Use a pleasant facial expression.
3. Smile.

❑ **D**emonstrate the behavior:

1. Demonstrate *smiling*.
2. Repeat the steps while demonstrating the behavior.
3. Demonstrate and discuss differences between smiling and laughing or smiling and frowning expressions.

❑ **E**ncourage the student to imitate:

1. Ask the student to imitate the behavior.
2. If necessary, repeat the steps or provide a mirror for the student.
3. Praise correct performance and provide corrective feedback if necessary.

❑ **L**ink the behavior:

1. Review the rationale for smiling when interacting with others.
2. Discuss opportunities for smiling in the classroom.
3. Discuss the consequences of not smiling at others and feelings when others do not smile at students.
4. Combine *smiling* with other behaviors such as *establishing eye contact* or *accepting help*.
5. Combine *smiling* with other social skills such as *making friends* or *working cooperatively*.
6. Discuss feelings of social self-confidence when students do smile at others.

❒ **I**ntegrate into classroom routine:

1. Expect students to carry a pleasant expression in the classroom. Do not tolerate sullen or pouting expressions.
2. Teach students to recognize facial expressions as indications of feelings.
3. Teach students that feelings of sadness or disappointment and accompanying facial expressions are sometimes legitimate. Show students ways to acknowledge and accept different types of feelings.

❒ **N**otice the behavior:

1. Praise students when they smile and use pleasant facial expressions and ignore students when they use negative, sullen expressions. Remember: reinforced behavior tends to be repeated, while ignored behavior tends to disappear when students want your attention.

❒ **G**eneralize the behavior:

1. Ask other school staff to praise students who smile and use pleasant expressions.
2. Take candid photographs of students smiling in other school situations. Post photographs in the classroom.

ACTIVITY A-2

ESTABLISHING EYE CONTACT

Rationale: When you establish eye contact with others, they are more apt to think you are interested in them. Consequently, they are more likely to ask you to join them and participate in their activities.

☐ **M**ake choices:

1. Select a behavior: establishing eye contact.
2. Select a model: the teacher.

☐ **O**rganize the behavior:

1. Face the person.
2. Establish a comfortable physical distance.
3. Look at the other person's eyes.

☐ **D**emonstrate the behavior:

1. Demonstrate the behavior to the student.
2. Verbalize steps 1–3 during demonstration, if necessary.
3. Demonstrate the difference between staring at a person and using eye contact.

☐ **E**ncourage the student to imitate:

1. Ask the student to imitate the behavior.
2. If necessary, repeat the steps for the student.
3. Praise correct performance and provide corrective feedback if necessary.

☐ **L**ink the behavior:

1. Discuss the rationale for establishing eye contact.
2. Discuss opportunities for establishing eye contact.
3. Discuss the consequences of not establishing eye contact and feelings when others do not establish eye contact with students.
4. Combine *establishing eye contact* with other social skills such as *participating in group discussions* or *making friends.*
6. Discuss feelings of social self-confidence after establishing eye contact.

☐ **I**ntegrate the behavior into classroom routine:

1. Expect students to establish eye contact during interactions with others.
2. Develop nonverbal cues, such as touching the corner of one's eye to help students remember to establish eye contact with others.
3. Have students maintain a chart to monitor when and how frequently they use the behavior.
4. When speaking to students, provide reminders such as "look at me."

(Activity A-2 Continued)

❏ **N**otice the behavior:

1. Praise students when they establish eye contact, with and without reminders.

❏ **G**eneralize the behavior:

1. Help students identify situations beyond the classroom in which they should be using eye contact.
2. Have students make a list of people with whom they will practice the behavior.
3. Have students report back on their successes (and failures) in practicing the behavior.
4. Send notes to other school staff and parents to ask them to reinforce students who use eye contact outside the classroom.

ACTIVITY A-3

MAINTAINING EYE CONTACT

Rationale: When you maintain eye contact with others, they are more apt to think you are interested in what they are saying. Consequently, they are more likely to ask you to join them and participate in their activities.

❏ **M**ake choices:

1. Select a behavior: maintaining eye contact.
2. Select a model: the teacher or a peer who is regarded as a friend.

❏ **O**rganize the behavior:

1. Establish eye contact (See Activity A-2).
2. Keep eyes focused for 5–8 seconds.
3. Pause and look away for 1–2 seconds.
4. Reestablish eye contact.
5. Repeat steps 2–4 until the interaction is complete.

❏ **D**emonstrate the behavior:

1. Review the steps for maintaining eye contact.
2. Demonstrate maintaining eye contact.
3. Repeat the steps for maintaining eye contact while demonstrating the behavior.
4. Demonstrate other behaviors to use when pausing, such as nodding, smiling, or briefly looking down. Pausing within the maintaining eye contact sequence allows the student to break the intensity of the interaction, which is helpful when first learning to maintain eye contact.
5. Discuss the difference between maintaining eye contact and staring.

❏ **E**ncourage the student to imitate:

1. Have the student imitate maintaining eye contact with the teacher or a peer.
2. If necessary, repeat the steps. Use key words such as focus, pause, refocus.
3. Praise correct performance and provide corrective feedback if necessary.

❏ **L**ink the behavior:

1. Review the rationale for maintaining eye contact when interacting with others.
2. Discuss opportunities for maintaining eye contact in the classroom.
3. Discuss the consequences and feelings when eye contact is not maintained during an interaction.
4. Combine *maintaining eye contact* with other behaviors such as *introducing oneself* or *maintaining a conversation*.
5. Combine *maintaining eye contact* with other social skills such as *maintaining a friendship* or *maintaining a conversation*.
6. Discuss feelings of social self-confidence when students are able to maintain eye contact with others.

❐ **I**ntegrate the behavior into classroom routine:

1. Teach students to *establish eye contact* with others before teaching students to *maintain eye contact.*
2. Expect students to maintain eye contact with others during interactions in the classroom.
3. Use nonverbal cues, such as touching the corner of your eye to remind a student to maintain eye contact.
4. When speaking to students, provide reminders such as *look at me.*

❐ **N**otice the behavior:

1. Praise students when they are able to maintain eye contact.
2. Teach students to praise one another when they maintain eye contact.

❐ **G**eneralize the behavior:

1. Ask students to list people with whom they feel comfortable using eye contact. They might practice maintaining eye contact with one or two of the people on their lists.
2. Ask students to report their successes and problems when practicing the behavior.
3. Ask other school personnel, peers, and parents to provide opportunities for students to practice maintaining eye contact and to praise students when they are successful.

ACTIVITY A-4

GREETING OTHERS

Rationale: When you greet others, it makes people feel good; it tells other people that you want to be friendly. It also tells people that you are glad to see them. People may be more apt to ask you to join in activities when you greet them. When you fail to greet others, they may think that you do not like them or care to be with them.

☐ **M**ake choices:

1. Select a behavior: greeting others
2. Select a model: the teacher or a peer who is regarded as a friend.

☐ **O**rganize the behavior:

1. Move toward the other person.
2. Face the other person.
3. Establish eye contact.
4. Smile.
5. Say a greeting (see below).

☐ **D**emonstrate the behavior:

1. Demonstrate greeting others while saying the five steps aloud.
2. Move toward the other person, face the person, establish eye contact, smile and say, "Hello."
3. Use verbal cues such as *move, face, eye contact, smile,* and *greet* to help the student remember the steps.
4. Tell the student that different greetings may be used at different times of the day. The first greetings of the day are usually, "Good morning," while "hello" or "hi" is used later in the day. Students may work with the teacher to develop lists of appropriate greetings—one for peers and another for adults.

☐ **E**ncourage the student to imitate:

1. After the sequence has been demonstrated and the student has rehearsed the cues, encourage the student to imitate greeting others by practicing with the teacher (model).
2. At first, use verbal cues such as *move, face, eye contact, smile,* and *greet* (if necessary); then, gradually fade the cues.
3. Praise the students as each correct step in the sequence is completed. Use a checklist to show students when a step is missed.

☐ **L**ink the behavior:

1. Review the rationale for greeting other people.
2. Discuss opportunities for greeting other people in the classroom.
3. Discuss the consequences and feelings when someone does not greet another person.
4. Combine *greeting others* with other behaviors such as *initiating a conversation* or *establishing eye contact.*

5. Combine *greeting others* with other social skills such as *joining an ongoing competitive game* or *making friends*.
6. Discuss feelings of social self-confidence when students are able to greet others successfully.

❐ **I**ntegrate the behavior into classroom routine:

1. Help students recognize the many opportunities to greet people during a school day: getting on the bus in the morning, arriving in the schoolyard, entering a classroom, approaching a peer group during freetime, joining other students in the lunchroom, reentering the classroom after speech therapy.
2. Make a list of the different situations in which students might greet others.
3. Make a list of the different types of greetings that are appropriate in each situation.
4. Expect students to greet others in the classroom.
5. Use nonverbal cues, such as a wave, to remind a student to greet another person.

❐ **N**otice the behavior:

1. Praise students when they do greet others.
2. If a student is having a difficult time remembering to greet others, make a checklist of specific times the behavior is to be used. Give the student a checkmark each time s/he remembers to use the behavior.
3. Once a student earns ten checkmarks, s/he earns a sticker or other reward.
4. Teach students to praise one another when they greet others.

❐ **G**eneralize the behavior:

1. Make another list of situations beyond the school setting (at home and in the community) when greeting others is important.
2. Alert other teachers who work with the student that s/he is practicing greeting others and ask them to encourage and praise the student when s/he uses the behavior.
3. Send notes home to parents and others so they may help the student to begin to greet others at home.
4. Ask students to list people whom they feel comfortable greeting. They might practice maintaining greeting others with one or two of the people on their lists.
5. Ask students to report their successes and problems when practicing the behavior.

ACTIVITY A-5

INITIATING A CONVERSATION

Rationale: By initiating conversations with others, you are telling them you want to be friendly with them. If you are unable to start a conversation, you may not make many friends. People might think you are self-centered if you never start conversations.

☐ **M**ake choices:

1. Select a behavior: initiating a conversation
2. Select a model: a teacher and other staff or students

☐ **O**rganize the behavior:

1. Think of a topic of conversation.
2. Approach the other person: respect the other person's personal space.
3. Greet the person.
   a. Face the person.
   b. Establish eye contact.
   c. Smile.
   d. Greet the person.

☐ **D**emonstrate the behavior:

1. Demonstrate *initiating a conversation* by following the steps. Since initiating a conversation is a complex behavior that encompasses several social behaviors such as respecting space, eye contact, greeting, it may be necessary to review each of the component behaviors.
2. Demonstrate the behavior with different students, asking a different question of each. This shows the variety of questions which may be used to start a conversation.

☐ **E**ncourage the student to imitate:

1. If necessary, practice listening skills, maintaining eye contact, nodding, and maintaining a pleasant expression.
2. Review the behavior of greeting others which entails moving toward the person, facing the person, eye contact, smiling, and saying a greeting.
3. Have the student demonstrate initiating a conversation while verbalizing the cues. Later have the student verbalize the cues him or herself while demonstrating the behavior.
4. Praise the student as each correct step in the sequence is completed.
5. Let students brainstorm types of questions that are good conversation starters and then role play these with classmates.

☐ **L**ink the behavior:

1. Review the rationale for initiating a conversation.
2. Define a conversation: What it *is* and what *is not.* Discuss the fact that a conversation entails at least two people interacting. It entails both listening and speaking.
3. Identify opportunities for initiating conversations in the classroom.
4. Discuss the importance of using this social behavior and the consequences of not using the behavior.

5. Combine *initiating a conversation* with other social behaviors such as *maintaining a conversation* or *asking for help.*
6. Combine *initiating a conversation* with other social skills such as *making friends* or *joining an ongoing competitive game.*
7. Discuss feelings of social self-confidence when students are able to initiate a conversation successfully.

❒ **I**ntegrate into classroom routine:

1. Help students recognize the many opportunities for initiating conversations that exist in the classroom: beginning a project with a group, asking to borrow materials, asking for information, etc.
2. Expect students to initiate and carry on conversations with one another as part of their regular school day.
3. Use role playing or simulation exercises during social studies or math lessons in which students will have to initiate conversations with one another.
4. Help students develop a repertoire of questions to use to start conversations.
5. Practice this behavior as part of a formal language arts lesson on listening and speaking.

❒ **N**otice the behavior:

1. Praise students when they initiate conversations.
2. Teach students to praise one another when they initiate conversations.

❒ **G**eneralize the behavior:

1. Discuss the various times when starting a conversation would be used in and out of the school setting. Have the student choose a time during school in which to practice the behavior. Have the student make a list of various conversation starters to use on this occasion. Have student report back to the class on her/his success with using the behavior.
2. Once students can successfully initiate conversations in school, have them decide on a time to use the behavior outside the school setting. Have them list the following: with whom they used the behavior, the setting (time and place), what was said, how it worked, what they could have done differently, what they did that worked out well, whether they will try this again and why. This could be organized for the students on a form for them to complete and could be used as a homework assignment.

ACTIVITY A-6

MAINTAINING A CONVERSATION

Rationale: Knowing how to maintain conversation helps you to meet other people and makes other people feel more comfortable when they are with you. Also, you may learn interesting things by maintaining conversation with other people.

☐ **M**ake choices:

1. Select a behavior: maintaining a conversation
2. Select a model: a teacher with other students or other staff members

☐ **O**rganize the behavior:

1. Initiate or join a conversation.
   a. Think of what to say.
   b. Approach the person.
   c. Greet the person.
   d. Initiate a conversation.
2. Show you are interested: smile and nod as the person talks and listen.
3. Ask questions based on what the person has said. try to ask a question that needs more than a *yes* or *no* answer.
4. Listen to the response and respond by asking another question related to the response.
5. Again, listen to the response and keep the conversation going by asking another question.

☐ **D**emonstrate the behavior:

1. Review and demonstrate the steps for initiating or joining a conversation.
   a. Think of a topic of conversation.
   b. Approach the person: respect the person's personal space.
   c. Greet the person.
   d. Initiate the conversation by asking a question.
2. Demonstrate *maintaining a conversation.*

☐ **E**ncourage the student to imitate:

1. Review the behaviors of eye contact, listening, greeting and initiating conversations with the student.
2. Have the student review the steps for maintaining conversations by using the cues, I (initiate), L (listen), A (Ask).
3. Ask the student to imitate the behavior.

☐ **L**ink the behavior:

1. Review the rationale for maintaining a conversation: discuss why being adept at conversations is an important social behavior.
2. Discuss opportunities for maintaining conversation in the classroom.
3. Have students discuss how not knowing ways to *maintain conversation* would be a hindrance in developing social skills and in making friends.

3. Have students discuss how not knowing ways to *maintain conversation* would be a hindrance in developing social skills and in making friends.
4. Combine *maintaining conversation* with other social behaviors such as smiling or *maintaining eye contact.*
5. Combine *maintaining conversation* with other social skills such as *maintaining friendship* or *working cooperatively.*
6. Discuss feelings of social self-confidence when students are able to maintain a conversation.

❏ **I**ntegrate into classroom routine:

1. Students may practice thinking about conversation skills when introduced to quotation marks. Have students write a conversation using quotations to show the speaker's words. These writings may then be used as scripts for students to practice conversation skills.
2. Maintaining conversations may be made a part of a general language unit on listening and speaking skills.

❏ **N**otice the behavior:

1. Provide encouragement and praise as students try to use the behavior.

❏ **G**eneralize the behavior:

1. Have students brainstorm various times, places, and events which call for maintaining conversation.
2. Have students list times—at school, in the neighborhood, with siblings and parents—that conversation skills are used.
3. Send a note home to let parents know that students are practicing this behavior. Ask parents to take some time during the day to work with the students on the behavior.

ACTIVITY A-7

ENDING A CONVERSATION

Rationale: Ending a conversation tells people that you are interested in what they have to say, but that you can't continue—perhaps because you have other obligations. It tells other people that you are polite and a nice person. It makes other people feel more friendly toward you.

☐ **M**ake choices:

1. Select a behavior: ending a conversation
2. Select a model: a teacher with other students or other staff members.

☐ **O**rganize the behavior:

1. Initiate or join a conversation.
2. Maintain the conversation.
3. Know the reason that you need to end the conversation.
4. Think of what to say.
5. Wait for a lull in the conversation.
6. End the conversation pleasantly.

☐ **D**emonstrate the behavior:

1. Discuss with the students reasons that conversations must be ended. List these reasons on a chart.
2. Review steps for initiating (or joining) a conversation.
   a. Think of what to say.
   b. Approach the person.
   c. Greet the person.
   d. Initiate a conversation.
3. Review the steps for maintaining the conversation.
   a. Smile and nod as the person talks and listen.
   b. Ask questions based on what the person said.
   c. Ask questions: try to ask questions that need more than a *yes* or *no* answer.
4. Demonstrate ending the conversation.
   a. Think of what to say.
   b. Wait for a lull.
   c. End the conversation pleasantly.

☐ **E**ncourage the student to imitate:

1. Review the steps for ending a conversation.
2. Have the student recall friendly things to say when ending a conversation. Have the student select one or two of these things to use.
3. Have the student demonstrate ending a conversation while the teacher provides verbal cues. As the student is successful, fade the verbal cues.
4. Praise the student as each of the steps is successfully imitated.

☐ **L**ink the behavior:

1. Review the rationale for ending a conversation.
2. Identify opportunities for ending conversations in the classroom.

3. Discuss the importance of using this social behavior and the consequences of not being able to end a conversation pleasantly.
4. Combine ending a conversation with other social behaviors such as *maintaining a conversation* or *leaving others*.
5. Combine ending a conversation with other social skills such as *maintaining friendships* or *dealing with peer pressure*.
6. Discuss feelings of social self-confidence when students are able to end a conversation pleasantly.

❏ **I**ntegrate into classroom routine:

1. Have students role play situations in which they must end conversations.
2. Discuss times when students need to have conversations with people with whom they might not really be interested in talking. Having appropriate ways to escape the conversation will get them away from the situation in a way that makes the other person still feel friendly toward them.

❏ **N**otice the behavior:

1. Praise students when they end conversations pleasantly.
2. Teach students to praise one another when they end conversations pleasantly.

❏ **G**eneralize the behavior:

1. Have students practice different ways to end conversations with peers and adults. Show how these might differ.
2. Have students keep a log of conversation skills. Have them note with whom they maintain and end conversations, the setting (time and place), the topic of the conversation, and the ways in which the conversations ended. Then have students rate themselves. Have students list ways in which they might improve this social behavior.
3. Have students practice ending a conversation with a friend, a neighbor, a friend of his/her parent, or an older relative. Have students focus on not interrupting, but waiting for the appropriate moment to end the conversation.

ACTIVITY A-8

INTRODUCING ONESELF

Rationale: It is important to introduce yourself to people so that they will know what to call you. When people know your name, they will feel more comfortable with you. It also makes others feel that you are interested in knowing them. Introducing yourself breaks the ice. It is the first step in making a friend.

❐ **M**ake choices:

    1. Select a behavior: introducing oneself
    2. Select a model: a teacher or a peer

❐ **O**rganize the behavior:

    1. Quietly approach the other person.
    2. Establish eye contact.
    3. Smile.
    4. Greet the person.
    5. Tell your name.
    6. Make a gesture of greeting: a wave, a nod, or shaking hands (if appropriate).

❐ **D**emonstrate the behavior:

    1. Demonstrate the behavior of introducing oneself by first following the steps for greeting someone, establishing eye contact, smiling, and greeting the person.
    2. Point out that respecting the other person's space is an important part of approaching another person.
    3. Say your name and make a gesture of greeting. Point out to students that certain gestures are appropriate in certain situations.
    5. Point out that maintaining eye contact throughout the interaction is important.

❐ **E**ncourage the student to imitate:

    1. Review the behaviors of greeting someone, establishing eye contact, and smiling, if necessary.
    2. Teacher may use the mnemonic, GREETS, to help the student to imitate the behavior:

        Go up to the person.

        Respect their space.

        Establish eye contact.

        Exhibit a smile.

        Tell your name.

        Shake hands.

    2. Have the student practice the mnemonic until s/he is able to repeat it from memory.
    3. Have the student imitate the behavior while repeating the steps to himself/herself.

4. Have the students practice speaking in a clear voice so that others can hear her/his name.
5. Discuss how introductions might vary depending on the age of the person you are introducing yourself to. Adults would be treated more formally and would be given a handshake more often than peers might be.

❏ **L**ink the behavior:

1. Review the rationale for introducing oneself.
2. Discuss opportunities for introducing oneself in the classroom.
3. Discuss what might happen if someone doesn't know what to call you.
4. Discuss how students might miss out on events if others do not know their names.
5. Discuss when students might not want to give their names to a stranger.
6. Try to differentiate situations in which using this behavior might be inappropriate.
7. Combine *introducing oneself* with other social behaviors such as *maintaining conversations* or *making friends*.
8. Combine *introducing oneself* with other social skills such as *making friends* or *joining an ongoing competitive game*.
9. Discuss feelings of social self-confidence when students are able to introduce themselves.

❏ **I**ntegrate into classroom routine:

1. Have students introduce themselves to each other.
2. Make introductions a part of the classroom routine so that new students are made to feel comfortable in the class.

❏ **N**otice the behavior:

1. Praise students for using the behavior. Let them know how helpful it is when introductions are made.

❏ **G**eneralize the behavior:

1. Have students think of a situation in which using the skill of introducing oneself would be appropriate.
2. Have students think of a situation in which they would like to practice the skill outside of the classroom. Perhaps they would like to introduce themselves to a potential friend. Have students try out the skill and report back to the class.

ACTIVITY A-9

ASKING FOR HELP

Rationale: Knowing how to ask for help can help you solve all sorts of problems. As a result, you will feel better and be able to calm down if you are upset.

☐ **M**ake choices:

1. Select a behavior: asking for help
2. Select a model: a teacher or a peer who is regarded as a friend

☐ **O**rganize the behavior:

1. Gain the attention of the teacher or other person appropriately
   a. Approach quietly or,
   b. Raise hand.
2. Establish eye contact.
3. Maintain a serious expression.
4. State your problem.
5. Request help.

☐ **D**emonstrate the behavior:

1. Use the mnemonic device HELP.
   Hand (raise your hand).
   Eye contact (establish eye contact).
   Lead-in (state the problem).
   Pose the request (ask for help).
2. Model the behavior with another student or adult, using the mnemonic cues. Verbalize the cues aloud; then, gradually fade the cues.
3. Discuss how to use questions to ask for help; discuss the difference between commands and requests for help.
4. Have student differentiate between commands and questions.

☐ **E**ncourage the student to imitate:

1. Have student write out the mnemonic cues as an aid to remembering them.
2. Ask the student to imitate the behavior.
3. Cue the student while s/he imitates the behavior of asking for help.

☐ **L**ink the behavior:

1. Review the rationale for asking for help.
2. Discuss instances in which students may need to ask for help in the classroom.
3. Discuss feelings evoked when help is needed (frustration, anger, helplessness).
4. Discuss how not knowing how to ask for help could interfere with one's ability to get along with others in the classroom.
5. Discuss the consequences for using commands versus questions when asking for help.
6. Discuss differences and similarities when asking adults versus peers for help.
7. Combine *asking for help* with other social behaviors such as *interrupting appropriately* or *establishing eye contact*.

8. Combine *asking for help* with other social skills such as *working cooperatively* or *responding to frustration*.
9. Discuss feelings of social self-confidence when students are able to ask for help.

☐ **I**ntegrate into classroom routine:

1. Establish routines or signals for students to use when asking for help in the classroom.
2. Delineate times for students when raising hand versus approaching the teacher would be appropriate in the classroom.
3. Differentiate when students may ask peers for help.

☐ **N**otice the behavior:

1. Use praise and encouragement as students begin to use the behavior.
2. Keep a chart for individual students or for groups of students who have particular difficulty with this behavior.
3. Establish a quiet time at the end of the day to review who used the behavior and how well it was performed.

☐ **G**eneralize the behavior:

1. Discuss times during the schoolday, at home, and in the community when students need to use the behavior.
2. Send a note home to let parents know that the student is working on this behavior.
3. Assign homework to the students to use the behavior-to write down what they did and how it worked out.

ACTIVITY A-10

ACCEPTING HELP

Rationale: Knowing how to accept help makes you feel better about yourself and also alleviates the frustration and/or other negative feelings associated with not knowing what to do. If you accept help, you also enable the helper to feel good because offering help is a friendly thing to do. If you are unable to accept help, your frustration may increase, you may fail to solve the problem you have, and you may feel less confident about your ability to interact with others in certain situations.

❏ **M**ake choices:

    1. Select a behavior: accepting help
    2. Select a model: a teacher and a peer who is regarded as a friend to act as the helper.

❏ **O**rganize the behavior:

    1. Establish eye contact with the helper.
    2. Use a pleasant facial expression.
    3. Say, "Yes, thank you for the help."
    4. Listen.
    5. Ask for clarification, if needed.
    6. Thank the helper.

❏ **D**emonstrate the behavior:

    1. Demonstrate *accepting help* by following the steps.
    2. Then, demonstrate good *listening*.
        a. Maintain eye contact.
        b. Nod and maintain a pleasant expression when he or she under stands.
        c. Ask for clarification if needed.
        d. Thank the helper.
    3. Discuss various ways to ask for clarification, such as, "I don't understand that part,' "Why do you say that?", "Could I do it this way?"
    4. Model ways to thank the helper.
        a. Maintain eye contact.
        b. Use a pleasant expression.
        c. Use polite language that tells the person exactly why he or she is being thanked.

❏ **E**ncourage the student to imitate:

    1. Review *listening*.
    2. Review steps for accepting help and practice various ways to verbalize accepting help.
    3. Review different ways to thank the helper.
    4. Ask the student to imitate the behavior.

❏ **L**ink the behavior:

    1. Review the rationale for accepting help. Discuss why accepting help is an important social behavior.
    2. Discuss various situations in the classroom in which peers help each other.

3. Discuss times when students need to accept help from teachers.
4. Discuss when refusing help might be appropriate or inappropriate.
5. Combine *accepting help* with other social behavior such as *maintaining a conversation* or *maintaining eye contact*.
6. Combine *accepting help* with other social skills such as *working cooperatively* or *dealing with frustration*.
7. Discuss various feelings associated with accepting help and how students may socially feel more self confident if they are able to accept help from others.

❐ **I**ntegrate into classroom routine:

1. Have the students work in cooperative groups where helping each other is a part of the project. Show students that learning to accept help from each other makes working in groups more pleasant.
2. Since some students have a difficult time accepting help, they may need much encouragement and reinforcement in order to begin to use this behavior. These students may initially find it easier to accept help from other students than from adults in the classroom.

❐ **N**otice the behavior:

1. Provide encouragement and praise students who accept help.
2. Do not try to *talk* a student into accepting your help when he or she feels particularly frustrated over a lesson. It is better not to give the student much attention at this time, but rather the student *cool off* and relax before approaching with help. Later, discuss with the student how she or he might have better handled the frustration by practicing how to accept help.
3. Teach students to praise one another when their peers accept their help.

❐ **G**eneralize the behavior:

1. Have students practice this behavior in other areas of the school.
2. Have students keep a checklist of times when they are able to accept help. When students receive a predetermined number of checks, they earn a small reward.
3. Set up a specific contract with students who demonstrate low tolerance for frustration and who have difficulty accepting help. This may help them to begin to generalize this behavior to other situations.

ACTIVITY A-11

OFFERING HELP

Rationale: Knowing how to offer help to others may make everyone feel better. Other people will think that you care about them and that you want to be a friend. Offering help to others is an important part of friendship. Not offering help may make them believe that you do not want to be their friends.

❐ **M**ake choices:

    1. Select a behavior: offering help
    2. Select a model: a teacher or a peer who is regarded as a friend

❐ **O**rganize the behavior:

    1. Notice when another person needs help.
    2. Approach the person.
    3. Establish eye contact.
    4. Inquire whether the person would like help; if the person refuses help, move away.
    5. Offer your help.
    6. Use a pleasant, but serious expression.

❐ **D**emonstrate the behavior:

    1. Demonstrate offering help to a student using the six steps.
    2. Point out the acronym for offering help **N-AEIOU**, as a remembering device.
    3. Being careful to respect the other person's space, approach a student or another teacher to demonstrate the behavior.
    4. Using the person's name while establishing eye contact may help to deflect the person's anger and enable her/him to accept the offer of help.
    5. Formulate a question, inquiring whether help is needed. Model a variety of appropriate questions.
    6. Demonstrate moving away if help is refused. Discuss reasons why someone may refuse help.
    7. Give help with a serious, not gloating or superior, facial expression. Discuss the rationale for this.

❐ **E**ncourage the student to imitate:

    1. Have the student imitate the steps while the teacher verbalizes the cues.
    2. Have the student practice with other students and offer help in a variety of ways such as helping with math work, helping with a stuck zipper, helping to carry belongings.
    3. Have the student practice situations in which help is refused or accepted.

❐ **L**ink the behavior:

    1. Review the rationale for knowing how to offer help to others.
    2. Discuss the *signs* that tell us someone needs help. These might include nonverbal behaviors such as holding their head in their hands or verbal behaviors such as loud sighs.

3. Have students list situations in the classroom in which they may help their peers, teachers, or younger students. Sharing the lists may be helpful to those students who do not realize that they help in many ways throughout the day.

4. Discuss the fact that sometimes students may need to help, even when they do not feel like helping. Discuss the advantages of offering help in this situation.

5. Have students discuss why others might refuse their help and why this is appropriate at times. Also discuss facial expressions and body gestures that might act as clues that a person should not be approached for help.

6. Discuss the term very *helpful*. Discuss the problem of offering help too frequently and the consequences of this behavior.

7. Combine *offering help* with other social behaviors such as *initiating conversation* or *respecting another person's space*.

8. Combine *offering help* with other social skills such as *making friends* or *joining a group in the classroom*.

9. Discuss feelings of social self-confidence when students are able to offer help to one another.

❐ **I**ntegrate into classroom routine:

1. Make offering help to others a special rule within the classroom that is built into the general expectations for the class.

2. At first, it may be helpful to tell students when to help each other. Develop a hand signal or other nonverbal cue to let students know that you or someone else needs help.

❐ **N**otice the behavior:

1. Praise and encourage students when they offer to help each other.

2. When a student offers to help another, write the student's name on a cut-out construction paper shape of a hand. Place the hand on a bulletin board entitled *Helping Hands Make Good Friends*.

❐ **G**eneralize the behavior:

1. Have students keep a logbook or journal in which they keep track of offering and helping others.

2. Let parents know that students are working on offering help and ask them to reinforce thisbehavior at home.

3. Let other school staff know that students are working on the behavior. Try to set up situations for students to practice, for example, helping the librarian carry books.

ACTIVITY A-12

ACCEPTING PRAISE

Rationale: Knowing how to accept praise tells a person giving praise you care about what s/he has said or that s/he has made you feel good. Learning how to accept praise may help you feel more comfortable when someone praises you and may increase your self-esteem.

❒ **M**ake choices:

1. Select a behavior: accepting praise
2. Select a model: a teacher or a peer who is regarded as a friend.

❒ **O**rganize the behavior:

1. Establish eye contact with the person giving the praise.
2. Wait until he or she has finished talking.
3. Smile.
4. Say, "Thank you, I appreciate hearing that."

❒ **D**emonstrate the behavior:

1. Set up a situation in which one teacher gives praise to another teacher. (The teacher receiving praise establishes eye contact, waits for the other teacher to finish talking, smiles, and thanks the teacher who gave the praise.)
2. Use key words such as *eye contact, wait, smile* and *thank* to help students learn each step of the behavior.
3. Demonstrate a variety of appropriate verbalizations to use when thanking someone.
4. Keep these verbalizations concise.

❒ **E**ncourage the student to imitate:

1. Encourage the student to repeat the steps and imitate the behavior.
2. Have the student verbalize the key words to him or herself while practicing accepting praise.

❒ **L**ink the behavior:

1. Review the rationale for accepting praise.
2. Discuss opportunities for accepting praise in the classroom.
3. Discuss some inappropriate ways that people deal with praise, such as making excuses, denying the worthiness of the praise, etc.
4. Discuss how accepting praise from peers or adults may differ.
5. Combine *accepting praise* with other social behaviors such as *establishing eye contact* or *smiling*.
6. Combine *accepting praise* with other social skills such as *participating in a group discussion* or *making conversation*.
7. Discuss feelings of self-esteem and social self-confidence when students are able to accept praise.

❏ **I**ntegrate into classroom routine:

1. Brainstorm with students to determine times when students may need to know how to accept praise.
2. Have students practice this behavior often by giving students praise and immediately using the opportunity to review with students how they managed the behavior.

❏ **N**otice the behavior:

1. Tell students when you notice that they have accepted praise appropriately.
2. When they continue to have trouble with the behavior, encourage students to say thank you when given praise.

❏ **G**eneralize the behavior:

1. Have students recall when they were given praise. Discuss how the students handled the praise.
2. Talk with other teachers and school staff and *set up* situations in which students receive praise from another adult in the building.

ACTIVITY A-13

RESPECTING ANOTHER PERSON'S SPACE

Rationale: Knowing how to respect another person's space lets others know that you are interested in them and also you respect them. Standing too close to others may make them uncomfortable and they may move away from you.

☐ **M**ake choices:

1. Select a behavior: respecting another person's space
2. Select a model: a teacher or a peer who is regarded as a friend

☐ **O**rganize the behavior:

1. Approach the other person.
2. Stop about 2-feet in front of the other person.
3. Maintain your distance.

☐ **D**emonstrate the behavior:

1. Demonstrate the behavior appropriately, then . . . .
2. Demonstrate space that is too close.
3. Demonstrate that maintaining an appropriate space may mean moving with the person, if the other person moves.

☐ **E**ncourage the student to imitate:

1. Ask the student to approach the teacher.
2. Ask the student to repeat the behavior with a peer s/he has chosen.
3. Ask the student to repeat the behavior with a peer chosen by the teacher.

☐ **L**ink the behavior:

1. Review the rationale for respecting another person's space.
2. Discuss when the behavior is used in the classroom.
3. Ask students to recall times when their personal space was not respected and discuss how they felt.
4. Discuss how differences in relationships may determine how much space is appropriate. Discuss the differences in space that would be used with parents, siblings, peers, and teachers. Students may make a chart to show these relationships.
5. Combine *respecting another person's space* with other social behaviors such as *greeting others* or *interrupting appropriately.*
6. Combine *respecting another person's space* with other social skills such as *joining an ongoing competitive game* or *joining an ongoing conversation.*
7. Discuss feelings of social self-confidence when students are able to respect another person's space.

☐ **I**ntegrate into classroom routine:

1. Remind students to respect the space of others until the behavior becomes part of the classroom routine.
2. Make it a classroom rule to *respect others.*

(*Activity A-13 Continued*)

❏ **N**otice the behavior:

1. Recognize when students are practicing this behavior. Reward students periodically for following classroom rules, such as, *respecting others.*

❏ **G**eneralize the behavior:

1. Expect students to respect the space of others in other classrooms, on the playground, in the lunchroom, etc.
2. If a particular student has difficulty with this behavior, establish a contract between the teacher and the student to focus on this behavior. A home-school program may also help the student to practice the behavior at home.

GIVING COMPLIMENTS

Rationale: Knowing how to give compliments makes others feel good. It tells them that you noticed something special about them. When you give compliments, you say something nice about another person. You tell others that you like something about them or about something they have done. Giving compliments is a friendly thing to do.

❐ **M**ake choices:

1. Select a behavior: giving compliments
2. Select a model: a teacher or a peer

❐ **O**rganize the behavior:

1. Decide what you want to say to the person.
2. Decide how you want to say the compliment.
3. Use pleasant nonverbal behaviors such as establishing eye contact, smiling, respecting the person's space, and greeting the person.
4. Be sure that the time and place are appropriate for giving the compliment.
5. Give the compliment.

❐ **D**emonstrate the behavior:

1. Demonstrate the behavior.
2. Review the nonverbal behaviors of respecting the other person's space, using eye contact, greeting the person, and smiling.
3. Set up various situations in which giving compliments to others might be appropriate.
4. Discuss different ways to phrase compliments in various situations.
5. Discuss times and places that may not be appropriate for giving compliments.

❐ **E**ncourage the student to imitate:

1. Have the student imitate giving a compliment while repeating the steps.
2. Have the student practice speaking in a clear voice.
3. Ask the student to write compliments for a variety of situations.
4. Have the student practice giving compliments using the steps you have outlined and the phrases that s/he has written out.
5. Discuss with the student the affect his/her compliment may have on others, what feelings the compliment may evoke, and how that may be expressed differently by different people.
6. Provide many opportunities for the student to practice this behavior in order for the compliment to appear to be a sincere statement.

❐ **L**ink the behavior:

1. Review the rationale for giving a compliment.
2. Discuss opportunities for giving compliments in the classroom. Students often have difficulty recognizing opportunities to give compliments.

3. Discuss with students times when it might be better to *not* give a compliment. Try to differentiate situations in which using this behavior might be inappropriate.
4. Discuss with students times that might be appropriate for giving compliments. Try to differentiate situations in which using this behavior might be appropriate.
5. Make a list of instances and compliments that students may use in a variety of situations.
6. Combine *giving compliments* with other social behaviors such as *initiating a conversation* or *maintaining eye contact*.
7. Combine *giving compliments* with other social skills such as *maintaining a friendship* or *participating in group discussions*.
8. Discuss feelings of social self-confidence when students are able to give compliments to others. Students who have difficulty giving compliments are often students who have low self-esteem and poor social skills. Sometimes they feel that if they don't deserve a compliment, others shouldn't be given them either. Often students who have difficulty giving compliments have such low self-esteem that they view someone else receiving compliments as reinforcement for their own low self-esteem. Take care in working with these students on this behavior.

❒ **I**ntegrate into classroom routine:

1. Establish a general classroom rule such as *Be kind to each other*.
2. Remember to give compliments to students throughout the day.

❒ **N**otice the behavior:

1. Notice when students are able to give compliments.
2. Praise students for using the behavior.
3. Choose a person of the week or person of the day. Each student is given the assignment to give that person a compliment each day. At the end of the day or week, have the "person of the week" describe his/her experiences.

❒ **G**eneralize the behavior:

1. Have students think of situations outside the classroom in which giving compliments would be appropriate.
2. Have students think of a situation in which they would like to practice the behavior outside of the classroom. Have students think of a person to whom they would like to give a compliment. Have students decide what to compliment and what to say. Then have the students find the right time to give the compliment.
3. Set up homework assignments so that the behavior is used outside the classroom.

INTERRUPTING APPROPRIATELY

Rationale: Knowing how to interrupt appropriately may help students get their needs met more effectively. A student who rudely interrupts a teacher to ask a favor or a question is less likely to receive a favorable response than a student who patiently waits to be acknowledged. Interrupting appropriately tells a person that you appreciate the importance of their present interaction.

❐ **M**ake choices:

1. Select a behavior: interrupting appropriately.
2. Select a model: a teacher or a peer who is regarded as a friend

❐ **O**rganize the behavior:

1. Approach the person quietly.
2. Wait quietly for the person to acknowledge you.
   a. Maintain distance.
   b. Show good posture.
   c. Be still.
   d. Watch for the person to see you.
3. Establish eye contact.
4. Smile.
5. Say, "Excuse me."
6. State the reason for interrupting.

❐ **D**emonstrate the behavior:

1. Set up a situation in which two people are talking. Demonstrate the behavior with another student or teacher.
2. Teach *waiting,* if necessary. Students who demonstrate impulsive behavior may have greater difficulty to learn how to wait.
   a. Maintain a distance from the person that is close enough to gain attention but does not invade the other person's space.
   b. Stand straight and be still. Extraneous movements are distracting and inappropriate while waiting.
   c. Establish eye contact; once established, use eye contact as a signal that the time is right to interrupt.
3. Use key words such as *approach, wait, eye contact,* and *talk,* when teaching students to interrupt appropriately.

❐ **E**ncourage the student to imitate:

1. Ask the student to imitate the behavior.
2. Use key words (first by the teacher, then by both the student and the teacher, and finally only by the student), to help the student incorporate all the steps.
3. Some students may need to learn the nonverbal aspects of waiting before attempting the behavior of interrupting appropriately.

❐ **L**ink the behavior:

1. Review the rationale for interrupting appropriately.

2. Discuss opportunities for interrupting appropriately in the classroom—such as asking for clarification of directions or help when the teacher is busy with another child, another teacher, or the principal.
3. Combine *interrupting appropriately* with other social behaviors such as *establishing eye contact* or *maintaining eye contact*.
4. Combine *interrupting appropriately* with other social skills such as *joining a group in the lunchroom* or *participating in a group discussion*.
5. Discuss feelings of social self-confidence when students are able to interrupt appropriately.

❑ **I**ntegrate into classroom routine:

1. Expect students to interrupt appropriately.
2. Permit interruptions when they are made appropriately.
3. Student with special needs who spend time in general education classrooms may need to interrupt more frequently than their peers, since they may move in and out of classrooms many times throughout the day. These students may need special adaptations (such as a peer who provides information) when they are late for class and miss the directions given to the rest of the students.
4. Ignore students who interrupt inappropriately.

❑ **N**otice the behavior:

1. Acknowledge when a student uses the behavior of interrupting appropriately. Students should be given feedback regarding each step of the behavior.
2. Give particular notice to the waiting aspect of this behavior, as this may be the most difficult step for students to master.

❑ **G**eneralize the behavior:

1. Assign homework in which the students are asked to practice and evaluate the behavior. Have students report back and discuss which aspects of the behavior they have mastered and those with which aspects they had trouble.
2. Send students on errands to other classrooms. In this way, other teachers and staff within the school building may help the student practice and generalize the behavior outside the classroom.

ACTIVITY A-16

ASKING FOR PERMISSION

Rationale: Knowing how to ask for permission is viewed by others as a polite, considerate behavior. If you are polite, you are more likely to obtain permission than if you use demanding or commanding language. By asking for permission, you may also avoid inappropriate or unpleasant interactions with teachers, other adults, or peers.

❒ **M**ake choices:

1. Select a behavior: asking for permission
2. Select a model: a teacher or a peer who is regarded as a friend

❒ **O**rganize the behavior:

1. Approach the person.
2. Wait to be acknowledged.
3. Establish eye contact.
4. Smile.
5. Ask for permission.
   a. Use polite language (May I . . . , Would you mind if I . . . , Please . . .).
   b. Use questions.

❒ **D**emonstrate the behavior:

1. Set up a situation in which a student would have to ask for permission. For example, a student might ask another adult for permission to borrow a pen.
2. Review other behaviors such as *interrupting appropriately* and *waiting appropriately;* these may be embedded in the behavior of asking for permission.
3. Demonstrate the behavior (asking for permission).
4. Use key words such as *wait, ask,* and *thank you* to help the student remember the sequence of behaviors used in asking for permission.

❒ **E**ncourage the student to imitate:

1. Ask the student to imitate the behavior using the key words as an aid for remembering the sequence of behaviors used in asking for permission.
2. Some students may need to practice formulating a variety of questions that are suitable to use when asking for permission.

❒ **L**ink the behavior:

1. Review the rationale for asking permission.
2. Discuss opportunities for students to ask for permission in the classroom: to get out of their seats, sharpen pencils, use materials, or play certain games. Clarify those activities for which students must have permission.
3. Discuss inappropriate ways to ask for permission, such as saying "I'm going to use the markers, OK?"
4. Combine *asking for permission* with other social behaviors such as *establishing eye contact* or *interrupting appropriately.*

5. Combine *asking for permission* with other social skills such as *joining a group in the classroom* or *working cooperatively.*
6. Discuss feelings of social self-confidence when students are able to ask for permission.

❐ **I**ntegrate into classroom routine:

1. Expect students to ask for permission in the classroom.
2. Use nonverbal cues such as a raised finger to remind students to ask for permission.

❐ **N**otice the behavior:

1. Notice when students ask for permission appropriately.
2. Encourage students who try the behavior and give corrective feedback on those aspects with which the students have difficulty.
3. Ignore students who fail to ask for permission.

❐ **G**eneralize the behavior:

1. Assign students the task of asking for permission at home and in various situations in school. For example, students may be assigned the task of asking a parent for permission to participate in an activity.
2. Have students construct a list of the steps used in asking for permission and use this list to evaluate their performance at other times and in other situations.
3. Have students discuss whether they received permission and evaluate why they did or did not succeed.
4. Help students generalize this behavior to other situations through the use of role play activities that they create to use the behavior. In this way, students can practice some of the situations in which asking for permission in a polite manner may get them something they want.
5. Discuss how rules and routines may vary in other classrooms and in various parts of the school building. It may be that students are allowed to walk around in the library, but need to ask permission to walk around in the classroom or cafeteria.
6. To help students realize the importance of asking for permission in their lives, have them brainstorm times when asking for permission is required.

ACTIVITY A-17

FORMING A LINE

Rationale: Knowing how to form a line helps students move from one activity to another without disruptions and unproductive social interactions. When you form a line properly, you demonstrate to your peers that you respect them and can interact with them appropriately. Waiting, listening, and respecting the space between one another are behaviors that are needed to form a line and demonstrate kindness and patience—attributes needed to form and maintain friendships.

❏ **M**ake choices:

    1. Select a behavior: forming a line
    2. Select a model: a teacher or a peer who is regarded as a friend

❏ **O**rganize the behavior:

    1. Wait to be called to line up (form a line).
    2. Walk to the line.
    3. Keep a *balloon* space between yourself and others.
    4. Keep hands to yourself.
    5. Face forward.
    6. Wait quietly for directions.

❏ **D**emonstrate the behavior:

    1. Verbalize each step for students before asking them to move.
    2. Use key words for each step: *wait, walk, balloon, be still, listen.*
    3. Demonstrate each step for the students while verbalizing the steps.
    4. Discuss what is meant by keeping a *balloon* space between yourself and others. Using the notion of *not popping the balloons* between them may help students to visualize how much space they need to maintain between themselves and others.

❏ **E**ncourage the student to imitate:

    1. Ask the student to imitate the behavior.
    2. Following and modeling a peer may be helpful.

❏ **L**ink the behavior:

    1. Review the rationale for knowing how to form a line.
    2. Identify opportunities for using the behavior in the classroom.
    3. Discuss the importance of using the steps to form a line appropriately. Have students identify a rationale for each step.
    4. Have students examine the consequences of not following each step in the behavior sequence.
    5. Combine *forming lines* with other social behaviors such as *walking in line* or *asking permission.*
    6. Combine *forming lines* with other social skills such as *joining a group* or *dealing with loneliness.*
    7. Discuss feelings of social self-confidence when students are able to form a line.

❐ **I**ntegrate into classroom routine:

1. Review the routine (either verbally or through modeling the behavior) each time the tudents need to use the behavior, until the students practice the behavior without reminders.
2. Expect students to form a line appropriately.
3. Model the behavior each time students need to use the behavior.
4. Choose a student to show the class what is expected.

❐ **N**otice the behavior:

1. Praise students who model forming lines as well as students who learn to use the behavior appropriately.
2. Have students return to seats if they do not follow the sequence of steps. Have them practice with corrective support until they are able to follow the steps.
3. For students who are having trouble, review the steps before you call on them and be sure to praise when they demonstrate the behavior appropriately.

❐ **G**eneralize the behavior:

1. Discuss how other teachers may expect students to form a line in different ways; discuss similarities and differences among teachers.
2. Share with other teachers your expectations for this behavior and ask them to remind students before they are put in line, and to praise them when they practice the behavior.
3. Discuss various times outside of the school setting when forming lines is expected: at checkout lines, banks, cafeterias, restaurants, movies, etc.
4. Have students select three situations in which they will practice the behavior and report back to the class.

ACTIVITY A-18

WALKING IN LINE

Rationale: Knowing how to walk in line helps students move from one activity to another without disruptions and unproductive social interactions. When you are able to walk in line, you demonstrate to your teachers and your peers that you respect their space and are willing to coperate for the sake of the group. Cooperation and respect are attributes that are important in friendships and productive social relationships.

☐ **M**ake choices:

1. Select a behavior: walking in line
2. Select a model: a teacher or a peer who is regarded as a friend

☐ **O**rganize the behavior:

1. Use lining up behaviors.
   a. Keep a *balloon* space between yourself and others
   b. Keep hands to yourself
   c. Face forward
   d. Wait quietly for directions
2. Watch the person in front of you.
3. When that person moves, you move in the same way.
4. Watch where you are going.
5. Keep your *balloon* from touching anyone.
6. Keep quiet.

☐ **D**emonstrate the behavior:

1. Review the steps for lining up with others. Demonstrate these steps; use key words: *wait, walk, balloon,* and *listen.*
2. Demonstrate walking in line with other students.

☐ **E**ncourage the student to imitate:

1. Have students practice being attentive by playing *Follow the Leader* game. The activity would require students to follow a classmate, without breaking his/her *balloon.*
2. Students may use the mnemonic WALK to help remember the sequence of steps:

   Watch your space.
   Aim forward.
   Look where you are going.
   Keep quiet.

☐ **L**ink the behavior:

1. Review the rationale for knowing how to form lines.
2. Identify times during the day when the behavior is used in the classroom.
3. Discuss the consequences of bumping into others in line.
4. Combine *walking in line* with other social behaviors such as *forming a line* or *respecting another person's space.*
5. Combine *walking in line* with other social skills such as *dealing with covert rejection* or *making friends.*

(Activity A-18 Continued)

6. Discuss feelings of social self-confidence when students are able to walk in line.

☐ **I**ntegrate into classroom routine:

1. Review the sequence of steps for lining up and walking in line each time the class needs to line up and walk from one part of the building to another.
2. Routinely review how to walk in line before each transition.
3. Review the mnemonic WALK before leaving the room; place a chart with the WALK mnemonic above the door to act as a reminder to the students.

☐ **N**otice the behavior:

1. As students move in line, praise those students who are walking in line appropriately. Describe the specific part/s of the behavior that they are demonstrating correctly. This is often an effective way to decrease inappropriate behavior without directly calling attention to it.
2. Praise students as frequently as possible as you move with them throughout the building.

☐ **G**eneralize the behavior:

1. Once students have mastered the behavior of walking in line with others, they may be ready to generalize this behavior to walking in a more informal manner with peers. Students should discuss how their behavior might be different when walking with two other students, versus an entire class.
2. Discuss times when students walk with others outside of the school building. Relate walking with others in lines to other lines students walk in, i.e., at stores, movies, etc. Discuss the consequences of inappropriate behavior in lines outside of the school building.
3. Allow students to move throughout the building without an adult—first, have them move by themselves, later, let them walk with a peer.
4. Alert school staff that students are working on this behavior. Ask school staff to reinforce this behavior by giving praise and encouragement to students.

ACTIVITY A-19

LEAVING OTHERS

Rationale: Leaving others appropriately tells others that you are sorry to leave them, but that you care about them. Leaving a group without saying good-bye may confuse others and make them wonder why you left the group. People may be more apt to consider you a friend if you take the time to say good-bye politely when you must leave.

❐ **M**ake choices:

1. Select a behavior: leaving others
2. Select a model: a teacher or a peer who is regarded as a friend

❐ **O**rganize the behavior:

1. Look around the group.
2. Establish eye contact with one group member.
3. Have a neutral expression.
4. Tell the group or the group member that you need to leave.
5. Wait for a response.
6. Say *good-bye* while looking around the group.
7. Use nonverbal behaviors such smiling, nodding, or waving, as you walk away.

❐ **D**emonstrate the behavior:

1. Form a group.
2. Look around to get a group member's attention.
3. Establish eye contact with this group member.
4. Maintain a neutral expression.
5. Use the member's name to preface the statement that you must leave the group; say, "John, I've got to go now."
6. Wait for John to respond.
   a. If John asks a question, respond to the question.
   b. If John does not respond, say a general *good-bye,* and *wave.*

❐ **E**ncourage the student to imitate:

1. Encourage students to verbalize the steps.
2. Encourage students to verbalize the steps using the key words.
3. Practice the behavior with small classroom groups.
4. Have students practice the behavior while verbalizing the steps.

❐ **L**ink the behavior:

1. Review the rationale for leaving others appropriately.
2. Identify opportunities to use the behavior in the classroom such as leaving the classroom for tutoring, or responding to a teacher request.
3. Discuss why using this behavior might be important.
4. Discuss the consequences of not leaving others appropriately.
5. Combine *leaving others* with other social behaviors such as *interrupting appropriately* or *ending a conversation.*
6. Combine *leaving others* with other social skills such as *participating in group discussions* or *dealing with peer pressure.*

7. Discuss feelings of social self-confidence when students are able to leave others appropriately.

❏ **I**ntegrate into classroom routine:

1. Expect students to leave groups appropriately.
2. Make a chart, listing a few specific times when using the behavior of leaving others could be practiced in the classroom. List students' names on the chart and record when students use the behavior.
3. Maintain the list until students are practicing the behavior at a high and consistent rate.

❏ **N**otice the behavior:

1. Refer to the chart at the start of the school day, reminding students when to use the behavior.
2. Take time during the day to complete the chart; at these times, praise and encourage students who are trying to use the behavior.
3. Tally the chart at the end of the day; comment to students on their progress.
4. Give students praise and encouragement when you see them practice the behavior.

❏ **G**eneralize the behavior:

1. Once the behavior is occurring at high rates in the classroom, have students discuss other times (home, school, community) when they might practice the behavior.
2. Make a contract with individual students; have the student list two or three times during the day when s/he will try to remember to practice the behavior.
3. Have the student list the times and report back on his/her progress when practicing the behavior.

COACHING ACTIVITIES

ACTIVITY B-1

JOINING A GROUP IN THE CLASSROOM (ACADEMIC)

Rationale: Knowing how to join a group that is completing an academic task in the classroom will enable you to join a group as a participant. If other students see you use cooperative and polite behaviors, they will be more likely to ask you to join with them in their activity. You need to enter these groups if you are late for school, coming from another classroom, or changing activities at the request of your teacher.

❐ Construct a hypothetical social problem (use Figure B-1):

> *Nancy is returning from her early session in the Resource Room. All the other students are busily engaged at different learning centers. All the old familiar anxieties surface as she pauses at the classroom door. Just then, her teacher says, "Nancy, join a group and get to work." Nancy says, "OK," but her stomach is doing flip-flops. They all understand what they're doing and I've missed the first part. Which group should I join? Wht if nobody lets me in?"*
> *What should Nancy do to join a group?*

❐ Organize a discussion:

1. Select a heterogenous group of students to discuss the problem.
2. Include students who are socially competent as well as those who need to develop social knowledge and become more socially skilled.
3. Read the hypothetical social problem and/or show the picture to the students.

❐ Ask the coaching questions:

Understand Concepts:	What is fear? When does fear happen? Why is it important to overcome fear?
Perceive Situations:	
Recognitize the situation:	What's going on here? What's happening in this story?
Identify the participants:	Who are the people in the story?
Identify the goal:	What are the members of the class trying to do?
Identify behaviors:	What are the other students doing? What else were they doing?
Identify the social problem:	What's the problem in this situation? What is Nancy trying to do?
Identify the perspective of others:	How does Nancy feel? How do the other members of the class feel? How does the teacher feel?

Solve Problems:

Recall past experiences:	Have you ever been in a situation like this?
Identify previous behaviors	What did you do? What did other people do?
Identify consequences:	What happened when you _____? or _____ ?
Identify behaviors to use in this situation:	What could Nancy do in this situation? What might happen? What else could she do? What could the other students do? What might happen? What is the best idea to solve this problem?

❐ **C**hoose students to play roles:

1. Select students of varying social abilities to play key roles.
2. Give students opportunities to practice new ways of behaving if they wish.
3. Provide other students with the experience of being treated differently by their peers.
4. Allow students to role play the situation using the strategies they have selected.
5. Provide students with as much direction as is needed.
6. Assign other students roles as observers.

❐ **H**elp students to evaluate the effectiveness of behaviors used:

1. Ask students the following questions.
   a. What happened? What did you do? What did the others do?
   b. Were the behaviors you selected effective? Why? or Why not? Was the goal achieved?
   c. What else could you have done? Would that have been more effective?
   d. How did you feel? How do you think the others feel?
2. Permit students to reenact the situation using different behaviors or actors if they wish. Ask, Do you want to do it again?"
3. Ask evaluation questions again and compare results.

❐ **I**ntegrate into classroom routine:

1. Provide many opportunities for students to join the small groups in the classroom.
2. Cue students to think bout behaviors before joining a group.

❐ **N**otice interactions:

1. Praise and give other positive reinforcement to students when they use successful behaviors to join groups appropriately.
2. Teach students to praise one another when they use effective behaviors.
3. Teach students to discuss why certain behaviors are not effective and encourage one another to try again.

❐   **G**eneralize social knowledge:

1. Work with other staff members to provide opportunities for students to use social knowledge to join an academic group appropriately in situations outside the classroom.
2. Cue peers to help others join their groups outside the classroom.

FIGURE B-1

ACTIVITY B-2

JOINING AN ONGOING CLASSROOM ACTIVITY (PLAY)

Rationale: Knowing how to join an ongoing classroom activity will enable you to join a group as a participant. If other students see you use cooperative and polite behaviors, they will be more likely to ask you to join them in their activities.

❐ **C**onstruct a hypothetical social problem:

> *Linda and Brian were assembling a new puzzle during indoor recess. Both Linda and Brian enjoy puzzles and usually play well together. When they were halfway through the puzzle, Karl approached them, sat down, and began to break apart a section of the puzzle they had already finished. Linda and Brian told him to stop and go away, but Karl continued to take the puzzle apart and put it together his own way. Then Brian tried to take the puzzle pieces away from Karl but he held onto them refused to leave.*
> *What should Karl do?*

❐ **O**rganize a discussion:

1. Select a heterogenous group of students to discuss the problem.
2. Include students who are socially competent as well as those who need to develop social knowledge and become more socially skilled.
3. Read the hypothetical social problem to the students.

❐ **A**sk the coaching questions to develop social knowledge:

Understand Concepts:	What is interrupting? Why is it important to know how to interrupt appropriately?
Perceive Situations:	
Recognize the situation:	What's going on here?
	What's happening in this story?
Identify the participants:	Who are the people in the story?
Identify the goal of the group:	What are Linda and Brian trying to do?
Identify behaviors:	What were Linda and Brian doing before Karl tried to join them?
	What else were they doing?
	What's the problem in this situation?
Identify the social problem:	What is Karl trying to do?
Identify the perspective of others:	How does Karl feel?
	How do Linda and Brian feel?
Solve Problems:	
Recall past experiences:	Have you ever been in a situation like this?
Identify previous behaviors:	What did you do? What did other people do?
Identify consequences:	What happened when you _____? or _____ ?

Identify behaviors to use
in this situation:

What could Linda and Brian do
in this situation?
What might happen?
What else could they do?
What is the best idea to solve this
problem?

☐ **C**hoose students to play roles:

1. Select students of varying social abilities to play key roles.
2. Give students opportunities to practice new ways of behaving if they wish.
3. Provide other students with the experience of being treated differently by their peers.
4. Allow students to role play the situation using the strategies they have selected.
5. Provide students with as much direction as is needed.
6. Assign other students roles as observers.

☐ **H**elp students to evaluate the effectiveness of behaviors used:

1. Ask students the following questions:
   a. What happened? What did you do? What did the others do?
   b. Were the behaviors you selected effective? Why? or Why not?
   c. What else could you have done? Would that have been more effective?
   d. How did you feel? How do you think the others feel?
2. Permit students to reenact the situation using different behaviors or actors if they wish.
3. Ask evaluation questions again and compare results.

☐ **I**ntegrate into classroom routine:

1. Provide many opportunities for students to join an ongoing activity in the classroom in small groups.
2. Cue students to use their social knowledge (understanding perception and problem-solving) before joining an ongoing game or activity and to evaluate their behavior.

☐ **N**otice interactions:

1. Praise and give other positive reinforcement to students when they use successful social knowledge to join ongoing classroom activities appropriately.
2. Teach students to praise one another when they use social knowledge effectively.
3. Teach students to discuss why certain behaviors are not effective and encourage one another to try again.

☐ **G**eneralize social knowledge:

1. Work with other staff members to provide opportunities for students to use social knowledge to join ongoing activities apropriately in situations outside the classroom.
2. Ask parents to provide opportunities for students to practice joining ongoing informal activities at home and to praise students when they use their social knowledge.

ACTIVITY B-3

JOINING A CLASSROOM ACTIVITY (ACADEMIC)

Rationale: Knowing how to join peers who are working on an academic task in the classroom may enable you to join the group as a participant. If other students see you use appropriate behaviors, they may view you as a competent person and will be more likely to ask you to join them in their activities. You may need to join others while they are working to complete your own assignments.

❏ **C**onstruct a hypothetical social problem:

Sandy and Paul were working together at the computer on a story they had written together. They hoped to finish making corrections so they could print the story in time for the teacher to put it in the class book. Sandy and Paul like working at the computer and always seem to work well together. When they were halfway through making their corrections, Carla walked over and asked if they would show her what they were doing so she could use the computer too. The boys didn't even look up as they both said, "No," and continued working. Sandy told Carla that there was only room for two people to work at the computer and that she would have to find someone else to help her.
What should Carla do?

❏ **O**rganize a discussion:

1. Select a heterogenous group of students to discuss the problem.
2. Include students who are socially competent as well as those who need to develop social knowledge and become more socially skilled.
3. Read the hypothetical social problem to the students.

❏ **A**sk the coaching questions:

Understand Concepts:	What is rejection? Why is it important to be able to deal with rejection?
Perceive Situations:	
Recognize the situation:	What's going on here? What's happening in this story?
Identify the participants:	Who are the people in the story?
Identify the goal:	What are Sandy and Paul trying to do?
Identify behaviors:	How are they doing this? What else are they doing?
Identify the social problem:	What's the problem in this situation? What is Carla trying to do? Do you think Sandy and Paul acted fairly? Why?
Identify the perspective of others:	How does Carla feel? How do the boys feel?
Solve Problems:	
Recall past experiences:	Have you ever been in a situation like this? How did you feel?

Identify previous behaviors:	What did you do?
Identify consequences:	What did other people do? What happened when you _____ ? or _____ ?
Identify behaviors to use in this situation:	What could Carla do in this situation? What might happen? What else could she do? What could the others do? What might happen? What is the best idea to solve this problem?

❐ **C**hoose students to play roles:

1. Select students of varying social abilities to play key roles.
2. Give students opportunities to practice new ways of behaving.
3. Provide other students with the experience of being treated differently by their peers.
4. Allow students to role play the situation using the behaviors they have selected.
5. Provide students with as much direction as is needed.
6. Assign other students roles as observers.

❐ **H**elp students to evaluate the effectiveness of behaviors used:

1. Ask students the following questions.
   a. What happened? What did you do? What did the others do?
   b. Were the behaviors you selected effective? Why? or Why not?
   c. What else could you have done? Would that have been more effective?
   d. How did you feel? How do you think the others feel?
2. Permit students to reenact the situation using different behaviors or actors if they wish.
3. Ask evaluation questions again and compare results.

❐ **I**ntegrate into classroom routine:

1. Provide many opportunities for students to join an ongoing activity in the classroom in small groups.
2. Cue students to think about behaviors before interrupting an activity.

❐ **N**otice interactions:

1. Praise and give other positive reinforcement to students when they use successful behaviors to join classroom activities appropriately.
2. Teach students to praise one another when they use effective behaviors.
3. Teach students to discuss why certain behaviors are not effective and encourage one another to try again.

❐ **G**eneralize social knowledge:

1. Work with other staff members to provide opportunities for students to use social knowledge to join groups appropriately in other classrooms.
2. Cue peers to help others join their groups outside the classroom.

ACTIVITY B-4

PARTICIPATING IN GROUP DISCUSSIONS

Rationale: Knowing how to participate in group discussions will enable you to become a more visible member of the group. If other students see you contributing appropriately, they may view you as a competent person and will be more likely to ask you to join with them in other activities. Your teacher may also use your participation in group discussions as a measure of your ability to get along with your classmates as well as your ability to understand the topic of the discussion.

☐ **C**onstruct a hypothetical social problem:

> *The science class was having a lively discussion on the lifecycle of the Monarch Butterfly. Everyone seemed to understand the material pretty well, but Sarah really knew more than the other students. She was reluctant to participate in the discussion because she was afraid that the others would think she was a know-it-all. She was sure of her facts and she wanted to share, but she held back because she was intimidated by other members of the group who seemed to talk more easily and often.*
> *What should Sarah do?*

☐ **O**rganize a discussion:

1. Select a heterogenous group of students to discuss the problem.
2. Include students who are socially competent as well as those who need to develop social knowledge and become more socially skilled.
3. Read the hypothetical social problem to the students.

☐ **A**sk the coaching questions:

Understand Concepts:	What is fear? When does fear occur? Why is it important to overcome fear?
Perceive Situations:	
Recognize the situation:	What's going on here? What's happening in this story?
Identify the participants:	Who are the people in the story?
Identify the goal:	What is the class trying to do?
Identify behaviors:	How are they doing this? What else are they doing? What's the problem in this situation?
Identify the social problem:	What is Sarah trying to do?
Identify the perspective of others:	How does Sarah feel? How do the others in the class feel? How does the teacher feel?
Solve Problems:	
Recall past experiences:	Have you ever been in a situation like this?
Identify previous behaviors:	What did you do? What did other people do?
Identify consequences:	What happened when you _____? or _____ ?

Identify behaviors to use in this situation:

What could Sarah do in this situation?
What might happen?
What else could she do?
What could the others do?
What might happen?
What is the best idea to solve this problem?

❏ **C**hoose students to play roles:

1. Select students of varying social abilities to play key roles.
2. Give students opportunities to practice new ways of behaving.
3. Provide other students with the experience of being treated differently by their peers.
4. Allow students to role play the situation using the behaviors they have selected.
5. Provide students with as much direction as is needed.
6. Assign other students roles as observers.

❏ **H**elp students to evaluate the effectiveness of behaviors used:

1. Ask students the following questions.
   a. What happened? What did you do? What did the others do?
   b. Were the behaviors you selected effective? Why? or Why not?
   c. What else could you have done? Would that have been more effective?
   d. How did you feel? How do you think the others feel?
2. Permit students to reenact the situation using different behaviors or actors if they wish.
3. Ask evaluation questions again and compare results.

❏ **I**ntegrate into classroom routine:

1. Provide many opportunities for students to talk in the classroom: in small groups of 2–6 students and in larger whole-class discussions.
2. Let students who may have difficulty participating in group discussions work in smaller groups at first to practice using different strategies.

❏ **N**otice interactions:

1. Praise and give other positive reinforcement to students when they use successful behaviors to participate class discussions appropriately.
2. Teach students to praise one another when they use effective behaviors.
3. Teach students to discuss why certain behaviors are not effective and encourage one another to try again.

❏ **G**eneralize social knowledge:

1. Work with other staff members to provide opportunities for students to use social knowledge to participate in discussions in other classrooms.
2. Cue peers to help others join their conversations and discussions outside the classroom.

ACTIVITY B-5

JOINING AN ONGOING CONVERSATION

Rationale: Knowing how to join an ongoing conversation will help you become a more visible member of the group. If other students see you contributing appropriately, they may view you as a competent person and will be more likely to ask you to join with them in other activities.

☐ **C**onstruct a hypothetical social problem:

> *Tom and Matt were talking in the hallway before school. Tom was telling Matt about a video he had seen last weekend. Matt had seen the video too and agreed that it was one of the funniest ever. Tom and Matt were laughing and becoming sillier by the moment.*
>
> *Dan walked up to the two boys and said, "Hi." Since Tom and Matt were still talking about parts of the video, they continued to laugh instead of responding to Dan's greeting. Dan didn't understand what was happening, thought they were laughing at him, and became very angry. He said, "What's so funny, you guys? You two are always laughing at me." With that, Dan stomped off down the hall.*
>
> *What should Dan do?*

☐ **O**rganize a discussion:

1. Select a heterogenous group of students to discuss the problem.
2. Include students who are socially competent as well as those who need to develop social knowledge and become more socially skilled.
3. Read the hypothetical social problem to the students.

☐ **A**sk the coaching questions:

Understand Concepts:	What is rejection? Why is it important to know how to deal with rejection?
Perceive Situations:	
Recognize the situation:	What's going on here? What's happening in this story?
Identify the participants:	Who are the people in the story?
Identify the goal:	What are Tom and Matt trying to do?
Identify behaviors:	How are they doing this? What else are they doing? What's the problem in this situation?
Identify the social problem:	What is Dan trying to do?
Identify the perspective of others:	How does Dan feel? How do Tom and Matt feel?
Solve Problems:	
Recall past experiences:	Have you ever been in a situation like this?
Identify previous behaviors:	What did you do? What did other people do?
Identify consequences:	What happened when you _____? or _____ ?

(Activity B-5 Continued)

Identify strategies to
use in this situation:

What could Dan do in this situation?
What might happen?
What else could he do?
Could Dan have avoided this
   problem?
What could Tom and Matt do?
What might happen?
What is the best idea to solve this
   problem?

☐ **C**hoose students to play roles:

1. Select students of varying social abilities to play key roles.
2. Give students opportunities to practice new ways of behaving.
3. Provide other students with the experience of being treated differently by their peers.
4. Allow students to role play the situation using the behaviors they
   have selected.
5. Provide students with as much direction as is needed.
6. Assign other students roles as observers.

☐ **H**elp students to evaluate the effectiveness of behaviors used:

1. Ask students the following questions.
   a. What happened? What did you do? What did the others do?
   b. Were the behaviors you selected effective? Why? or Why not?
   c. What else could you have done? Would that have been more
      effective?
   d. How did you feel? How do you think the others feel?
2. Permit students to reenact the situation using different behaviors or
   actors if they wish.
3. Ask evaluation questions again and compare results.

☐ **I**ntegrate into classroom routine:

1. Provide many opportunities for students to join an ongoing conversation in the classroom.
2. Expect students to use appropriate behaviors and problem–solving
   techniques to solve social problems.
3. Encourage students to help one another as they try to solve social
   and academic problems.

☐ **N**otice interactions:

1. Praise and give other positive reinforcement to students when they
   use successful behaviors to join ongoing conversations appropriately.

☐ **G**eneralize social knowledge:

1. Work with other staff members to provide opportunities for students to use social knowledge to join ongoing conversations in other
   classrooms and situations throughout the school.
2. Cue peers to encourage others to join their conversations outside
   the classroom.

ACTIVITY B-6

MAKING CONVERSATION

Rationale: Knowing how to make conversation will enable you to become a more visible member of a group. If other students see you contributing appropriately, they may view you as a competent person and will be more likely to ask you to join them in other activities.

❑ **C**onstruct a hypothetical social problem:

All Ron ever wanted to talk about was wrestling. Each day when he arrived at school, he would approach anyone who would listen with news about wrestlers and their trick holds. He described body slams, claw holds, death grips, tomahawk chops, and atomic drops.

At first, several of the boys in his class were interested in Ron's conversation. But after a while they grew tired of hearing lectures about wrestling day after day. It seemed that whenever they hung around Ron, they never had a chance to talk. Now, when they see Ron coming, they walk the other way. Sometimes Ron acts as if he doesn't notice how the other students are acting. When people walk away, he seems to find someone new to talk to.

What should Ron do?

❑ **O**rganize a discussion:

1. Select a heterogenous group of students to discuss the problem.
2. Include students who are socially competent as well as those who need to develop social knowledge and become more socially skilled.
3. Read the hypothetical social problem to the students.

❑ **A**sk the coaching questions:

Understand Concepts:	What is tolerance?
	Why is tolerance important?
Perceive Situations:	
Recognize the situation:	What's going on here?
	What's happening in this story?
Identify the participants:	Who are the people in the story?
Identify the goal:	What are the boys in the class trying to do?
Identify behaviors:	How are they doing this?
	What else are they doing?
Identify the social problem:	What's the problem in this situation?
	What is Ron trying to do?
	Do you think Ron knows he has a problem? Why?
Identify the perspective of others:	How does Ron feel?
	How do the other boys feel?
Solve Problems:	
Recall past experiences:	Have you ever been in a situation like this?
	Have you ever been so excited about your own story that you talked and talked about it?
	How did your listeners act when you did this?

Identify previous behaviors:	What did you do?
	What did other people do?
	What kind of things do people do or say to help you know that they are interested in what you have to say?
Identify consequences:	What happened when you _____? or _____ ?
	If Ron does not correct this problem, what kinds of difficulties might he have in the future?
Identify behaviors to use in this situation:	What could Ron do in this situation?
	What might happen?
	What else could he do?
	What might happen?
	What is the best idea to solve this problem?

☐ **C**hoose students to play roles:

1. Select students of varying social abilities to play key roles.
2. Give students opportunities to practice new ways of behaving.
3. Provide other students with the experience of being treated differently by their peers.
4. Allow students to role play the situation using the behaviors they have selected.
5. Provide students with as much direction as is needed. You may direct the students who are Ron's listeners to use the nonverbal and verbal cues that students mentioned in the previous discussion to give Ron the idea that they are not interested in what he has to say.
6. Assign other students roles as observers.

☐ **H**elp students to evaluate the effectiveness of behaviors used:

1. Ask students the following questions.
   a. What happened? What did you do? What did the others do?
   b. Were the behaviors you selected effective? Why? or Why not?
   c. What else could you have done? Would that have been more effective?
   d. How did you feel? How do you think the others feel?
2. Permit students to reenact the situation using different behaviors or actors if they wish. Students may role play a successful conversation between Ron and the others, one in which each party is interested in what the other has to say.
3. Ask evaluation questions again and compare results.

☐ **I**ntegrate into classroom routine:

1. Provide many opportunities for students to practice making conversation in the classroom.
2. Expect students to use appropriate behaviors and problem-solving techniques to solve social problems.
3. Encourage students to help one another as they try to solve social and academic problems.

❐ **N**otice interactions:

1. Praise and give other positive reinforcement to students when they use successful behaviors to make conversation with one another.
2. Teach students to praise one another when they use effective behaviors and make interesting and appropriate conversation.
3. Teach students to discuss why certain behaviors are not effective and encourage one another to try again.

❐ **G**eneralize social knowledge:

1. Work with other staff members to provide opportunities for students to use social knowledge to make conversation in other classrooms and situations throughout the school.
2. Cue peers to encourage others to make conversations outside the classroom.

ACTIVITY B-7

WORKING COOPERATIVELY

Rationale: Knowing how to work cooperatively can help you complete your academic tasks. You can also learn how to get along socially with your peers.When you are cooperative, your peers will view you as a helpful and valued member of the group—a person who knows that, for the group to succeed, each person must contribute. Being accepted by peers provides you with opportunities to become more socially skilled and develop more meaningful peer relationships.

❐ **C**onstruct a hypothetical social problem (Use Figure B-7):

> *Sue is a good student and she is usually correct when the teacher calls on her. Also, she is usually the first to finish her work. Today when the class divided into groups, Sue found that the group didn't work very well together. First of all, the others didn't do their work as well or as neatly as she could have. Sue boasted, "I can do it. Let me do it my way." So, the others let Sue finish the project by herself; but, they start calling her smarty and bossy. Sue did all the group's work correctly, but, the next time the class formed groups, Sue had a hard time finding partners.*
> *What should Sue do?*

❐ **O**rganize a discussion:

1. Select a heterogenous group of students to discuss the problem.
2. Include students who are socially competent as well as those who need to develop social knowledge and become more socially skilled.
3. Read the hypothetical social problem and/or show the picture to the students.

❐ **A**sk the coaching questions:

Understand Concepts:	What is cooperation?
	Why is cooperation important?
Perceive Situations:	
Recognize the situation:	What's going on here?
	What's happening in this story?
Identify the participants:	Who are the people in the story?
Identify the goal:	What are the other students doing?
Identify behaviors:	How are they doing this?
	What else are they doing?
Identify the social problem:	What's the problem in this situation?
	What is Sue trying to do?
	What does Sue want to have happen?
Identify the perspective of others:	How does Sue feel?
	How do the others feel?
Solve Problems:	
Recall past experiences:	Have you ever been in a situation like this?
Identify previous behaviors:	What did you do?
	What did other people do?
Identify consequences:	What happened when you _____? or _____ ?

<table>
<tr><td>Identify behaviors to use
in this situation:</td><td>What could Sue do in this situation?
What might happen? What else could
she do?
What could the others do?
What might happen?
What is the best idea to solve this
problem?</td></tr>
</table>

❒ **C**hoose students to play roles:

1. Select students of varying social abilities to play key roles.
2. Give students opportunities to practice new ways of behaving.
3. Provide other students with the experience of being treated differently by their peers.
4. Allow students to role play the situation using the strategies they have selected.
5. Provide students with as much direction as is needed.
6. Assign other students roles as observers.

❒ **H**elp students to evaluate the effectiveness of behaviors used:

1. Ask students the following questions.
   a. What happened? What did you do? What did the others do?
   b. Were the behaviors you selected effective? Why? or Why not? Was the goal achieved?
   c. What else could you have done? Would that have been more effective?
   d. How did you feel? How do you think the others feel?
2. Permit students to reenact the situation using different behaviors or actors if they wish.
3. Ask evaluation questions again and compare results.

❒ **I**ntegrate into classroom routine:

1. Provide frequent opportunities for students to work cooperatively in groups in the classroom. Establish rules for group work.
2. Expect students to use appropriate behaviors and problem-solving techniques to solve conflicts.
3. Encourage studentrs to help one another as they try to solve social and academic problems.
4. Expect students to stay on-task and be respectful of the rights of others to complete their work.

❒ **N**otice interactions:

1. Praise and give other positive reinforcement to students when they work cooperatively.
2. Teach students to praise one another when they resolve conflict effectively.
3. Teach students to discuss why certain behaviors are not effective and encourage one another to try again.
4. Provide specific verbal praise to students when they try to work cooperatively.

❏   **G**eneralize social knowledge:

1. Ask students to think of other situations in which they might have to work cooperatively outside the classroom.
2. Work with other staff members to promote the idea of using problem-solving throughout the school.
3. Send a note home to parents to let them know that their child is learning to work cooperatively. Ask parents to think of ways in which new behaviors might be used to solve problems at home.
4. Ask the students to keep a log of times when they try to work cooperatively with others and use problem-solving including the date, time, composition of the group, behaviors used, effectiveness. Have students report back to the class.

FIGURE B-7

ACTIVITY B-8

ACCEPTING HELP

Rationale: Knowing how to accept help from others when offered is as important as offering help to others. Accepting help is responsible behavior that reinforces the idea of peers supporting one another and learning to think of each other as resources. With help, you will become a more skillful participant in group activities—and other group members may seek you out and ask you to join them in other activities.

❏ **C**onstruct a hypothetical social problem:

> *The third grade language arts teacher assigned a creative writing task yesterday. Bob usually has trouble completing writing assignments. Putting his ideas down on paper is very difficult for him. He prefers to work alone so that the other kids in his class don't notice how often he must erase to correct his handwriting and spelling mistakes. Today, the teacher paired students who had completed the writing assignment to assist a student who had not. Bob really did not want to work with anyone else. Just as he was opening his notebook, he noticed Freddie coming toward him to be his assistant.*
> *What should Bob do?*

❏ **O**rganize a discussion:

1. Select a heterogenous group of students to discuss the problem.
2. Include students who are socially competent as well as those who need to develop social knowledge and become more socially skilled.
3. Read the hypothetical social problem to the students.

❏ **A**sk the coaching questions:

Understand Concepts:	What is helpfulness?
	Why is helpfulness important?
Perceive Situations:	
Recognize the situation:	What's going on here?
	What's happening in this story?
Identify the participants:	Who are the people in the story?
Identify the goal:	What does the teacher want the students to do?
Identify behaviors:	How are they doing this?
	What else are they doing?
Identify the social problem:	What's the problem in this situation?
	What is Bob trying to do?
Identify the perspective of others:	How does Bob feel?
	How does Freddie feel?
Solve Problems:	
Recall past experiences:	Have you ever been in a situation like this?
Identify previous behaviors:	What did you do?
	What did other people do?
Identify consequences:	What happened when you _____?
	or _____ ?

Identify behaviors to use
in this situation:

What could Bob do in this situation?
What might happen?
What else could he do?
What could Freddie do?
What might happen?
What is the best idea to solve this
problem?

❒ **C**hoose students to play roles:

1. Select students of varying academic abilities to play key roles.
2. Give students opportunities to practice new ways of behaving if they wish.
3. Provide other students with the experience of being treated differently by their peers.
4. Allow students to role play the situation using the strategies they have selected.
5. Provide students with as much direction as is needed.
6. Assign other students roles as observers.

❒ **H**elp students to evaluate the effectiveness of behaviors used:

1. Ask students the following questions.
   a. What happened? What did you do? What did the others do?
   b. Were the behaviors you selected effective? Why? or Why not? Was the goal achieved?
   c. What else could you have done? Would that have been more effective?
   d. How did you feel? How do you think the others feel?
2. Permit students to reenact the situation using different behaviors or actors if they wish.
3. Ask evaluation questions again and compare results.

❒ **I**ntegrate into classroom routine:

1. Assess students' strengths and weaknesses. Then provide frequent opportunities for the students to assist each other. Each student has some strengths, however small they may be.
2. Expect students to use appropriate behaviors and problem-solving techniques to solve social problems.
3. Encourage students to help one another as they try to solve social and academic problems.

❒ **N**otice interactions:

1. Praise and give other positive reinforcement to students when they readily ask for and willingly accept help with their work.
2. Teach students to praise one another when they use effective behaviors.
3. Teach students to discuss why certain behaviors are not effective and encourage one another to try again.

❒ **G**eneralize social knowledge:

1. Work with other staff members to provide opportunities for students to ask for, give, and accept help in other classrooms and situations throughout the school.
2. Advertise the idea of Helping Others via posting school compositions, posters, artwork, bulletin boards, etc.

JOINING A GROUP IN THE LUNCHROOM

Rationale: Knowing how to join groups in less structured situations, such as a lunchroom, may be the most frequent—and most demanding—social situation. In more structured situations, such as the classroom, procedures, groups, and routines may be more established and consistent. In situations, such as the lunchroom, the situation and the structure of the group may change more frequently. Trying to enter a group in a less structured situation may be extremely stressful. When you are able to enter groups such as these successfully, you demonstrate your social skills and self-confidence and may be perceived as socially competent. As a result, you are more likely to be included in groups in the future.

❒ Construct a hypothetical social problem (Use Figure B-9):

> *It's lunchtime and most of the kids are eating their lunches with their friends around the table. Susan comes into the lunchroom and doesn't know where to sit or with whom she should sit. Betsy, the girl with whom she usually sits, is absent today. Susan does not like to eat her lunch alone. She remembers that once she tried to sit with a group of girls and they didn't want her there. She felt hurt then and doesn't want to feel that way again. Now she wants to try again but she doesn't know what to do.*
> *What should Susan do?*

❒ Organize a discussion:

1. Select a heterogenous group of students to discuss the problem.
2. Include students who are socially competent as well as those who need to develop social knowledge and become more socially skilled.
3. Read the hypothetical social problem and/or show the picture to the students.

❒ Ask the coaching questions:

Understand Concepts:	What is acceptance? What is kindness?
	Why is it important?
Perceiving Situations:	
Recognize the situation:	What's going on here?
	What's happening in this story?
Identify the participants:	Who are the people in the story?
Identify the goal:	What are most of the students doing?
Identify behaviors:	How are they doing this?
	What else are they doing?
Identify the social problem:	What's the problem in this situation?
	What is Susan trying to do?
Identify the perspective of others:	How does Susan feel?
	How do the other students feel?
Solve Problems:	
Recall past experiences:	Have you ever been in a situation like this?
Identify previous behaviors:	What did you do?
	What did other people do?

| Identify consequences: | What happened when you _____ ? or _____ ? |
| Identify behaviors to use in this situation: | What could Susan do in this situation? What might happen? What else could she do? What could the other students do? What might happen? What is the best idea to solve this problem? |

❏ **C**hoose students to play roles:

   1. Select students of varying academic abilities to play key roles.
   2. Give students opportunities to practice new ways of behaving.
   3. Provide other students with the experience of being treated differently by their peers.
   4. Allow students to role play the situation using the strategies they have selected.
   5. Provide students with as much direction as is needed.
   6. Assign other students roles as observers.

❏ **H**elp students to evaluate the effectiveness of behaviors used:

   1. Ask students the following questions.
      a. What happened? What did you do? What did the others do?
      b. Were the behaviors you selected effective? Why? or Why not? Was the goal achieved?
      c. What else could you have done? Would that have been more effective?
      d. How did you feel? How do you think the others feel?
   2. Permit students to reenact the situation using different behaviors or actors if they wish.
   3. Ask evaluation questions again and compare results.

❏ **I**ntegrate into classroom routine:

   1. Provide frequent opportunities for the students to be with one another, in formal and informal activities.
   2. Expect students to use appropriate behaviors and problem-solving techniques to solve social problems.
   3. Encourage students to help one another as they try to solve social and academic problems.

❏ **N**otice interactions:

   1. Praise and give other positive reinforcement to students when they use successful behaviors to join groups appropriately.
   2. Teach students to praise one another when they accept others into their groups.
   3. Teach students to discuss why certain behaviors are not effective and encourage one another to try again.

❏ **G**eneralize social knowledge:

   1. Have students think of situations throughout the school in which they need to enter groups in less structured situations.

2. Have students identify specific situations in which they would like to practice the skill of entering a group. Ask the students to keep a log of their activities including the date, time, composition of the group, behaviors used, and effectiveness. Have students report back to the class.

FIGURE B-9

COACHING ACTIVITIES   **201**

ACTIVITY B-10

JOINING A GROUP ON THE PLAYGROUND

Rationale: Knowing how to join groups in less structured situations, such as a playground, is among the most frequent and most demanding social situations. In more structured situations, such as the classroom, procedures, groups, and routines may be more established and consistent. In less structured situations, the situation and the structure of the group may change more frequently. Trying to enter a group in a less structured situation may be extremely stressful. When you can enter groups such as these successfully, you demonstrate your social skills and self-confidence and may be perceived as socially competent. You also build your self-esteem and self-efficacy. Participating in cooperative physical activity will also improve your interpersonal relationships. As a result, you are more likely to be included in groups in the future.

❒ **C**onstruct a hypothetical social problem:

> *Juan was late getting outside to recess. By the time he ran out to the playground, the children had already formed teams and were playing a softball game. Juan wanted to play too, but didn't know what to do to join in. For one thing, he knew he didn't play softball as well as the other children. He was afraid that if he asked them if he could play, they would say no or laugh at him. So Juan walked over the swings, sat down, and watched the game. He thought that maybe they would ask him to play tomorrow.*
> *What should Juan do?*

❒ **O**rganize a discussion:

1. Select a heterogenous group of students to discuss the problem.
2. Include students who are socially competent as well as those who need to develop social knowledge and become more socially skilled.
3. Read the hypothetical social problem to the students.

❒ **A**sk the coaching questions:

Understand Concepts:	What is acceptance?
	Why is acceptance important?
Perceive Situations:	
Recognize the situation:	What's going on here?
	What's happening in this story?
Identify the participants:	Who are the people in the story?
Identify the goal:	What are most of the children doing?
Identify behaviors:	How are they doing this?
	What else are they doing?
Identify the social	What's the problem in this situation?
problem:	What is Juan trying to do?
	What does Juan want to happen?
	What is a friend?
Identify the perspective	How does Juan feel?
of others:	How do the other children feel?
Solve Problems:	
Recall past experiences:	Have you ever been in a situation like this?

Identify previous behaviors:	What did you do? What did other people do?
Identify consequences:	What happened when you _____? or _____ ?
Identify behaviors to use in this situation:	What could Juan do in this situation? What might happen? What else could he do? What could the others do? What might happen? What is the best idea to solve this problem?

☐ **C**hoose students to play roles:

1. Select students of varying social abilities to play key roles.
2. Give students opportunities to practice new ways of behaving.
3. Provide other students with the experience of being treated differently by their peers.
4. Allow students to role play the situation using the strategies they have selected.
5. Provide students with as much direction as is needed.
6. Assign other students roles as observers.

☐ **H**elp students to evaluate the effectiveness of behaviors used:

1. Ask students the following questions.
   a. What happened? What did you do? What did the others do?
   b. Were the behaviors you selected effective? Why? or Why not? Was the goal achieved?
   c. What else could you have done? Would that have been more effective?
   d. How did you feel? How do you think the others feel?
2. Permit students to reenact the situation using different behaviors or actors if they wish.
3. Ask evaluation questions again and compare results.

☐ **I**ntegrate into classroom routine:

1. Provide frequent opportunities for the students to be with one another. Encourage students to interact in physical education games to develop confidence in group interactions and participation. Encourage students to try new activities.
2. Expect students to use appropriate behaviors and problem-solving techniques to solve social problems.
3. Encourage students to help one another as they try to solve social and academic problems.

☐ **N**otice interactions:

1. Praise and give other positive reinforcement to students when they join groups or make the effort to include others in their group.
2. Teach students to praise one another when they accept others into their groups.
3. Teach students to discuss why certain behaviors are not effective and encourage one another to try again.

❏ Generalize social knowledge:

1. Brainstorm with other staff members for ways the entire school could use physical activity for students to learn to interact more appropriately: intramural competition, annual olympics, afterschool sports, etc.
2. Ask the students to keep a log of their activities including the date, time, composition of the group, behaviors used, and effectiveness. Have students report back to the class.

ACTIVITY B-11

MAINTAINING FRIENDSHIPS

Rationale: Knowing how to maintain friendships is an essential social skill. Sometimes, maintaining friendships means that you have to be with a friend in more than one situation. Therefore, you may need to know and use different behaviors according to where you are. If you are able to maintain contact with peers who accept and like you, you will have the opportunities to develop the behaviors you need to become more socially self-confident and develop meaningful peer relationships.

☐ **C**onstruct a hypothetical social problem (Use Figure B-11):

> *Kathy is a quiet but steady worker in the classroom. When she works with one particular group of kids, she has a good time. Everyone cooperates with one another and gets the work done well. Kathy also wants to be included in this group at recess. The other kids are never really mean to her, but they never seem to pay any attention to her or include her once they get to the playground. Kathy knows that she will be working with this group again today; she wants to let them know how much she likes them and that she wants to be their friend.*
> *What should Kathy do?*

☐ **O**rganize a discussion:

1. Select a heterogenous group of students to discuss the problem.
2. Include students who are socially competent as well as those who need to develop social knowledge and become more socially skilled.
3. Read the hypothetical social problem and/or show the picture to the students.

☐ **A**sk the coaching questions:

Understand Concepts:	What is friendship?
	Why is friendship important?
Perceive Situations:	
Recognize the situation:	What's going on here?
	What's happening in this story?
Identify the participants:	Who are the people in the story?
Identify the goal:	What are others doing (in the classroom/at recess)?
Identify behaviors:	How are they doing this?
	What else are they doing?
Identify the social problem:	What's the problem in this situation?
	What is Kathy trying to do?
	What does Kathy want to have happen?
Identify the perspective of others:	How does Kathy feel?
	How do the other children feel?
Solve Problems:	
Recall past experiences:	Have you ever been in a situation like this?
Identify previous behaviors:	What did you do?
	What did other people do?
Identify consequences:	What happened when you _____?
	or _____ ?

Identify behaviors to use
in this situation:

What could Kathy do in this
situation?
What might happen?
What else could she do?
What could the others do?
What might happen?
What is the best idea to solve this
problem?

❏   **C**hoose students to play roles:

1. Select students of varying social abilities to play key roles.
2. Give students opportunities to practice new ways of behaving.
3. Provide other students with the experience of being treated differently by their peers.
4. Allow students to role play the situation using the strategies they
have selected.
5. Provide students with as much direction as is needed.
6. Assign other students role as observers.

❏   **H**elp students to evaluate the effectiveness of behaviors used:

1. Ask students the following questions.
a. What happened? What did you do? What did the others do?
b. Were the behaviors you selected effective? Why? or Why ot?
c. What else could you have done? Would that have been more effective?
d. How did you feel? How do you think the others feel?
2. Permit students to reenact the situation using different behaviors or
actors if they wish.
3. Ask evaluation questions again and compare results.

❏   **I**ntegrate into classroom routine:

1. Provide frequent opportunities for the students to be with one another in the classroom.
2. Expect students to use appropriate behaviors and problem-solving
techniques to solve social problems.
3. Encourage students to help one another as they try to solve social
and academic aproblems.
4. Expect students to work together in more than one type of classroom activity in different roles.

❏   **N**otice interactions:

1. Praise and give other positive reinforcement to other students when
they are friendly to one another or make the effort to include others
in their group.
2. Teach students to praise one another when they are friendly to one
another or make the effort to include others in their group.
3. Teach students to evaluate why certain behaviors are not effective
and encourage one another to try again.

❏   **G**eneralize social knowledge:

1. Ask students to think of other situations in which they might try to
be friendly.

2. Cue other members of the group to model ways to be friendly.
3. Send a note home to parents to let them know that their child is learning to solve problems. Ask parents to think of ways in which new behaviors might be used to solve problems at home.
4. Ask the students to keep a log of their activities including the date, time, composition of the group, behaviors used, and effectiveness. Have students report back to the class.

(Activity B-11 Continued)

FIGURE B-11

ACTIVITY B-12

DEALING WITH LONELINESS

Rationale: Everyone is alone at times. Being alone does not mean you feel lonely. When you feel lonely, you feel left out and often begin to think negative thoughts about yourself. Knowing how to deal with loneliness means that you take some action to make yourself feel better. To feel better—to deal with loneliness—you try to ignore the negative feelings and make some effort to be included with others in their activities. Being able to take action for yourself is important because you cannot always depend on others to reach out and include you.

❐ **C**onstruct a hypothetical social problem:

> *Alana moved to her new school in November when class friendships and cliques were already well-established. The teacher did his best to integrate her into the life of the classroom, but the children seemed hesitant to include Alana into their groups voluntarily. Alana was feeling very sad and alone. She longed for a friend.*
> *What should Alana do?*

❐ **O**rganize a discussion:

1. Select a heterogenous group of students to discuss the problem.
2. Include students who are socially competent as well as those who need to develop social knowledge and become more socially skilled.
3. Read the hypothetical social problem to the students.

❐ **A**sk the coaching questions:

Understand Concepts:	What is loneliness?
Perceiving Problems:	
Recognize the situation:	What's going on here?
	What's happening in this story?
Identify the participants:	Who are the people in the story?
Identify the goal:	What are others doing?
Identify behaviors:	How are they doing this?
	What else are they doing?
Identify the social problem:	What's the problem in this situation?
	What is loneliness?
	What is Alana trying to do?
	What does Alana want to have happen?
Identify the perspective of others:	How does Alana feel?
	How do the other children feel?
	How does the teacher feel:
Solve Problems:	
Recall past experiences:	Have you ever been in a situation like this?
Identify previous behaviors:	What did you do?
	What did other people do?
Identify consequences:	What happened when you _____?
	or _____ ?

Identify behaviors to use in this situation:	What could Alana do in this situation? What might happen? What are some nonverbal ways that she could use to show that she wants to be a friend? What else could she do? What could the others do? What might happen? What is the best idea to solve this problem?

❒ **C**hoose students to play roles:

1. Select students of varying social abilities to play key roles.
2. Give students opportunities to practice new ways of behaving.
3. Provide other students with the experience of being treated differently by their peers.
4. Allow students to role play the situation using the strategies they have selected.
5. Provide students with as much direction as is needed.
6. Assign other students roles as observers.

❒ **H**elp students to evaluate the effectiveness of behaviors used:

1. Ask students the following questions.
   a. What happened? What did you do? What did the others do?
   b. Were the behaviors you selected effective? Why? or Why not?
   c. What else could you have done? Would that have been more effective?
   d. How did you feel? How do you think the others feel?
2. Permit students to reenact the situation using different behaviors or actors if they wish.
3. Ask evaluation questions again and compare results.

❒ **I**ntegrate into classroom routine:

1. Provide many opportunities for the students to be with one another in the classroom.
2. Expect students to use appropriate behaviors and problem-solving techniques to solve social problems.
3. Encourage students to help one another as they try to solve social and academic problems.
4. Expect students to show kindness toward one another and to include one another in their groups.

❒ **N**otice interactions:

1. Praise and give other positive reinforcement to students when they are friendly to one another or make the effort to include others in their group.
2. Teach students to praise one another when they accept others into their groups.
3. Teach students to evaluate why certain behaviors are not effective and encourage one another to try again.

❐ **G**eneralize social knowledge:

1. Ask students to think of other situations in which they might try to include others and act as a friend toward a new person.
2. Cue other members of the group to model ways to include others into established groups.
3. Send a note home to parents to let them know that their child is learning to solve problems. Ask parents to think of ways in which new behaviors might be used to solve problems at home.
4. Ask the students to keep a log of their activities including the date, time, composition of the group, behaviors used, and effectiveness. Have students report back to the class.

ACTIVITY B-13

DEALING WITH PEER PRESSURE

Rationale: It is important to feel accepted by other people, especially your peers. Sometimes, however, it seems that peers ask each other to act in ways that may not feel right. At these times, you have to decide whether your own instincts and beliefs are more important than those of the group. Making these kinds of decisions can be difficult because you do not want to lose the companionship of your friends. However, if you are able to deal with peer pressure, you can become more self-confident as you learn to adapt your own behavior and stand up for yourself. Your peers may admire this quality and stand by you.

❐ Construct a hypothetical social problem:

> *Adam is a new boy in Seth's class. Although Seth doesn't know Adam very well yet, Seth already thinks he would like to be Adam's friend. Adam is interested in science and knows many magic tricks, two of Seth's favorite interests. Wayne and David, Seth's best friends, decided right away that Adam was a nerd. Whenever Adam tried to sit with the three boys at lunch, Wayne and David would move to another table. Seth wants to befriend Adam, but he doesn't know what to do about Wayne and David. He doesn't want to lose their friendship.*
> *What should Adam do?*

❐ Organize a discussion:

1. Select a heterogeneous group of students to discuss the problem.
2. Include students who are socially competent as well as those who need to develop social knowledge and become more socially skilled.
3. Read the hypothetical social problem to the students.

❐ Ask the coaching questions:

Understand Concepts:	What is friendship? How do you make a friend?
Perceive Situations:	
Recognize the situation:	What's going on here?
	What's happening in this story?
Identify the participants:	Who are the people in the story?
Identify the goal:	What are others doing (in the classroom/lunchroom)?
Identify behaviors:	How are they doing this?
	What else are they doing?
Identify the social problem:	What's the problem in this situation?
	What is Adam trying to do?
	What does Adam want to have happen?
Identify the perspective of others:	How does Adam feel?
	How does Seth feel?
	How do the other boys feel?
Solve Problems:	
Recall past experiences:	Have you ever been in a situation like this?

Identify previous behaviors:	What did you do? What did other people do?
Identify consequences:	What happened when you _____? or _____ ?
Identify behaviors to use in this situation:	What could Adam do in this situation? What might happen? What else could he do? What could the others do? What might happen? What is the best idea to solve this problem?

❒ **C**hoose students to play roles:

1. Select students of varying social abilities to play key roles.
2. Give students opportunities to practice new ways of behaving.
3. Provide other students with the experience of being treated differently by their peers.
4. Allow students to role play the situation using the strategies they have selected.
5. Provide students with as much direction as is needed.
6. Assign other students roles as observers.

❒ **H**elp students to evaluate the effectiveness of behaviors used:

1. Ask students the following questions.
   a. What happened? What did you do? What did the others do?
   b. Were the behaviors you selected effective? Why? or Why not? Was the goal achieved?
   c. What else could you have done? Would that have been more effective?
   d. How did you feel? How do you think the others feel?
2. Permit students to reenact the situation using different behaviors or actors if they wish.
3. Ask evaluation questions again and compare results.

❒ **I**ntegrate into classroom routine:

1. Provide frequent opportunities for the students to be with one another in the classroom.
2. Expect students to use appropriate behaviors and problem-solving techniques to solve social problems.
3. Encourage students to help one another as they try to solve social and academic problems.
4. Expect students to show kindness toward one another and to include one another in their groups

❒ **N**otice interactions:

1. Praise and give other positive reinforcement to students when they do not give in to peer pressure.
2. Teach students to praise one another when they resist peer pressure.
3. Teach students to discuss why certain behaviors are not effective and encourage one another to try again.

4. Develop bulletin boards and conduct class discussions on the topic of "Saying No to Peer Pressure."

❏ **G**eneralize social knowledge:

1. Ask students to think of other situations in which they might try to resist peer pressure.
2. Work with other staff members to promote the idea of resisting inappropriate peer pressure throughout the school. Identify key issues and collaborate on projects to help students confront these topics.
3. Send a note home to parents to let them know that their child is learning to solve problems. Ask parents to think of ways in which new behaviors might be used to deal with peer pressure.
4. Ask the students to keep a log of their activities including the date, time, composition of the group, behaviors used, and effectiveness. Have students report back to the class.

ACTIVITY B-14

DEALING WITH DISAPPOINTMENTS

Rationale: Knowing how to deal with disappointment will help you feel better about yourself and make you appear more competent to others. Dealing with disappointment means that you are able to accept failures, changes of plan, or the actions of others that might be painful to you. By using positive ways to relieve feelings of sadness, anxiety, or helplessness, that may be associated with disappointment, you can change the way you feel and the way you interact. These skills will enable you to interact with others more successfully.

❒ **C**onstruct a hypothetical social problem:

> *Mandy is an excellent student who enjoys school. She likes to read and is very interested in social studies and science. Mandy studies a lot, but she also enjoys talking and playing with her friends. Even though Mandy usually receives A's on all her school work, she cries when she doesn't get a perfect score on a paper. Last week, when Mandy had one error on a math test, she cried and tore up the paper even though she had a good grade. At the beginning of the year, Mandy's friends tried to be understanding whenever she cried. Now, a few of them are beginning to call her a crybaby.*
> *What should Mandy do?*

❒ **O**rganize a discussion:

1. Select a heterogenous group of students to discuss the problem.
2. Include students who are socially competent as well as those who need to develop social knowledge and become more socially skilled.
3. Read the hypothetical social problem to the students.

❒ **A**sk the coaching questions:

Understand Concepts:	What is disappointment?
Perceive Situations:	
Recognize the situation:	What's going on here?
	What's happening in this story?
Identify the participants:	Who are the people in the story?
Identify the goal:	What are the others doing?
Identify behaviors:	How are they doing this?
	What else are they doing?
Identify the social problem:	What's the problem in this situation?
	What is self-control?
	What is Mandy try to do?
	What does Mandy want to have happen?
Identify the perspective of others:	How does Mandy feel?
	How do the others feel?
Solve Problems:	
Recall past experiences:	Have you ever been in a situation like this?
Identify previous behaviors:	What did you do?
	What did other people do?
Identify consequences:	What happened when you _____?
	or _____ ?

Identify behaviors to use
in this situation:

What could Mandy do in this
  situation?
What might happen?
What else could she do?
What could the others do?
What might happen?
What is the best idea to solve this
  problem?

❏ **C**hoose students to play roles:

1. Select students of varying social abilities to play key roles.
2. Give students opportunities to practice new ways of behaving.
3. Provide other students with the experience of being treated differently by their peers.
4. Allow students to role play the situation using the strategies they have selected.
5. Provide students with as much direction as is needed.
6. Assign other students roles as observers.

❏ **H**elp students to evaluate the effectiveness of behaviors used:

1. Ask students the following questions.
   a. What happened? What did you do? What did the others do?
   b. Were the behaviors you selected effective? Why? or Why not?
   c. What else could you have done? Would that have been more effective?
   d. How did you feel? How do you think the others feel?
2. Permit students to reenact the situation using different behaviors or actors if they wish.
3. Ask evaluation questions again and compare results.

❏ **I**ntegrate into classroom routine:

1. Provide frequent opportunities for the students to be with one another in the classroom.
2. Expect students to use appropriate behaviors and problem-solving techniques to solve social problems.
3. Encourage students to help one another as they try to solve social and academic problems.
4. Expect students to show kindness toward one another.
5. Use the theme "Nobody's Perfect" in posters, bulletin boards, and writing assignments.

❏ **N**otice interactions:

1. Praise and give other positive reinforcement to students when they handle disappointing times in positive ways.
2. Teach students to praise one another when they deal with disappointment effectively.
3. Teach students to evaluate why certain behaviors are not effective and encourage one another to try again.
4. Provide specific verbal praise to students when they are facing disappointments.
5. Encourage students when they use self-control.

☐ **G**eneralize social knowledge:

1. Ask students to think of other situations in which they might try to deal with disappointment and use self-control.
2. Work with other staff members to promote the idea of using self-control throughout the school. Identify key issues and collaborate on projects to help students use self-control in situations outside the classroom.
3. Send a note home to parents to let them know that their child is learning to solve problems. Ask parents to think of ways in which new behaviors might be used to solve problems at home.
4. Ask the students to keep a log of their activities including the date, time, composition of the group, behaviors used, and effectiveness. Have students report back to the class.

ACTIVITY B-15

DEALING WITH OVERT REJECTION

Rationale: Knowing how to deal with rejection will help when it seems that other people do not want you to participate in their activities. Dealing with rejection means that you are able to face situations that might be painful to you. By using positive ways to relieve feelings of sadness, anger, or helplessness that may be associated with rejection, you can change the way you feel and the way you interact with others. These skills will enable you to interact with others more successfully.

❐ **C**onstruct a hypothetical social problem:

> *John and Mary were playing checkers during indoor recess. They were enjoying themselves until Paul arrived. Paul asked in a whiny voice if he could play the winner of the game. Both John and Mary refused. John said, "You always cheat when you play games, Paul. You're not much fun to play with. Go ask someone else to play with you."*
> *What should Paul do?*

❐ **O**rganize a discussion:

1. Select a heterogeneous group of students to discuss the problem.
2. Include students who are socially competent as well as those who need to develop social knowledge and become more socially skilled.
3. Read the hypothetical social problem to the students.

❐ **A**sk the coaching questions:

Understand Concepts:	What is rejection?
Perceiving Situations:	
Recognize the situation:	What's going on here?
	What's happening in this story?
Identify the participants:	Who are the people in the story?
Identify the goal:	What are John and Mary doing?
Identify behaviors:	How are they doing this?
	What else are they doing?
Identify the social	What's the problem in this situation?
problem:	What is Paul trying to do?
	What does Paul want to have happen?
Identify the perspective	How does Paul feel?
of others:	How do John and Mary feel?
	Were John and Mary being fair when they told Paul they didn't want to play with him?
Solve Problems:	
Recall past experiences:	Have you ever been in a situation like this?
Identify previous	What did you do?
behaviors:	What did other people do?
Identify consequences:	What happened when you _____?
	or _____ ?

Identify behaviors to
use in this situation:

What could Paul do in this situation?
What might happen?
What else could he do?
What could John and Mary do?
What might happen?
What is the best idea to solve this
problem?

❐ **C**hoose students to play roles:

1. Select students of varying social abilities to play key roles.
2. Give students opportunities to practice new ways of behaving.
3. Provide other students with the experience of being treated differently by their peers.
4. Allow students to role play the situation using the strategies they have selected.
5. Provide students with as much direction as is needed.
6. Assign other students roles as observers.

❐ **H**elp students to evaluate the effectiveness of behaviors used:

1. Ask students the following questions.
   a. What happened? What did you do? What did the others do?
   b. Were the behaviors you selected effective? Why? or Why not? Was the goal achieved?
   c. What else could you have done? Would that have been more effective?
   d. How did you feel? How do you think the others feel?
2. Permit students to reenact the situation using different behaviors or actors if they wish.
3. Ask evaluation questions again and compare results.

❐ **I**ntegrate into classroom routine:

1. Provide frequent opportunities for the students to be with one another.
2. Expect students to use appropriate behaviors and problem-solving techniques to solve social problems.
3. Encourage students to help one another as they try to solve social and academic problems.
4. Expect students to show kindness toward one another.

❐ **N**otice interactions:

1. Praise and give other positive reinforcement to students when they handle rejection by trying to resolve the conflict through discussion and cooperation.
2. Teach students to praise one another when they resolve conflict effectively.
3. Teach students to evaluate why certain behaviors are not effective and encourage one another to try again.
4. Provide specific verbal praise to students when they are dealing with rejection from peers.
5. Encourage students when they use self-control and problem-solving behaviors.

❏ **G**eneralize social knowledge:

1. Ask students to think of other situations in which they might have to deal with rejection from peers.
2. Work with other staff members to promote the idea of using problem-solving throughout the school. Identify areas of potential conflict in situations outside the classroom.
3. Send a note home to parents to let them know that their child is learning to solve problems. Ask parents to think of ways in which new behaviors might be used to solve problems at home.
4. Ask the students to keep a log of their activities including the date, time, composition of the group, behaviors used, and effectiveness. Have students report back to the class.

ACTIVITY B-16

DEALING WITH COVERT REJECTION

Rationale: Knowing how to deal with rejection will help when it seems that other people do not want you to participate in their activities. Dealing with rejection means that you are able to face situations that might be painful to you. By using positive ways to relieve feelings of sadness, anger, or helplessness, tht may be associated with rejection, you can change the way you feel and the way you interact with others. These skills will enable you to interact with others more successfully.

❐ **C**onstruct a hypothetical social problem (Use Figure B-16):

> *It's snack time and Jeff feels left out. When he sits down at a table with several other children, they start talking and moving around. Eventually, they end up at the other end of the table. Now Jeff is all alone with his snack. He wishes he had a giant magnet to draw the other kids to his end of the table. He really wants to join the others and feel like he belongs.*
> *What should Jeff do?*

❐ **O**rganize a discussion:

1. Select a heterogenous group of students to discuss the problem.
2. Include students who are socially competent as well as those who need to develop social knowledge and become more socially skilled.
3. Read the hypothetical social problem and/or show the picture to the students.

❐ **A**sk the coaching questions:

Understand Concepts:	What is rejection?
Perceive Situations:	
Recognize the situation:	What's going on here?
	What's happening in this story?
Identify the participants:	Who are the people in the story?
Identify the goal:	What are other students doing?
Identify behaviors:	How are they doing this?
	What else are they doing?
Identify the social problem:	What's the problem in this situation?
	What is Jeff trying to do?
	What does Jeff want to have happen?
Identify the perspective of others:	How does Jeff feel?
	How do the others feel?
Solve Problems:	
Recall past experiences:	Have you ever been in a situation like this?
Identify previous behaviors:	What did you do?
	What did other people do?
Identify consequences:	What happened when you _____? or _____ ?
Identify behaviors to use in this situation:	What could Jeff do in this situation? What might happen?
	What else could he do?

> What could the others do?
> What might happen?
> What is the best idea to solve this problem?

☐ **C**hoose students to play roles:

1. Select students of varying social abilities to play key roles.
2. Give students opportunities to practice new ways of behaving.
3. Provide other students with the experience of being treated differently by their peers.
4. Allow students to role play the situation using the strategies they have selected.
5. Provide students with as much direction as is needed.
6. Assign other students roles as observers.

☐ **H**elp students to evaluate the effectiveness of behaviors used:

1. Ask students the following questions.
   a. What happened? What did you do? What did the others do?
   b. Were the behaviors you selected effective? Why? or Why not?
   c. What else could you have done? Would that have been more effective?
   d. How did you feel? How do you think the others feel?
2. Permit students to reenact the situation using different behaviors or actors if they wish.
3. Ask evaluation questions again and compare results.

☐ **I**ntegrate into classroom routine:

1. Provide frequent opportunities for students to play with one another in the classroom.
2. Expect students to use appropriate behaviors and problem-solving techniques to solve social problems.
3. Encourage students to help one another as they try to solve social and academic problems.
4. Expect students to show kindness toward one another.

☐ **N**otice interactions:

1. Praise and give other positive reinforcement to students when they handle rejection by trying to resolve the conflict through discussion and cooperation.
2. Teach students to praise one another when they resolve conflict effectively.
3. Teach students to evaluate why certain behaviors are not effective and encourage one another to try again.
5. Encourage students when they use self-control and problem-solving strategies.

☐ **G**eneralize social knowledge:

1. Ask students to think of other situations in which they might have to deal with rejection from peers.
2. Work with other staff members to promote the idea of using problem-solving throughout the school. Identify areas of potential conflict in situations outside the classroom.

3. Send a note home to parents to let them know that their child is learning to solve problems. Ask parents to think of ways in which new behaviors might be used to solve problems at home.
4. Ask the students to keep a log of their activities including the date, time, composition of the group, behaviors used, and effectiveness. Have students report back to the class.

(Activity B-16 Continued)

FIGURE B-16

ACTIVITY B-17-1

RESPONDING TO TEASING

Rationale: Knowing how to respond to teasing will help you relieve feelings of sadness, anger, or helplessness that may occur when others make unkind remarks. Using appropriate responses to teasing may also indicate to your peers that the teasing is ineffective. By using effective responses, you can also change the way you feel and the way you interact. These skills will enable you to interact with others more successfully.

❒ **C**onstruct a hypothetical social problem:

> *During an outdoor physical education activity, a group of fourth graders is playing a game of kickball. Diane is at bat and strikes out for the third time in a row. Two of her teammates begin to yell at her. Wayne runs over to her, gets right in her face, and shouts, "You stupid klutz. You can't even kick! Figures—you're just a dumb girl."*
> *What should Diane do?*

❒ **O**rganize a discussion:

1. Select a heterogenous group of students to discuss the problem.
2. Include students who are socially competent as well as those who need to develop social knowledge and become more skilled.
3. Read the hypothetical social problem and/or show the picture to the students.

❒ **A**sk the coaching questions:

Understand Concepts:	What is teasing?
Perceive Situations:	
Recognize the situation:	What's going on here?
	What's happening in this story?
Identify the participants:	Who are the people in the story?
Identify the goal:	What are the other students doing?
Identify behaviors:	How are they doing this?
	What else are they doing?
Identify the social	What's the problem in this situation?
problem:	What is Diane trying to do?
	What does Diane want to have happen?
Identify the perspective	How does Diane feel?
of others:	How does Wayne feel?
Solve Problems:	
Recall past experiences:	Have you ever been in a situation like this?
Identify previous	What did you do?
behaviors:	What did other people do?
Identify consequences:	What happened when you _____? or _____ ?
Identify behaviors to	What could Diane do in this situation?
use in this situation:	What might happen?
	What else could she do?

What could Wayne or the others do?
What might happen?
What is the best idea to solve this
problem?

☐ **C**hoose students to play roles:

1. Select students of varying social abilities to play key roles.
2. Give students opportunities to practice new ways of behaving.
3. Provide other students with the experience of being treated differently by their peers.
4. Allow students to role play the situation using the strategies they have selected.
5. Provide students with as much direction as is needed.
6. Assign other students roles as observers.

☐ **H**elp students to evaluate the effectiveness of behaviors used:

1. Ask students the following questions.
   a. What happened? What did you do? What did the others do?
   b. Were the behaviors you selected effective? Why? or Why not?
   c. What else could you have done? Would that have been more effective?
   d. How did you feel? How do you think the others feel?
2. Permit students to reenact the situation using different behaviors or actors if they wish.
3. Ask evaluation questions again and compare results.

☐ **I**ntegrate into classroom routine:

1. Provide opportunities for students to play and work competitively.
2. Expect students to use appropriate behaviors and problem-solving techniques to solve social problems.
3. Encourage students to help one another as they try to solve social and academic problems.
4. Expect students to compete with kindness and respect for one another.

☐ **N**otice interactions:

1. Praise and give other positive reinforcement to students when they compete without making unkind remarks to one another.
2. Teach students to praise one another when they encourage one another to do their best.
3. Teach students to evaluate why certain behaviors are not effective and encourage one another to try again.
4. Provide specific verbal praise to students when they are dealing with rejection from peers.

☐ **G**eneralize social knowledge:

1. Ask students to think of other situations in which they might have to respond to teasing from peers.
2. Work with other staff members to promote the idea of using roblem-solving throughout the school. Identify areas of potential conflict in situations outside the classroom.

3. Send a note home to parents to let them know that their child is learning to solve problems. Ask parents to think of ways in which new behaviors might be used to solve problems at home.
4. Ask the students to keep a log of their activities including the date, time, composition of the group, behaviors used, and effectiveness. Have students report back to the class.

ACTIVITY B-18

MAKING FRIENDS

Rationale: Knowing how to make friends will enable you to practice your social behaviors in new settings with new people. As you expand your social environment, you will also expand your social network as you meet more people through your new friends. the opportunity to practice and refine social behaviors as well as to observe new behaviors will help you become more self-confident as you think of yourself as able to handle a variety of social situations. In this way, you also become a model for others who are learning social behaviors and trying to become more socially skilled and self-confident.

❐ **C**onstruct a hypothetical social problem:

> *During homeroom, Keith invites a classmate, Ed, to play at his house on Saturday. Although the two boys are not friends, Keith hopes that Ed will become his friend. But Ed isn't sure that he wants to be friends with Keith, even though he has always acted in a friendly way towards Keith. After all, they don't share any of the same interests. Ed really wants to refuse Keith's invitation, but also doesn't want to hurt Keith's feelings.*
> *What should Ed do?*

❐ **O**rganize a discussion:

1. Select a heterogenous group of students to discuss the problem.
2. Include students who are socially competent as well as those who need to develop social knowledge and become more socially skilled.
3. Read the hypothetical social problem to the students.

❐ **A**sk the coaching questions:

Understand Concepts:	What is friendship?
	Why is friendship important?
Perceive Situations:	
Recognize the situation:	What's going on here?
	What's happening in this story?
Identify the participants:	Who are the people in the story?
Identify the goal:	What are they trying to do?
Identify behaviors:	How are they doing this?
	What else are they doing?
Identify the social problem:	What's the problem in this situation?
	What is Ed trying to do?
	What does Ed want to happen?
Identify the perspective of others:	How does Ed feel?
	How does Keith feel?
Solve Problems:	
Recall past experiences:	Have you ever been in a situation like this?
Identify previous behaviors:	What did you do?
Identify consequences:	What happened when you _____?
	or _____ ?

Identify behaviors to use in this situation:

What could Ed do in this situation?
What might happen?
What else could he do?
What could Keith do?
What might happen?
What is the best idea to solve this problem?

❐ **C**hoose students to play roles:

1. Select students of varying social abilities to play key roles.
2. Give students opportunities to practice new ways of behaving.
3. Provide other students with the experience of being treated differently by their peers.
4. Allow students to role play the situation using the strategies they have selected.
5. Provide students with as much direction as is needed.
6. Assign other students roles as observers.

❐ **H**elp students to evaluate the effectiveness of behaviors used:

1. Ask students the following questions.
   a. What happened? What did you do? What did the others do?
   b. Were the behaviors you selected effective? Why? or Why not? Was the goal achieved?
   c. What else could you have done? Would that have been more effective?
   d. How did you feel? How do you think the others feel?
2. Permit students to reenact the situation using different behaviors or actors if they wish.
3. Ask evaluation questions again and compare results.

❐ **I**ntegrate into classroom routine:

1. Provide opportunities for students to develop friendships in the classroom.
2. Expect students to use appropriate behaviors and problem-solving techniques to solve social problems.
3. Encourage students to help one another as they try to solve social and academic problems.
4. Expect students to act in friendly ways in the classroom.
5. Promote the inclusion of students with special needs into regular classrooms.
6. Provide regular opportunities for different classrooms to intermingle—academically and socially, especially those from different cultures and those with other languages.

❐ **N**otice interactions:

1. Provide specific verbal praise and give other positive reinforcement to students when they offer friendship to one another.
2. Teach students to praise one another when they treat each other kindly.
3. Teach students to evaluate why certain behaviors are not effective and encourage one another to try again.

❐ **G**eneralize social knowledge:

1. Ask students to think of other situations to use friendship-making skills.
2. Work with other staff members to promote the idea of including various types of students together to provide oportunities for children to make new friends from various classrooms and backgrounds.
3. Send a note home to parents to let them know that their child is learning to solve problems. Ask parents to think of ways in which new behaviors might be used to solve problems at home.
4. Ask the students to keep a log of times when they make new friends.

ACTIVITY B-19

BEING ON-TASK IN A GROUP

Rationale: Knowing how to be on-task in a group will help you complete your tasks and also learn how to work cooperatively with your peers. When you use these behaviors appropriately, your peers will view you as a valued and acceptable member of the group—a person who knows that for the group to succeed, each person must contribute in positive ways. Being accepted by peers provides you with the opportunity to become socially skilled and develop more meaningful peer relationships.

❒ **C**onstruct a hypothetical social problem (Use Figure B-19):

> *Tim talked to the other boys in his class, but he never seemed to get along with them. In fact, the boys in the class thought he was somewhat of a busybody and a big talker. When they had to work in a group together, Tim would be so busy talking, he wouldn't even notice that he didn't have his work out and that he wasn't helping the group. Although the other boys would talk to Tim and have him in their groups, they really didn't like him.*
> *What should Tim do?*

❒ **O**rganize a discussion:

1. Select a heterogenous group of students to discuss the problem.
2. Include students who are socially competent as well as those who need to develop social knowledge and become more socially skilled.
3. Read the hypothetical social problem and/or show the picture to the students.

❒ **A**sk the coaching questions:

Understand Concepts:	What is cooperation?
	Why is cooperation important?
Perceive Situations:	
Recognize the situation:	What's going on here?
	What's happening in this story?
Identify the participants:	Who are the people in the story?
Identify the goal:	What are the other students doing?
Identify behaviors:	How are they doing this?
	What else are they doing?
Identify the social problem:	What's the problem in this situation?
	What is Tim trying to do?
	What does Tim want to have happen?
Identify the perspective of others:	How does Tim feel?
	How do the others feel?
Solve Problems:	
Recall past experiences:	Have you ever been in a situation like this?
Identify previous behaviors:	What did you do?
	What did other people do?
Identify consequences:	What happened when you _____?
	or _____ ?

Identify behaviors to use
in this situation:

What could Tim do in this situation?
What might happen?
What else could he do?
What could the others do?
What might happen?
What is the best idea to solve this
   problem?

❏ **C**hoose students to play roles:

1. Select students of varying social abilities to play key roles.
2. Give students opportunities to practice new ways of behaving.
3. Provide other students with the experience of being treated differently by their peers.
4. Allow students to role play the situation using the strategies they
   have selected.
5. Provide students with as much direction as is needed.
6. Assign other students roles as observers.

❏ **H**elp students to evaluate the effectiveness of behaviors used:

1. Ask students the following questions.
   a. What happened? What did you do? What did the others do?
   b. Were the behaviors you selected effective? Why? or Why not?
   c. What else could you have done? Would that have been more ef-
      fective?
   d. How did you feel? How do you think the others feel?
2. Permit students to reenact the situation using different behaviors or
   actors if they wish.
3. Ask evaluation questions again and compare results.

❏ **I**ntegrate into classroom routine:

1. Provide many opportunities for students to work cooperatively in
   groups in the classroom. Establish rules for group work.
2. Expect students to use appropriate behaviors and problem-solving
   techniques to solve conflicts.
3. Encourage students to help one another as they try to solve social
   and academic problems.
4. Expect students to stay on-task and be respectful of the rights of
   others to complete their work.
5. Use children's literature as a source of material for the discussion.
   The story *Ants and the Grasshopper* is a good example. Encourage
   students to express the emotions of the ants. Discuss their tolerance
   (or lack of) toward the grasshopper.

❏ **N**otice interactions:

1. Praise and give other positive reinforcement to students when they
   work without distracting one another.
2. Teach students to praise one another when they resolve conflict effectively.
3. Teach students to evaluate why certain behaviors are not effective
   and encourage one another to try again.
4. Provide specific verbal praise to students when they try to manage
   distracting behavior.

☐ **G**eneralize social knowledge:

1. Ask students to think of other situations in which they might have to deal with distractions.
2. Work with other staff members to promote the idea of using problem-solving throughout the school.
3. Send a note home to parents to let them know that their child is learning to solve problems. Ask parents to think of ways in which new behaviors might be used to solve problems at home.
4. Ask the students to keep a log of their activities including the date, time, composition of the group, behaviors used, and effectiveness. Have students report back to the class.

(Activity B-19 Continued)

FIGURE B-19

ADDITIONAL RESOURCES

ACTIVITY C-1

REFERENCES TO PUBLISHED ASSESSMENT INSTRUMENTS

Achenbach, T. M., & Edelbrock, C. (1983). Manual for the child behavior checklist for ages 4–16. San Antonio, TX: Psychological Corporation.

Barclay, J. R. (1982). *Barclay classroom assessment system.* Los Angeles, CA: Western Psychological Services.

Bracken, B. A. (1992). *Multidimensional self-concept scale.* Austin, TX: Pro-Ed.

Brown, L., & Hammill, D. (1978). *Behavior rating profile.* Austin, TX: Pro-Ed.

Brown, L., & Alexander, J. (1991). *Self-esteem index.* Austin, TX: Pro-Ed.

Burks, H. (1969). *Burks' behavior rating scale.* Los Angeles, CA: Western Psychological Services.

Cassel, R. N. (1962). *Child behavior rating scale (CTBS).* Los Angeles, CA: Western Psychological Services.

Conners, C. K. (1989). *Conner's teacher and parent rating scales.* Austin, TX: Pro-Ed.

Coopersmith, S. (1981). *Coopersmith self-esteem inventory.* San Francisco, CA: W. H. Freeman and Co. Self-Esteem Institute.

Elliott, S. N., Gresham, F. M., Freeman, T., & McClosky, G. (1988). *Social skills rating skills-T.* Circle Pines, MN: American Guidance Service.

Harter, S. (1985). *Perceived competence scale for children.* Denver, CO: University of Denver, Department of Psychology.

Hresko, W. P., & Brown, L. (1984). *Test of early socioemotional development.* Austin, TX: Pro-Ed.

Hutton, J., & Roberts, T. G. (1986). *Social-emotional dimension scale.* Austin, TX: Pro-Ed.

Jesness, C. F. *Jesness behavior checklist.* Palo Alto, CA: Consulting Psychologists Press.

Lambert, N., Windmiller, M., Cole, L., & Thinger, D. (1981). *AAMD adaptive behavior rating scale (School Edition).* Austin, TX: Pro-Ed.

Miller, L. C. (1977). *School behavior checklist.* Los Angeles, CA: Western Psychological Press.

McDaniel, E. L. (1973). *Inferred self-concept Scale.* Los Angeles, CA: Western Psychological Services.

Piers, E. V., & Harris, D. B. (1969). *The Piers-Harris self-concept scale.* Nashville, TN: Counselor Recordings and Tests.

Quay, H. C., & Peterson, D. R. (1977). *Manual for the revised behavior problem checklist.* Coral Gables, FL: University of Miami.

Spivack, G., & Spotts, J. (1966). *Devereux child behavior rating scale.* Devon, PA: Devereux Foundation Press.

(Activity C-2 Continued)

Spivack, G., & Spotts, J. (1966). *Devereux child behavior rating scale.* Devon, PA: Devereux Foundation Press.

Spivack, G., & Swift, M. (1967). *Devereux elementary school behavior rating scale.* Devon, PA: Devereux Foundation Press.

Waksman, S. A., & Loveland, R. J. (1980). *The Portland problem behavior checklist.* Portland, OR: Steven A. Waksman.

Waksman, S. A. (1985). *The Waksman social skills rating scale.* ASIEP Education Company.

Walker, H. M. (1970). *Walker problem behavior identification checklist.* Los Angeles, CA: Western Psychological Services.

Walker, H. M., & McConnell, S. R. (1988). *Walker-McConnell scale of social competence and school adjustment: A social skills rating scale for teachers.* Austin, TX: Pro-Ed.

Walker, H. M., & Severson, H. H. (1992). *Systematic screening for behavior disorders (SSBD).* Longmont, CO: Sopris West.

ACTIVITY C-2

REVISED CLASS PLAY-REVISED (RCP-R)

The Revised Class Play-Revised (RCP-R) enables teachers to measure peer perceptions of classmates' social behavior. Students are asked to select classmates to fill 12 roles that require either positive or negative characteristics (attributes). Of the 12 roles, six require positive attributes that are characteristic of sociability/leadership; the remaining six roles require negative attributes that are characteristic of either aggressiveness/ disruptiveness or sensitivity/isolation. By analyzing the data, it is possible to obtain pictures of student functioning within or across these three dimensions, substantiate other sociometric data, and associate specific behaviors or attributes to students according to their social category. The (RCP-R) is more appropriate for students in grades 3–6 than for students in lower grades. As students mature, their friendships become more stable and are based upon the attributes contained in the RCP-R.

ADMINISTRATION

List the names of all boys on RCP-R Form 1 and all girls on RCP-R Form 2. Then duplicate a copy for each student.

If you have not used peer assessment with your students before, read the general introductory script for peer assessment before distributing the forms to students. Otherwise, begin with the section titled *Instructions*.

GENERAL INTRODUCTORY SCRIPT

Have you ever heard of a survey? (Pause for student responses.) What do you know about surveys? (Pause for responses.) A survey usually consists of a list of questions that is used to ask people what they think or how they feel about something. For example, someone might telephone you to ask you to take part in a survey about the supermarkets in your community. The caller might ask you at which markets your family shops, and which one is your favorite and why. Your answers and the answers of other people may be used to improve a supermarket or to plan a new one.

Today I am going to give you a survey that will ask you to think about your classmates. The survey will take you about _____ minutes to finish. The information from the survey will help me organize groups of students who will work well together on class projects (or other activities).

There are several important things you should know about surveys. One is that your answers are private or secret. Another is that there are no right or wrong answers, so you can express your honest feelings and know they will not be shared with anyone except me.

INSTRUCTIONS

The survey I would like you to respond to is about the other students in this class. At the top of the survey, you will find a space for your name and a space for the date. When I give you your survey, write your name and today's date in the proper spaces. Today's date is written correctly for you on the black-board. (Distribute Form 1 to the boys and Form 2 to the girls.)

Now, I want each of you to pretend that you are a director of a play starring the students in this classroom. If you are a girl, you will be choosing girls for your play. If you are a boy, you will be choosing boys for your play. The director of a play has many jobs. The most important task is to select the right people to play each part. So your job is to pick the students you think best fit each part.

Since some students may fit more than one role, you may choose the same person for more than one part. For example, a student might make friends easily and also help others. You may also choose more than one student for each role. You may feel that two students are equally helpful. But if you choose more than one student for a role, you should be sure that each student is right for that role. Think very carefully about your choices.

As the director, you would be too busy to play a part, so you can't choose a part for yourself. Find your name and draw a line from your name straight down to the bottom of the page. (Demonstrate how this should be done.)

Each of you must choose people to play the roles without anyone's help. Don't show anyone else your choices. I will not share your choices with anyone either.

Look at the first role (on the left-hand side of the paper). Look at each name across the top of the paper and place a checkmark under the name or names of the students you think everyone likes to be with in real life. When you have finished, go on to the next role and continue in the same way.

When you have finished, check your answers carefully. Then turn your paper over and take out your (independent reading book).

Allow students 15–20 minutes to complete their surveys. Monitor students as they respond and praise those who are working appropriately. Collect all forms when all students have finished; check to be sure that they are properly identified and marked. Begin a structured whole-class activity immediately. This will prevent students from "sharing" their responses.

SCORING

Reproduce RCP-R Recording Form 3, one for the boys and one for the girls. List the girls's names alphabetically from left to right across the top of the appropriate RCP-R Recording Form. Then list the boys' names in the same way on the proper RCP-R Recording Form. Refer to the RCP-R Form 3— Sample (Figure C-2) to see how a completed form might look.

Separate completed RCP-R forms by gender. Transfer each student's responses from his or her form to the recording sheet by entering a tally mark under the name of each student selected for each role. Notice that the order of the roles on the RCP-R Recording Sheet has been rearranged and grouped according to the three dimensions of behavior being analyzed: Sociability/ Leadership, Aggressiveness/Disruptiveness, and Sensitivity/Isolation.

When you have finished recording students' role selections, total the number of each student's marks at the bottom of each of the three sections as shown in the sample Figure C-2 (Sample).

INTERPRETATION

Data obtained from administering the RCP-R may help teachers understand the nature of the interactions that occur among peers in the classroom. By comparing the totals for each student in each of the three dimensions (Sociability/ Leadership, Aggressiveness/Disruptiveness, and Sensitivity/Isolation), teachers may be able to associate specific behaviors with individual students. This information may either confirm previous observations, add insight as to why students may have been placed in specific social categories (popular, accepted, controversial, rejected, or isolated), or help teachers associate specific behaviors/ attributes with students placed in those social categories. The RCP-R may provide teachers with information that may be helpful in arranging classrooms to foster social competence (See Section I) or in helping individual students develop social competence (See Section II).

FIGURE C-2

(Form 1 – Boys)

Name _____   Date _____

Choose the boys in the class who:

1. everyone likes to be with													
2. are too bossy													
3. make new friends easily													
4. are often left out													
5. can be trusted													
6. interrupt													
7. help others													
8. get feelings hurt easily													
9. are usually happy													
10. get into fights													
11. wait their turn													
12. are usually sad													

FIGURE C-2

(Form 2 – Girls)

Name _____   Date _____

Choose the girls in the class who:

1. everyone likes to be with													
2. are too bossy													
3. make new friends easily													
4. are often left out													
5. can be trusted													
6. interrupt													
7. help others													
8. get feelings hurt easily													
9. are usually happy													
10. get into fights													
11. wait their turn													
12. are usually sad													

FIGURE C-2

(Form 3)

Sociability/Leadership

1. everyone likes to be with

3. make new friends easily

5. can be trusted

7. help others

9. are usually happy

11. wait their turn

   Totals:

Aggressive/Disruptive

2. are too bossy

6. interrupt

10. get into fights

   Totals:

Sensitive/Isolated

4. are often left out

8. get feelings hurt easily

12. are usually sad

   Totals:

FIGURE C-2

(Form 3 – Sample)

Sociability/Leadership

	Laura A.	Jennifer C.	Mary E.	Debbie F.	Carol J.	Megan K.	Suzanne L.	Diane L.	Sally O.	Elizabeth Q.	Lisa R.	Jean R.		
1. everyone likes to be with		9		7	8					4	9			
3. make new friends easily		10			5									
5. can be trusted	4			10						3	7			
7. help others		7	3			3								
9. are usually happy	6										9			
11. wait their turn	5			6		2		4						
Totals:	15	26	3	23	13	5		4		7	25			

Aggressive/Disruptive

	Laura A.	Jennifer C.	Mary E.	Debbie F.	Carol J.	Megan K.	Suzanne L.	Diane L.	Sally O.	Elizabeth Q.	Lisa R.	Jean R.		
2. are too bossy						2			10					
6. interrupt								4	11					
10. get into fights									10					
Totals:						2		4	32					

Sensitive/Isolated

	Laura A.	Jennifer C.	Mary E.	Debbie F.	Carol J.	Megan K.	Suzanne L.	Diane L.	Sally O.	Elizabeth Q.	Lisa R.	Jean R.		
4. are often left out	2				11				7					
8. get feelings hurt easily					9									
12. are usually sad			1		11									
Totals:	2		1		31				7					

ACTIVITY C-3

SOCIAL NETWORKS

This assessment may be administered either individually or to a group of students. Use the responses to get a sense of whether students have friendships that either exist apart from or extended beyond the classroom. With this instrument, it is possible to identify other individuals who are important members of a student's social network.

DIRECTIONS:

Instruct student/s to: *Consider each question carefully and tell me . . .*

A. Who you would talk to if:

1. you had a problem on the playground:

   _____

   _____

2. you had a problem on the bus:

   _____

   _____

3. you had a problem after school:

   _____

   _____

4. you had a problem at home:

   _____

   _____

5. something were really bothering you:

   _____

   _____

B. Who is the most important person in your life?

   _____

ACTIVITY C-4

SOCIAL SKILLS RATING SCALE (STUDENT VERSION)

The Social Skills Rating Scale can be used to evaluate whether students believe they exhibit these skills *usually, sometimes,* or *never.* It may be administered to students either individually or in a group.

DIRECTIONS:

GROUP ADMINISTRATION
Instruct students:

On this form, there is a list of social skills. Read each item on the list and decide whether you exhibit the skill. . . .

NEVER: You *never or hardly ever* exhibit the skill.
SOMETIMES: You *sometimes* exhibit the skill.
USUALLY: You exhibit the skill *consistently and appropriately* in *different* situations.

Place a checkmark under the appropriate column: (Never, Sometimes, Usually).

INDIVIDUAL ADMINISTRATION
Say to the student:

I am going to read a list of social skills to you. Tell me whether you demonstrate each one as follows:

NEVER: You *never* or *hardly ever* exhibit the social skill.
SOMETIMES: You can *sometimes* exhibit the social skill.
USUALLY: You *consistently* and *appropriately* exhibit the social skill in *different* situations.

Place a checkmark under the appropriate column: (Never, Some times, Usually).

INTERPRETATION:

Look over the list of social skills. Note the social skills that a student usually demonstrates (competencies), those demonstrated sometimes (inconsistencies), and those never demonstrated (incompetencies). Note social skills that are important, easy to teach, and naturally reinforced. Select/target behaviors for intervention and note in the TARGETED column.

Use this form to record dates when targeted skills are mastered and to reassess—measure—changes in social competence at a later date. Use different colors to record ratings completed at different times on the same form.

Student _____ Grade _____ Age _____

I.	Never	Sometimes	Usually	Targeted
join a group in the classroom	_____	_____	_____	_____
interrupt an ongoing activity	_____	_____	_____	_____
participate in group discussions	_____	_____	_____	_____
join ongoing conversations	_____	_____	_____	_____
make conversation	_____	_____	_____	_____
ask for help	_____	_____	_____	_____
accept help	_____	_____	_____	_____
join a group in the lunchroom	_____	_____	_____	_____
join a group on the playground	_____	_____	_____	_____
maintain friendships	_____	_____	_____	_____
deal with loneliness	_____	_____	_____	_____
deal with peer pressure	_____	_____	_____	_____
deal with disappointment	_____	_____	_____	_____
deal with covert rejection	_____	_____	_____	_____
deal with overt rejection	_____	_____	_____	_____
respond to teasing	_____	_____	_____	_____
make friends	_____	_____	_____	_____
am on-task in a group	_____	_____	_____	_____
work cooperatively	_____	_____	_____	_____
leave a group	_____	_____	_____	_____
avoid conflict	_____	_____	_____	_____
participate in discussions	_____	_____	_____	_____
play cooperatively	_____	_____	_____	_____
respond to being left-out	_____	_____	_____	_____
deal with embarrassment	_____	_____	_____	_____
accept a new group member	_____	_____	_____	_____
work in a large group	_____	_____	_____	_____
work in a small group	_____	_____	_____	_____
work with one other person	_____	_____	_____	_____

ACTIVITY C-5

SOCIAL BEHAVIOR RATING SCALE (STUDENT VERSION)

The Social Behavior Rating Scale can be used to evaluate whether students believe they exhibit these behaviors *usually, sometimes,* or *never.* It may be administered either individually or in a group.

DIRECTIONS:

GROUP ADMINISTRATION

Say to the students:

On this form, there is a list of social behaviors. Read each item on the list and decide whether you exhibit the skill. . . .

NEVER: You *never* or *hardly ever* exhibit the behaviors.
SOMETIMES: You CAN *sometimes* exhibit the behavior.
USUALLY: You *consistently* and *appropriately* exhibit the behavior in *different* situations.

Place a checkmark under the appropriate column: (Never, Sometimes, Usually).

INDIVIDUAL ADMINISTRATION

Say to the student:

I am going to read a list of behaviors to you. Tell me whether you demonstrate each one as follows:

NEVER: You *never* or *hardly ever* exhibit the behavior.
SOMETIMES: You can *sometimes* exhibit the behavior.
USUALLY: You *consistently* and *appropriately* exhibit the behavior in *different* situations.

Place a checkmark under the appropriate column: (Never, Sometimes, Usually).

INTERPRETATION:

Look over the list of behaviors. Note the behaviors that a student usually demonstrates (competencies), those demonstrated sometimes (inconsistencies), and those never demonstrated (incompetencies). Note behaviors that are important, easy to teach, and naturally reinforced. Select/ target behaviors for intervention and note in the TARGETED column.

Use this form to record dates when targeted skills are mastered and to reassess—measure—changes in social competence at a later date. Use different colors to record ratings completed at different times on the same form.

Student ———————————————— Grade ————— Age ————

I.	Never	Sometimes	Usually	Targeted
smile	———	———	———	———
establish eye contact	———	———	———	———
maintain eye contact	———	———	———	———
greet others	———	———	———	———
initiate a conversation	———	———	———	———
maintain a conversation	———	———	———	———
end a conversation	———	———	———	———
introduce myself	———	———	———	———
listen	———	———	———	———
ask for help	———	———	———	———
accept help	———	———	———	———
offer help	———	———	———	———
accept praise	———	———	———	———
respect another's space	———	———	———	———
give compliments	———	———	———	———
interrupt appropriately	———	———	———	———
ask for permission	———	———	———	———
form a line	———	———	———	———
walk in line	———	———	———	———
leave others appropriately	———	———	———	———
give praise	———	———	———	———
say nice things	———	———	———	———
negotiate	———	———	———	———
share materials	———	———	———	———
take turns	———	———	———	———
share ideas	———	———	———	———
give criticism	———	———	———	———
accept criticism	———	———	———	———
tell the truth	———	———	———	———
keep secrets	———	———	———	———
am assertive	———	———	———	———
ask for a favor	———	———	———	———
ignore unkind remarks	———	———	———	———
wait my turn	———	———	———	———
take care of belongings	———	———	———	———
eat with others	———	———	———	———
make suggestions	———	———	———	———
make an apology	———	———	———	———
acknowledge feelings of others	———	———	———	———
keep hands and feel to myself	———	———	———	———

ACTIVITY C-6

TIME SAMPLE RECORDING

DIRECTIONS
1. Select a behavior.
2. Select an observation period of several minutes or more.
3. Divide the observation period into equal intervals.
4. Observe student during each entire interval.
5. Record whether behavior occurred (+) or did not occur (–) at the *end* of the interval (Do not record the number of times the behavior occurred during the interval).
6. Calculate the percentage of intervals in which the student demonstrated the behavior.
   a. Count the number of intervals in which the behavior occurred.
   b. Divide by the total number of intervals.

$$\text{Ex: } \frac{\text{number of intervals behavior occurred}}{\text{number of intervals}} = 4/7 = 57\% \text{ of intervals}$$

Student _____ Date _____

Behavior _____

Observation Period _____

Interval Length _____

ACTIVITY C-7

INTERVAL RECORDING

DIRECTIONS
1. Select a behavior.
2. Select an observation period of several minutes or more.
3. Divide the observation period into equal intervals.
4. Observe student during each entire interval.
5. Record whether behavior occurred (+) or did not occur (–) *at any time* during the interval.
6. Calculate the percentage of intervals in which the student demonstrated the behavior.
   a. Count the number of intervals in which the behavior occurred.
   b. Divide by the total number of intervals.

$$\text{Ex: } \frac{\text{number of intervals behavior occurred}}{\text{number of intervals}} = 4/7 = 57\% \text{ of intervals}$$

Student _____ Date _____

Behavior _____

Observation Period _____

Interval Length _____

ACTIVITY C-8

DURATION RECORDING

DIRECTIONS
1. Select a behavior.
2. Determine a total observation time.
3. Each time a behavior occurs, record the time the behavior starts and stops.
4. Calculate the duration of the behavior.
5. Repeat Steps 3 and 4 when the behavior reoccurs.
6. Calculate the percentage of time that the student was engaged in the behavior.
   a. Total durations.
   b. Divide total durations by the length of the observation period.

Ex: $\dfrac{\text{Total durations}}{\text{length of observation period}} = 10/25 = 40\%$ of the time observed

Student _____ Date _____

Behavior _____

Start	Stop	Duration
_____	_____	_____
_____	_____	_____
_____	_____	_____
_____	_____	_____
_____	_____	_____
_____	_____	_____
_____	_____	_____
_____	_____	_____
_____	_____	_____
_____	_____	_____
_____	_____	_____
		Total: _____

ACTIVITY C-9

LATENCY RECORDING

DIRECTIONS
1. Select a behavior.
2. Determine a total observation time.
3. Record the time at which a signal for a behavior is given.
4. Record the time at which the student responds to the signal.
5. Record the time span between signal and the student's response (response latency).
6. Calculate the average response latencies for the time period observed.
   a. Total the total response latencies for the time period observed.
   b. Divide total response latencies for the time period observed by the number of recorded opportunities to obtain the average response latency.

   Ex: $\dfrac{\text{total response latencies}}{\text{number of opportunities}} = 32/7 = 4.6$ minutes

---

Student _____ Date _____

Behavior _____

Start	Stop	Duration
_____	_____	_____
_____	_____	_____
_____	_____	_____
_____	_____	_____
_____	_____	_____
_____	_____	_____
_____	_____	_____
_____	_____	_____
_____	_____	_____
_____	_____	_____
_____	_____	_____
_____	_____	_____
		Total: _____

ACTIVITY C-10

EVENT RECORDING

DIRECTIONS
1. Select a behavior.
2. Select an observation period.
3. Observe student throughout the observation period.
4. Record (tally) the number of times (occurrences) the behavior is observed.
5. Calculate the ratio of behavior occurrences per length of time observed.
    a. Total the number of occurrences (See Step 4).
    b. State ratio as number of occurrences per length of time observed.

Ex: 32 occurrences per 40 minute period of time.

Student _____ Date _____

Behavior _____

Observation Period _____

ACTIVITY C-11

ANECDOTAL RECORDING

DIRECTIONS
1. Select a student and an observation period.
2. Record, in narrative form, all behaviors demonstrated by student during the observation period.
3. When a behavior occurs, record antecedent conditions (events immediately preceding behavior) and consequences (events immediately following behavior).
4. Observe student across settings, activities, and behaviors.
5. Collate data to determine patterns.

Student _____	Date _____
Time Period _____	

Antecedent Conditions	Behavior	Consequences

ACTIVITY C-12

WHAT IS A FRIEND?

PURPOSE

Use this activity to determine whether the student understands this concept. You may also use this activity to determine whether the student understands cooperation, honesty, truthfulness, etc. Simply rephrase the questions.

DIRECTIONS

Always ask the questions in the following order. Questions followed by an asterisk are optional questions with which to probe for additional information. Tape record the session; then write student responses below.
Say to the student:

Listen carefully. We are going to talk about friendship today. I am going to ask you some questions about friends. There are no right or wrong answers. I am going to tape record your responses so that I won't have to write down everything you say and I will be able to remember what you say. Are you ready?

Can you tell me what you think a friend is?

Is there something else that you can tell me about what a friend is?

Who are your best friends?

Do you have friends in your class at school?

Why are they your friends?

Can you tell me more?

What is it about them that makes them your friends?

Who is your very best friend?

What makes that person your best friend?

Why did you choose each other as friends?

What are some things you might do with your friends?

How do you feel when you are with your friends?

REFERENCES TO PUBLISHED CURRICULA

Camp, B. W., & Bash, M. A. (1981). *Think Aloud—Increasing Social and Cognitive Skills: A Problem Solving Program*. Champaign, IL: Research Press.

Cartledge, G., & Kleefeld, J. (1991). *Taking Part: Introducing Skills to Children*. Circle Pines, MN: American Guidance Service.

Dinkmeyer, D., & Dinkmeyer, D., Jr. (1982). *DUSO-1 (Revised)*. Circle Pines, MN: American Guidance Service.

Dinkmeyer, D., & Dinkmeyer, D., Jr. (1982). *DUSO-2 (Revised)*. Circle Pines, MN: American Guidance Service.

Dupont, H., Gardner, O. S., & Grody, D. S. (1974). *Toward Affective Development (TAD)*. Circle Pines, MN: American Guidance Service.

Elliott, S. N., & Gresham, F. M. (1991). *Social Skills Intervention Guide*. Circle Pines, MN: American Guidance Service.

Freed, M., & Freed, A. (1982). *TA for Kids (and Grown-ups too): The New Revised Edition*. Rolling Hills Estates, CA: Jalmar.

Hazel, J. S., Schumaker, J. B., Sherman, J. A., & Sheldon-Wildgen, J. (1981). *ASSET*. Champaign, IL: Research Press.

Hops, H., Walker, H. M., & Greenwood, C. R. (1979). PEERS: A Program for Remediating Social Withdrawal at School. Behavior Systems for the Developmentally Disabled. In L. A. Hammerlynck (Ed.). *School and family environments*. New York: Bruner/Mazel.

Jackson, N. F., Jackson, D. A., & Monroe, C. (1983). *Getting Along with Others*. Champaign, IL: Research Press.

McGinnis, E., & Goldstein, A. (1984). *Skillstreaming the Elementary School Child*. Champaign, IL: Research Press.

Page, P., & Cieloha, D. (1992). *Getting Along*. Circle Pines, MN: American Guidance Service.

Schumaker, J. B., Hazel, J. S., & Pederson, C. S. (1988). *The Social Skills for Daily Living Curriculum*. Circle Pines, MN: American Guidance Serivice.

Sheinker, J., & Sheinker, A. (1988). *Metacognitive Approach to Social Skills Training*. Rockville, MD: Aspen.

Spengler, G. (1986). *Improving Your Self-Concept*. Kalamazoo, MI: Educational Program.

Stephens, T. M. (1978). *Social Skills in the Classroom*. Columbus, OH: Cedars Press.

Walker, H. M., McConnell, S., Holmes, D., Tadis, B., Walker, J., & Golden, N. (1983). *The Walker Social Skills Curriculum: The ACCEPTS Program*. Austin, TX: Pro-Ed.

Wiig, E. H. (1982). *Let's Talk: Developing Prosocial Communication Skills*. Columbus, OH: Merrill.

ACTIVITY C-14

PEER TUTORING PLANNING GUIDE

DIRECTIONS
Answer the following questions to begin organizing an effective peer tutoring program. Each question may be answered in a variety of ways, depending on the situation.

1. Which goals and objectives do you want peer tutoring to accomplish?

   _____

   _____

   _____

2. Which skills should be targeted for instruction?

   Academic   Social

   _____   _____

   _____   _____

   _____   _____

3. What materials will be needed?

   _____   _____

   _____   _____

   _____   _____

4. Who will be the tutors?   the tutees?

   _____   _____

   _____   _____

   _____   _____

5. When will tutoring sessions take place?
   Days: _____   Time: _____

6. How much time will be needed to master each objective?
   a. _____   b. _____   c. _____   d. _____
   e. _____   f. _____   g. _____   h. _____

7. How will tutor/tutee interactions be monitored?

   _____

   _____

   _____

8. How will student progress be evaluated?

_____

_____

_____

9. Describe how tutors will be trained.

_____

_____

10. How will student motivation and enthusiasm be monitored?

_____

_____

_____

_____

INSTRUCTIONAL GOALS AND OBJECTIVES FOR INDIVIDUALIZED EDUCATIONAL PLANS (IEPs)

ACTIVITY D-1

MAKING FRIENDS

A. **Current Performance Levels**

Student does not understand the concept of friend/friendship
Student does not have a friend
Student can discuss friend/friendship
Student can identify characteristics of a friend/friendship
Student practices social conventions of friendship
Student can identify multiple aspects of similarities and differences in people
Student can recognize the effect of labels on relationships
Students can recognize the effects of stereotypes
Student can differentiate judgmental/non-judgmental attitudes towards others
Student recognizes the relationship between language and feelings
Student recognizes the relationship between feelings and events
Student recognizes the relationship between feelings and behaviors
Student recognizes the relationships among feelings, thoughts, events, and behaviors
Student demonstrates self-esteem

B. **General Student Centered Goals**

Student will be able to:
understand concepts of friend/friendship
recognize characteristics of a friend, i.e., know, like, trust
develop social conventions of friendship
develop awareness of thoughts and actions that occurs when making a friend
recognize attitudes needed in developing friendships
develop effective interpersonal communication skills
recognize the relationship between events and feelings
recognize the relationship between behaviors and feelings
recognize the relationship between physical reactions and feelings
distinguish between fact and belief
recognize and replace *junk thoughts*
recognize the relationships among feelings, thoughts, events, and behaviors

C. **Behavioral Objectives**

Student will be able to:
define and discuss meaning of self-esteem

identify own qualities (nature)
identify own characteristics
identify own strengths
identify own weaknesses
recognize growth and change
recognize ambivalance of change
recognize personal responses to environment, associations, and expectations of others
recognize the difference between wants and needs
recognize that mistakes do not equal a person's worth
recognize the characteristics of self-esteem in others
distinguish physical from emotional hurt
develop and comprehend a vocabulary of feeling words
recognize that feelings come from thoughts
recognize that feelings are different from behaviors
develop and comprehend a vocabulary of behavior words
identify many ways to express feelings
distinguish between pleasant and unpleasant feelings
differentiate between healthy and unhealthy feelings
recognize that feelings help and hinder
recognize that feelings differ in intensity
recognize the connection between feelings and physical reactions
identify and develop a vocabulary of physical reactions to feelings
identify feelings that cause particular physical reactions
recognize the relationship between language and feelings
recognize that what *we think* happened is more important than *what did happen*
realize there is a choice of feelings in response to a given situation
identify language that leads to negative emotions and low self-esteem
identify and give examples of fact, belief, rational belief, irrational belief
recognize the four different kinds of *junk thoughts* (demanding, overgeneralizing, copping-out and catastrophizing)
expand the ability to recognize irrational thinking in both language and actions
expand awareness of irrational thinking in music, advertisements, peer pressure and other aspect of culture
determine the presence of irrational thinking and which irrational beliefs are operating
replace irrational language with new language free of demands and *junk thoughts*
recognize that feelings change when thoughts change
recognize that past behavior does not influence present but relates to growth and change
integrate skills and use rational beliefs to continue to improve self-esteem

ACTIVITY D-2

SELF-ESTEEM

A. Current Performance Levels

Student is aware of concept of self-esteem
Student can define self-esteem
Student can identify own qualities (nature)
Student can identify own characteristics
Student can identify own strengths
Student can identify own weaknesses
Student can recognize individual growth and change
Student recognizes personal responses to environments
Student recognizes personal responses to associations
Student recognizes personal responses to expectations of others
Student has a vocabulary of feelings and emotions
Student comprehends a vocabulary of feelings and emotions
Student differentiates between wants and needs
Student can accept mistakes
Student recognizes characteristics of self-esteem in others
Student recognizes the relationship between thoughts and feelings
Student recognizes the relationship between language and feelings
Student recognizes the relationship between feelings and events
Student recognizes the relationship between feelings and behaviors
Student recognizes the relationships among feelings, thoughts, events, and behaviors
Student demonstrates self-esteem

B. General Student Centered Goals

Student will be able to:
develop an awareness of self-esteem
recognize individual uniqueness
develop a vocabulary of feelings and emotions
develop a comprehension of a vocabulary of feelings and emotions
differentiate between wants and needs
recognize mistakes/performance do not equal a person's worth
recognize the self-esteem of others
recognize the relationship between language and feeling
recognize the relationship between events and feelings
recognize the relationship between behaviors and feelings
distinguish between fact and belief
recognize and replace junk thoughts
recognize the relationships among feelings, thoughts, events, and behaviors

C. Behavioral Objectives

Student will be able to:
define and discuss meaning of self-esteem
identify own qualities (nature)
identify own characteristics
identify own strengths
identify own weaknesses
recognize growth and change
recognize ambivalence of change

recognize personal responses to environment, associations, and expectations of others

recognize the difference between wants and needs

recognize that mistakes do not equal a person's worth

recognize the characteristics of self-esteem in others

distinguish physical from emotional hurt

develop and comprehend a vocabulary of feeling words

recognize feelings come from thoughts

recognize feelings are different from behaviors

develop and comprehend a vocabulary of behavior words

learn many ways to express feelings

distinguish between pleasant and unpleasant feelings

differentiate between healthy and unhealthy feelings

recognize that feelings help and hinder

recognize that feelings differ in intensity

recognize the connection between feelings and physical reactions

identify and develop a vocabulary of physical reactions to feelings

identify feelings that cause particular physical reactions

recognize the relationship between language and feelings

recognize that what WE THINK happens is more important than *what actually happens*

realize there is a choice of feelings in response to a given situation

identify language that leads to negative emotions and lowered self-esteem

identify and give examples of fact, belief, rational belief, irrational belief

recognize the four different kinds of *junk thoughts* (demanding, over-generalizing, copping-out and catastrophizing)

expand the ability to recognize irrational thinking in both language and actions

expand awareness of irrational thinking in music, advertisements, peer pressure and other aspects of culture

determine the presence of irrational thinking and which irrational beliefs are operating

replace irrational language with new language free of demands and *junk thoughts*

recognize that feelings change when thoughts change

recognize that past behavior does not influence present but relates to growth and change

integrate skills and use rational beliefs to continue to improve self-esteem

RECOGNIZING AND RESPECTING PRIVACY

A. Current Performance Levels

Student can discuss need for privacy
Student can discuss occasions of privacy
Student can discuss, recognize concepts of private time, personal space
Student practices social conventions
Student practices recognizing another's right to privacy and private property

B. General Student Centered Goals

Student will be able to:
  recognize occasions of privacy
  recognize need for privacy
  practice social conventions of privacy
  practice respecting another's right to privacy and private property

C. Behavioral Objectives

Student will be able to:
  discuss meaning of privacy
  develop a vocabulary of privacy
  demonstrate comprehension of vocabulary
  discuss when privacy is needed
  discuss occasions requiring privacy
  discuss and recognize need for private time
  verbally request private time/privacy as needed in an appropriate manner
  respect another's private time by asking only appropriate questions
  respect another's privacy by refraining from unnecessary comments
  discuss and recognize concept of personal space
  practice using personal space
  maintain appropriate distances between self and others in all occasions
  practice identifying private property
  ask permission to see, touch, use items belonging to others
  return private property
  refrain from destroying another's property

ACTIVITY D-4

SHARING/TAKING TURNS/PLAYING FAIRLY

A. Current Performance Levels

Student can discuss the meaning of sharing
Student can discuss the meaning of public property
Student can discuss the meaning or private property
Student can recognize occasions of sharing
Student can recognize taking turns is sharing
Student can recognize game/play as situations of sharing
Student can recognize rules of game/play
Student can participate in choosing partners/teams
Student can accept outcome of play/game
Student can apply social conventions to play/game situations
Student participates in activities requiring taking turns
Student can recognize things to be shared
Student can recognize the possibility of effecting a compromise if it is
  beneficial, appropriate
Student can recognize the need to share
Student can share

B. General Student Centered Goals

Student will be able to:
  understand the concepts of sharing
  recognize the occasions of sharing
  recognize things to share
  recognize the possibility of compromise
  recognize taking turns is sharing
  recognize game/play as sharing
  participate in play/game situations
  recognize rules are necessary and important
  practice appropriate social conventions
  demonstrate sharing skills

C. Behavioral Objectives

Student will be able to:
  discuss and demonstrate recognition of the vocabulary of sharing
  demonstrate comprehension of sharing vocabulary
  discuss and demonstrate recognition of the vocabulary of public
    property
  demonstrate comprehension of public property vocabulary
  demonstrate comprehension of private property vocabulary
  recognize occasion of sharing
  recognize things to share
  recognize taking turns is a sharing
  recognize need for taking turns
  recognize importance of taking turns in different settings/environments
  wait for a turn in an appropriate manner
  recognize games/play as a sharing situation
  practice play/playing games according to rules
  participate in choosing partners/teams

appropriately accept winners/losers in play/game situations

accept outcome of play/game situation

apply social conventions to play/game situations

ask to share in a polite, acceptable manner

respond to a request to share in a polite acceptable manner

share when requested or offer a reasonable refusal

respond appropriately to a refusal by asking again, walking away, asking someone else

negotiate a compromise if it is appropriate, beneficial, not a response to pressure

use appropriate language when sharing: please, thank you, may I, etc.

recognize the need to share time and attention

recognize the need to share physical and verbal space

ACTIVITY D-5

ASKING FOR AND ACCEPTING HELP

A. Current Performance Levels

Student recognizes need for help
Student recognizes why help is needed
Student can determine appropriate time to request help
Student appropriately communicates needs to others
Student can accept help

B. General Student Centered Goals

Student will be able to:
  recognize need for help
  recognize why help is needed
  recognize an offer of help
  communicate needs appropriately
  determine appropriate time to request help

C. Behavioral Objectives

Student will be able to:
  discuss instances when help is needed
  recognize feelings evoked when the reason for needing help is
    understood
  discuss relationship of needing help and the concept of private time
    and personal space
  learn appropriate language to request help
  learn and understand the vocabulary associated with needing,
    requesting, accepting and offering help
  apply the vocabulary

ACTIVITY D-6

COOPERATING WITH AUTHORITY

A. Current Performance Levels

Student cannot identify authority figure
Student cannot identify authority role
Student can identify authority figure
Student can identify authority role
Student can identify purpose of authority figure/role
Student can understand obligations and responsibilities of authority figure
Student can understand the purpose of authority figure
Student can identify circumstances/situations where authority may be disregarded
Student can relate to authority figures

B. General Student Centered Goals

Student will be able to:
  identify authority figures
  identify authority roles
  understand obligations and responsibilities of authority figures
  understand the purpose of authority
  identify the circumstances/situations in which authority can be disregarded
  establish and practice a positive relationship with authority

C. Behavioral Objectives

Student will be able to:
  identify authority figures
  identify authority roles
  recognize vocabulary associated with authority figures and roles
  understand obligations and responsibilities of various authority figures
  understand purpose of authority's rules, regulations in different environments
  recognize situations/circumstances when authority can be disregarded
  develop a relationship with authority
  appropriately get attention of an authority figure by using the social conventions of correct timing, addressing adult by preferred name/title, respectful tone of voice
  respond to a request by answering promptly and politely, coming to an agreement, and acting
  develop appropriate technique for disagreeing with authority by choosing appropriate time, stating the problem, listening to authority position, and coming to an agreement

ACTIVITY D-7

DEALING WITH FRUSTRATION

A. Current Performance Levels

Student becomes frustrated and is unable to direct/control behavior

Student can recognize feelings of frustration

Student comprehends frustration and related emotions/behaviors

Student can identify source of frustration

Student can recognize strategies to manage emotions/behaviors attendant to frustration

Student can implement strategies to cope with frustration

B. General Student Centered Goals

Student will be able to:

recognize emotion of frustration

comprehend vocabulary of frustration and related emotions/behaviors

recognize source of frustration

develop strategies for managing frustration

practice/implement strategies of managing frustration

C. Behavioral Objectives

Student will be able to:

understand frustration as a feeling of discouragement, bafflement that prevents the accomplishment of a purpose, task, goal

understand vocabulary of frustration: thwart, foil, balk

understand the other emotions and behaviors arise from frustration

discontinue/remove self from situation of frustration and not destroy work

identify source of frustration i.e., lack of listening, difficulty with directions, lack of understanding concept, lack of materials, etc.

use skills of asking for and accepting help

Student/teacher will assess situation

Student/teacher will decide to make changes

Student/teacher will implement changes

BIBLIOGRAPHY

Anderson, L. M., Stevens, D. D., Prawat, R. S., & Nicerson, J. (1988). Classroom task environment and students' task-related beliefs. *Elementary School Journal, 88,* 281–296.

Aronson, E., Blaney, N., Stephan, C., Sikes, J., & Snapp, M. (1978). *The Jigsaw classroom.* Beverly Hills, CA: Sage.

Asher, S. R., & Hymel, S. (1981). Children's social competence in peer relations: Sociometric and behavioral assessment. In J. D. Wine & M. D. Syme (Eds.), *Social Competence* (pp. 125–157), New York: Guilford Press.

Asher, S. R., & Taylor, A. R. (1982). Social outcomes of mainstreaming: Sociometric assessment and beyond. In P. S. Strain, (Ed.), *Social development of exceptional children.* Rockville, MD: Aspen.

Asante, M. K., & Gudykundst, W. B. (1989). *Handbook of international and intercultural communication.* Newbury Park: Sage.

Baruth, L., & Manning, M. (1992). *Multicultural education of children and adolescents.* Needham Heights, MA: Allyn and Bacon.

Brophy, J. E. (1983). Classroom organization and management. *Elementary School Journal, 83,* 254–285.

Brophy, J. E. (1983). Research on the self-fulfilling prophecy and teacher expectations. *Journal of Educational Psychology, 75,* 631–661.

Brophy, J., & Good, T. L. (1986). Teacher behavior and student achievement. In M. C. Wittrock (Ed.), *Handbook of Teaching* (3rd ed., pp. 328–375). New York: Macmillan.

Buchanan, L. (Sept., 1992). Tips for building self-esteem in students who are "not quite perfect." *Connect: A newsletter supporting educational practitioners.* Longmont, CO. p. 1 & 10.

Bulgren, J. A., & Carta, J. J. (1992). Examining the instructional contexts of students with learning disabilities. *Exceptional Children, 59,* 182–191.

Burns, P. E. (1975), *How to ask the right questions.* Washington, D.C.: National Science Teachers Association.

Cohen, E. (1986). *Designing groupwork: Strategies for the heterogeneous classroom.* New York: Teachers College Press.

Coie, J. D., & Dodge, K. A. (1988). Multiple sources of data on social behavior and social status in the school: A cross-age comparison. *Child Development, 59,* 815–829.

Colvin, B., & Sugai, G. (1988). Proactive strategies for managing social behavior problems: An instructional approach. *Education and Treatment of Children, 11,* 341–348.

Cooper, L., Johnson, D., Johnson, R., & Wilderson, F. (1980). Effects of cooperative, competitive, and individualistic experiences on interpersonal attraction among heterogeneous peers. *Journal of Social Psychology, 111,* 243–252.

Dansereau, D. F. (1980). Cooperative learning strategies. In D. E. Weinstein, E. T. Gietz, and P. A. Alexander (Eds.), *Learning and study strategies: Issues in assessment, instruction, and evaluation* (pp. 103–102). New York: Academic Press.

Deno, S. L., & Fuchs, L. S. (1987). Developing curriculum-based measurement systems for data-based special education problem solving. *Focus on Exceptional Children, 19*(8), 1–16.

DeVries, D. L., & Edwards, K. (1973). Learning games and student teams: Their effects on classroom process. *American Educational Research Journal, 10,* 307–318.

DeVries, D. L., & Slavin, R. E. (1978). Teams-Games-Tournament (TGT): Review of ten classroom experiments. *Journal of Research and Development in Education, 12,* 28–38.

Dodge, K. A. (1985). Facets of social interaction and the assessment of social competence. In B. H. Schneider, K. H. Rubin, & J. E. Ledingham, (Eds.), *Children's peer relations: Issues in assessment and intervention.* New York: Springer-Verlag.

Doyle, W. (1986). Classroom organization and management. In M. C. Wittrock (Ed.), *Handbook of Research on Teaching* (3rd ed., pp. 392–431). New York: Macmillan.

Gage, N. L., & Needels, M. C. (1989). Process-product research on teaching: A review of criticisms. *Elementary school Journal, 89,* 253–300.

Good, T. L. (1983). Classroom research: A decade of progress. *Educational Psychologist, 18*, 127–144.

Graves, N., & Graves, T. (1985). Creating a cooperative learning environment: An ecological approach. In R. E. Slavin, S. Sharan, S. Kagan, R. Hertz-Lazarowitz, C. Webb, & R. Schmuck (Eds.), *Learning to cooperate, cooperating to Learn.* New York: Plenum.

Greenwood, C. R., Delquadri, J., Stanley, S. O., Terry, B., & Hall, R. V. (1985). Assessment of ecobehavioral interaction in school settings. *Behavioral Assessment, 7*, 331–347.

Gresham, F. (1985). Utility of cognitive-behavioral procedures for social skill training with children: A critical review. *Journal of Abnormal Child Psychology, 13*, 411–423.

Gunter, P., Fox, J. J., & Brady, M. P. (1984). Social skills training of handicapped children in less restrictive environments: Research implications for classroom teachers. *The Pointer, 29*, 3–10.

Heshius, L. (1991). Curriculum-based assessment and direct instruction: Critical reflections on fundamental assumptions. *Exceptional Children, 57*, 315–328.

Humphreys, B., Johnson, R., & Johnson, D. W. (1982). Effects of cooperative, competitive, and individualistic learning on students' achievement in science class. *Journal of Research in Science Teaching, 19*, 351–356.

Johnson, D. W., & Johnson, R. T. (1974). Instructional structure: Cooperative, competitive or individualistic. *Review of Educational Research, 44*, 213–240.

Johnson, D. W., & Johnson, R. T. (1975). *Learning together and alone.* Englewood Cliffs, NJ: Prentice-Hall.

Johnson, D. W., & Johnson, R. T. (1980). Integrating handicapped children into the mainstream. *Exceptional Children, 47*, 90–98.

Johnson, D. W., & Johnson, R. T. (1981a). Effects of cooperative and individualistic learning experiences on interethnic interaction. *Journal of Educational Psychology, 73*, 444–449.

Johnson, D. W., & Johnson, R. T. (1981b). The integration of the handicapped into the regular classroom: Effects of cooperative and individualistic instruction. *Contemporary Educational Psychology, 6*, 344–355.

Johnson, R. T., & Johnson, D. W. (1983). Effects of cooperative, competitive, and individualistic learning experiences on social development. *Exceptional Children, 49*, 323–330.

Johnson, D. W., & Johnson, R. T. (1985). The internal dynamics of cooperative learning groups. In R. E. Slavin, S. Sharan, S. Kagan, R. Hertz-Lazaroitz, C. Webb, & R. Schmuck (Eds.), *Learning to cooperate, cooperating to learn.* New York: Plenum.

Johnson, D. W., & Johnson, R. T. (1986). *Learning together and alone* (2nd ed.). Englewood Cliffs, NJ: Prentice-Hall.

La Greca, A. M., & Stark, P. (1986). Naturalistic observations of children's social behavior. In P. S. Straw, M. J. Guralnick, & H. M. Walker, (Eds.), *Children's social behavior* (pp. 181–213). Orlando, FL: Academic Press.

Lampert, M. (1990). When the problem is not the question and the solution is not the answer: Mathematical knowledge and teaching. *American Educational Research Journal, 27*, 29–64.

Lyman, F. (1981). The responsive classroom discussion. In A. S. Anderson (Eds.), *Mainstreaming Digest.* College Park: University of Maryland, College of Education.

Madden, N. A., & Slavin, R. E. (1983). Effects of cooperative learning on the social acceptance of mainstreamed academically handicapped students. *Journal of Special Education, 17*, 171–182.

Madden, N. A., Slavin, R. E., & Stevens, R. J. (1986). *Cooperative integrated reading and comparison: Teachers manual.* Baltimore: Johns Hopkins University Center for Research in Elementary and Middle Schools.

Manning, B. H. (1989). Application of cognitive behavior modification: First and third graders' self-management of classroom behaviors. *American Educational Research Journal, 2*, 193.

McCloskey, M. L., & Quay, L. C. (1987). Effects of coaching on handicapped children's social behavior and teachers' attitudes in mainstreamed classrooms. *The Elementary School Journal, 87*, 425–435.

McGinnis, E., & Goldstein, A. P. (1984). *Skillstreaming the elementary school child.* Champaign, IL: Research Press.

Moll, L. C. (1990). In L. C. Moll (Ed.). *Vygotsky and education: Instructional implications and applications of sociohistorical psychology* (pp. 1–27). Cambridge, MA: Cambridge University Press.

Morvitz, E., & Motta, R. W. (1992). Predictors of self-esteem: The roles of parent–child perceptions, achievement, and class placement. *Journal of Learning Disabilities, 25*, 72–80.

Moskowitz, J. M., Malvin, J. H., Schaeffer, G. A., & Schaps, E. (1983). Evaluation of a cooperative learning strategy. *American Educational Research Journal, 20*, 687–696.

Moskowitz, J. M., Malvin, J. H., Schaeffer, G. A., & Schaps, E. (1985). Evaluation of Jigsaw, a cooperative learning technique. *Contemporary Educational Psychology, 10*, 104–112.

Oden, S., & Asher, S. R. (1977). Coaching children in social skills and friendship making. *Child Development, 48*, 495–506.

Padilla, A. M. (1990). Bilingual education: Issues and perspectives. In A. M. Padilla, H. H. Fairchild, & C. M. Valadez (Eds.), *Bilingual education: Issues and strategies.* Newbury Park, CA: Sage. (pp. 15–26).

Palinscar, A. S., & Brown, A. L. (1984). Reciprocal teaching of comprehension-fostering and comprehension-monitoring activities. *Cognition and Instruction, 1*, 117–175.

Reid, D. K., & Stone, C. A. (1991). *Why is cognitive instruction effective? Underlying learning mechanisms. RASE, 12*(3), 8–19.

Reith, H. J., & Evertson, C. (1988). Variables related to the effective instruction of difficult-to-teach children, *Focus on Exceptional Children, 20*(5), 1–8.

Roberts, C., & Zubrick, S. (1992). Factors influencing the social status of children with mild academic disabilities in regular classrooms. *Exceptional Children, 59*, 192–202.

Rosenkoetter, S. E., & Fowler, S. A. (1986). Teaching mainstreamed children to manage daily transitions. *Teaching Exceptional Children, 19*, 20–23.

Rosenshine, B., & Stevens, R. (1986). Teaching functions. In M. C. Wittrock (Eds.), *Handbook of Research on Teaching* (3rd ed.), (pp. 376–391). New York: MacMillan.

Rowe, M. B. (1986). Wait time: Slowing down may be a way of speeding up! *Journal of Teacher Education, 17*, 43–50.

Sainato, D. M., Maheady, L., & Shook, G. L. (1986). The effects of a classroom manager role on the social interaction patterns and social status of withdrawn kindergarten students. *Journal of Applied Behavior Analysis, 19*, 187–195.

Schmuck, R. A., & Schmuck, P. A. (1983). *Group processes in the classroom.* Dubuque, IA: C. Brown.

Schniedewind, N., & Salend, S. J. (1987). Cooperative learning works. *Teaching Exceptional Children, 20*, 22–25.

Sharan, S., & Hertz-Lazarowitz, R., & Ackerman, Z. (1980). Academic achievement of elementary school children in small group vs. whole class instruction. *Journal of Experimental Education, 48*, 125–129.

Sharan, S., & Sharan, Y. (1976). *Small-group teaching.* Englewood Cliffs, NJ: Educational Technology Publications.

Shenkle, A. (1988). The making of a meta teacher: Shaping the classroom landscape. *Learning, 17*(2), 61–64.

Sherman, L. W., & Thomas, M. (1986). Mathematics achievement in cooperative versus individualistic goal-structured high school classrooms. *Journal of Educational Research, 79*, 169–172.

Siperstein, G. N., Bopp, M. J., & Bak, J. J. (1978). Social status of learning disabled children. *Journal of Learning Disabilities, 11*, 49–53.

Slavin, R. E. (1977). Classroom reward structure: An analytic and practical review. *Review of Educational Research, 47*, 633–650.

Slavin, R. E. (1978). Student teams and achievement divisions. *Journal of Research and Development in Education, 12*, 39–49.

Slavin, R. E. (1979). Effects of biracial learning teams on cross-racial friendships. *Journal of Educational Psychology, 71*, 381–387.

Slavin, R. E. (1980). Effects of student teams and peer tutoring on academic achievement and time-on task. *Journal of Experimental Education, 48*, 252–257.

Slavin, R. E. (1983). When does cooperative learning increase student achievement? *Psychological Bulletin, 94*, 429–445.

Slavin, R. E. (1984). Team Assisted Individualization: Cooperative learning and individualized instruction in the mainstreamed classroom. *Remedial and Special Education, 5*(6), 33–42.

Slavin, R. E. (1985). Team-Assisted Individualization: Combining learning and individualized instruction in mathematics. In R. E. Slavin, S. Sharan, S. Kagan, R. Hertz-Lazarowitz, C. Webb, J. R. Schmuck (Eds.), *Learning to Cooperate, Cooperating to Learn,* (pp. 177–209). New York: Plenum.

Slavin, R. E. (1986). *Using student team learning* (3rd ed.). Baltimore: Johns Hopkins University, Center for Research on Elementary and Middle Schools.

Slavin, R. E. (1987). Cooperative learning: Can students help students learn? *Instructor, 96*(7), 74–78.

Slavin, R. E. (1989). Cooperative learning and student achievement. In R. Slavin (Ed.), *School and classroom organization.* Hillsdale, NJ: Erlbaum.

Slavin, R. E. (1990). Cooperative learning: Theory, research, and practice. Englewood Cliffs, NJ: Prentice-Hall.

Slavin, R. E., & Leavey, M. B., & Madden, N. A. (1984). *Team Accelerated Instruction: Mathematics.* Watertown, MA: Charlesbridge.

Slavin, R. E., & Karweit, N. L. (1985). Effects of whole-class, ability grouped, and individualized instruction on mathematics achievement. *American Educational Research Journal, 22,* 351–367.

Stainback, W., Stainback, S., & Froyen, L. (1987). Structuring the classroom to prevent disruptive behaviors. *Teaching Exceptional Children, 19*(4), 12–17.

Sugai, G. (1992). Applications of teaching social behavior. *LD Forum, 17,* 20–23.

Tharp, R. G., & Gallimore, R. (1988). *Rousing minds to life: Teaching, learning and schooling in social context.* New York: Cambridge University Press.

Wassermann, S. (1987). Enabling children to develop personal power through building self-respect. *Childhood Education, 63,* 293–294.

Weigel, R. H., Wiser, P. L., & Cook, S. W. (1975). Impact of cooperative learning experiences on cross-ethnic relations and attitudes. *Journal of Social Issues, 31*(1), 219–245.

Wheeler, R., & Ryan, F. L. (1973). Effects of cooperative and competitive classroom environments on the attitudes and achievement of elementary school students engaged in social studies inquiry activities. *Journal of Educational Psychology, 65,* 402–407.

Yager, S., Johnson, R. T., Johnson, D. W., & Snider, B. (1986). The impact of group processing on achievement in cooperative learning. *Journal of Social Psychology, 126,* 389–397.

Ysseldyke, J. E., & Christenson, S. L. (1987). Evaluating students' instructional environments. *Remedial and Special Education, 8*(3), 17–24.

Ziegler, S. (1981). The effectiveness of cooperative learning teams for increasing cross-ethnic friendship: Additional evidence. *Human Organization, 40,* 264–268.